Praise for Mike Riera

"Connecting to your teenager is a process not unlike building up muscles. As parents, you need to work on your timing and build up strength in your relationship. This book gives you the 'machinery' on which to exercise . . . it will change the way you think about teenagers and transform the way you relate to them."—Michael Gurian, author, *The Wonder of Boys* and *The Wonder of Girls*

"This book offers a wealth of down-to-earth and practical advice. No detached academic author here! Dr. Riera is in the trenches with hands-on experience to pass on to frustrated parents and teens alike."—Dr. Dean Edell

STAYING CONNECTED
TO YOUR
TEENAGER

STAYING CONNECTED

TO YOUR
TEENAGER

*How to Keep Them Talking to You and
How to Hear What They're Really Saying*

MICHAEL RIERA, PhD

Da Capo
LIFE
LONG

Note: The names and identifying details of people associated with events described in this
book have been changed. Any similarity to actual persons is coincidental.

Copyright © 2017 by Michael Riera

Set in 11 point Goudy Old Style by Perseus Books

Cataloging-in-Publication data for this book is available from the Library of Congress.

Da Capo Press revised edition 2017
ISBN: 978-0-7382-1955-4 (paperback)
ISBN: 978-0-7382-1956-1 (e-book)

Published by Da Capo Press

www.dacapopress.com

Note: The information in this book is true and complete to the best of our knowledge.
This book is intended only as an informative guide for those wishing to know more about
health issues. In no way is this book intended to replace, countermand, or conflict with the
advice given to you by your own physician. The ultimate decision concerning care should be
made between you and your doctor. We strongly recommend you follow his or her advice.
Information in this book is general and is offered with no guarantees on the part of the
authors or Da Capo Press. The authors and publisher disclaim all liability in connection with
the use of this book. The names and identifying details of people associated with events
described in this book have been changed. Any similarity to actual persons is coincidental.

LSC-C

10 9 8 7 6 5 4 3 2 1

For Megan, Lucia, and Sam —
the most important connections in my life.

The real art of conversation is not only to say the right thing at the right place but to leave unsaid the wrong thing at the tempting moment.

—DOROTHY NEVILLE

If the only tool you have is a hammer, you tend to see every problem as a nail.

—ABRAHAM MASLOW

I've learned that people will forget what you said, people will forget what you did, but people will never forget how you made them feel.

—MAYA ANGELOU

Contents

Acknowledgments

Anyone who has ever written a book knows that it's always more than a one-person task. There are the numerous people who challenge, support, cajole, tease, and cheer you along the way, and who, because of their input, transform the book into something more than one person's work. This is most assuredly the case with this book. And because of their connections to this project, there are a few people I want to thank and acknowledge publicly.

First, thanks to my home team: Megan, Lucia, and Sam. You're the best. Let's always keep our connections to one another first and foremost. Thanks also to my colleague and best buddy, Joe Di Prisco—your questions and musings linger longer than you know.

Thanks to my esteemed literary agent and friend, Liz Trupin-Pulli. Your support and advice are of the highest value.

Thanks to my editor, Marnie Cochran, and my publisher, David Goehring of Perseus Publishing, for your instant and unwavering enthusiasm for this project, from start to finish. Thanks especially to you, Marnie, and not just for your superior editing skills but also as much for your heartfelt feedback throughout the writing.

For this second edition I want to thank all the folks at Da Capo Lifelong Books who helped me to make this an even better and more comprehensive book than the first edition. Thanks to publisher John Radziewicz and designer Kerry Rubenstein. And special thanks to Claire Schulz who in her role as associate editor shepherded this edition from start to finish.

I also want to acknowledge Marianne Jacobbi and the folks at the Ceridian Corporation who several years ago asked me to make a recorded talk for them on talking with your teenager. That was when I first began to focus on the idea of a book based on the connection between teenagers and their parents.

And a special thanks to the crew at MAR's Architecture for putting up with a moody writer in their midst.

Finally, thank you to all the parents and teenagers who have shared their stories with me. In the end you are the impetus for this book. Listening to your stories and recognizing the savvy understanding of the deep issues at play during adolescence has been inspiring. I just hope I have done you all justice.

Introduction

I respect teenagers a great deal, and I respect the parents of teenagers even more. Nothing in a parent's life is more trying, confusing, and frustrating than raising a teenager. They are moody, self-centered, and full of mixed messages; at least that's the way normal, healthy teenagers behave. That will not change. As the parent of a teenager, you know all too well that your job entails setting limits, having big talks, enforcing consequences, helping them learn from their mistakes, and putting them on course for a happy and successful adulthood. Talk about an exhausting task.

What I find curious, however, is that hardly anyone ever mentions the importance of staying connected to our teenagers throughout their adolescence. Given the enormous to-do list from the previous paragraph, why isn't anybody addressing practical ways of staying connected to our teenagers throughout this trying time? From a practical perspective, all the items on your to-do list are handled more efficiently, more effectively, and more pleasantly when you are connected to your teenager. For instance, research has shown that the emotional connection between adolescent girls and their parents (especially their mothers) significantly delays the onset of sexual activity. When you are connected, everything else comes more easily and naturally. And when they do misbehave—as they will—nothing worthwhile can happen until your connection is reestablished. The number one complaint of the parents of teenagers is a lack of communication with their teenagers, but, even in the face of this, if you are paying attention, thinking creatively, and maintaining your curiosity, your connection will hold steadfast despite the lack of regular heart-to-heart talks.

Beyond effectiveness, there is another reason to maintain your connection with your teenager: It's fun. Teenagers, for better and worse, are some of the most creative and fun people on the planet, and when you stay connected you, too, enjoy these aspects of your teenager; and in doing so, you regularly replenish your parenting batteries. Besides, sharing humor itself promotes connection. Or, as the humorist Victor Borge once said, "Laughter is the shortest distance between two people."

Therefore, I find it surprising that although there are many good books on the market about setting limits and such, there are still none about how to maintain the connection with your teenager despite everything else that is going on and that is demanded of you. This book fills that gap. *Staying Connected to Your Teenager* deals exclusively with all that you can do to strengthen and deepen your relationship with your teenager even as you attend to the more standard parental duties. I'll leave the rest of the to-do list to the other books. More than ever before, as your children become teenagers, you yearn for a deep connection, and with good reason. First, regardless of the ages of your kids, as a parent you always see the five-year-old in them, and, from this frame of reference, no five-year-old is ready for puberty and beyond. Second, society appears to have changed for the worse. And even though generations have been saying this since probably before the invention of the written word—the cover of a 1954 *Newsweek* stated: "Let's Face It, Our Teenagers Are Out of Control"—it now, somehow, feels different. The devastation and aftereffects of terrorist attacks in San Bernardino and Paris continue to wash over us. Add to that the implicit bias that has revealed itself in how law enforcement treats African Americans and we see that each event in its own way has forced us to reconsider the previously safe havens of school, work, and church. Third, over time, adolescence has become stretched out. These days, teenagers are dependent on their parents well past the teen years, at least until the end of college for most, and beyond that for many others.

As a result, parents desperately want a connection that affords them continued influence in their teenager's life, just as they have had since birth and through childhood. Parents wonder to themselves, and sometimes even out loud, *Why does my relationship with my child need to change now, during adolescence, when he could most benefit from my expertise?* After all, from the parental perspective, life has worked out quite well for your children when you have taken the lead. Whether in choosing a school, providing limited choices for school attire, or trimming the guest list for the upcoming birthday party, children do well and seem to enjoy going along with, for the most part, their parents' wishes and desires. In short, children are open to and welcoming of their parents' influence.

Teenagers, however, are adamant about wanting to change the terms of their parents' influence over and engagement with their lives. Most teenagers want to run their own lives. Most parents have a difficult time hearing and understanding this shift in power. Thus the proverbial battle lines are drawn. But, with teenagers, nothing is quite as it appears at first glance. With a more discerning second look, you begin to see, to the surprise of most adults, that teenagers still want their parents involved in their decisions. It's just a matter of degree. Parents generally want more control than teenagers are ready to, able to, or should relinquish. That is, parents want the same relationship that existed through the first twelve years of their children's lives to continue throughout adolescence. However, in the spirit of growing up, establishing an identity, and becoming an adult, teenagers cannot allow this old relationship to continue unfettered. Therefore, if your reason for reading this book is to figure out how to get your teenager to comply with your wishes and sage advice, then, alas, this is the wrong book for you. These opposing perspectives will not shift after reading this book. These differences are givens. With that in mind, the real question is how to reach across this gap for meaningful contact with one another, which is what this book is all about—how to stay connected to your teenager even though you have different agendas.

As your child enters adolescence, the challenges you both face are enormous. For instance, if you give up on trying to stay involved in your teenager's life, she will suffer enormously from what is essentially your abandonment of her. At the same time, if your teenager relinquishes control of her life to you, she will never grow up and will still live with you well into her forties. Fortunately, there is plenty of room for creative and useful parental stances in between these two extremes of abandonment and micromanagement.

Rethinking an Old Metaphor

Psychologists and various social scientists often talk about the theoretical concept of separation, and the need for adolescents to separate from their parents and families and establish their independence. Adolescence is thought of as a time when teenagers venture out on their own to discover themselves, so that they can come back to their families as fully individuated adults. Fat chance. The simplistic notion of independence versus dependence in the context of separation is outdated and inaccurate—if indeed it ever was a reflection of reality—and it needlessly pits parents and teenagers against one another. Connection is the foundation of a healthy parent–teenager relationship—a connection that is based on interdependence.

Therefore, you need to erase the idea of separation from your mind and replace it with the concept of extension. That is, during adolescence teenagers need to extend away from their parents, all the while staying connected to their parents. Their job is to extend; your job is to connect.

During infancy, our kids are not only within our sight but also within our reach. In childhood, they are within sight and sometimes within reach, and, at the very least, always within the sight and reach of some trusted adult. In adolescence, they are often out of sight and out of reach of us, or any other adult for that matter. Of course, adolescence is also when the stakes go way up. The fallen bike is replaced with the crashed car. The cookie thief is gone in favor of the anorexic. The running round and round in circles to get dizzy and fall down is transformed into the six-pack on Saturday night. It is during adolescence, as much as if not more than at any other time of life, that our teenagers need to feel our connection to them and their connection to us. The difficulty is that, at least at first glance, normal, healthy adolescent development seems to obviate this type of relationship. (For proof of this last point, just reflect on how "talkative and sharing" your teenager is with you when he gets home after school on just about any day.) But this stereotype of teenagers not wanting anything to do with their parents is wrong. In fact, healthy adolescent growth is predicated on a solid relationship with parents. To be clear, this book does not advocate that you give up your parental responsibilities and obligations so that you can stay friends with your kids. Far from it. Teenagers need their parents as parents first and friends second. Sometimes your relationship will include aspects of friendship and at other times it will feel nothing at all like friendship. (In fact, it will feel strangely familiar, kind of like the perpetual limit-setting role you had when your child was two.) The payoff to staying the parent first and the friend second is that your teenager stands a much better chance of successfully navigating adolescence with a parent at his side rather than a grown-up who behaves like a kid trailing behind him. Sure, there are lots of moments of friendship between a parent and a teenager, but there are also those critical moments when he needs parents who are willing to fall out of favor for his overall well-being, and, believe it or not, staying connected, all the while.

From Manager to Consultant

In an earlier book, *Uncommon Sense for Parents with Teenagers* (2012), I wrote about how the parent–child relationship changes during adolescence. The metaphor employed was that of manager and consultant. During the first ten to twelve years of children's lives, their parents are the managers of their lives. For the most part, children like their parents in this role. This is when children spontaneously express their love and fondness for parents: "Daddy, you're the best daddy in the world!" "Mommy, you're the smartest person in the world!" "I love our family, and when I grow up I am going to live right next door to you."

Not only is the role of manager appreciated, but parents also get to make the major decisions for their children: where they go to school, play dates, extracurricular activities, sleepovers, doctors' appointments.

However, once children become adolescents, all this changes. To continue the metaphor, in the beginning stages of adolescence, teenagers fire their parents as the managers of their lives. And, according to normal adolescent development, this is exactly what teenagers should do, which leaves parents in an unenviable quandary—stop parenting (giving up or abandonment) or refuse to be fired (an endless power struggle and countless gray hairs). Over the past ten years, another unhealthy option has emerged for parents frustrated at getting fired and losing control: agent/lawyer. In this role, parents hold the successes of their teenagers up as an extension of themselves. When their sons and daughters are faced with a difficulty or failure, they kick into legal mode to defend their children, which ultimately robs these teenagers of ever learning from mistakes and developing a genuine sense of resilience. Fortunately, there is another way. Give up the role of manager or lawyer and get yourself rehired as the consultant to your teenager's life. From this perspective, more to the side than face-to-face, parents have tremendous influence in their teenagers' lives; that is, if they understand how the relationship between them and their teenager has changed and what that means when it comes to their daily influence with their teenager. *Uncommon Sense* goes on to illustrate and explain this changed relationship in the context of the standard parent concerns: drinking, driving, romance, friendship, curfew, schoolwork.

Staying Connected to Your Teenager picks up on these themes by focusing solely on the connection between parents and teenagers. Given all the changes in the relationship, and given all the decisions teenagers are faced with every day, it is more important than ever that parents have a solid connection with their teenagers—a connection that both parent and teenager appreciate, count on, and value. But the way to establish and maintain this connection is not as straightforward as the connections made during childhood. Now much is dependent on the creativity and perseverance of parents. The good news is that not only is a connection with your teenager viable, but it is also something your teenager craves, though she will never say this in so many words.

Adolescence

Adolescence is really two distinct phases of life merged into one. That is, in each teenager there are two different people: the regressed child and the emergent adult. The emergent adult lives at school, on the field, in the music room, at work, in community service, and in front of his friends' parents. The regressed child lives at home, in front of you (and often behind the closed door of his room). The danger for parents is that you only get to know the regressed child part of your teenager—the person who teases his younger sister, who leaves her messy dishes in her room for days on end, who throws a tantrum when someone borrows his charger, who challenges your authority when you remind her to do her homework. Unless you're on the lookout, it is likely that you will miss ever getting to spot, let alone to know, the emergent adult in your teenager; you will have to depend on the random comments of other adults—teachers, coaches, other parents—who at times, much to your astonishment, extol the virtues of your teenager. And yes, of course, you nod your head as this person praises your teenager, but you never dare ask whether your Johnny or Susie is actually meant or if it's just a case of mistaken identity, as you strongly suspect. This is tragic for both you and your teenager.

You need to get to know this emergent adult to appreciate that the efforts you are putting in as a parent are paying off. You also need to connect to your teenager in some more adult ways. Your teenager needs you to see this part of her to begin to believe in herself. That is, when she looks into your eyes, she needs to know that you see and recognize the adult in her. At the same time, and I know this is perplexing, you need to connect with your teenager in some childish ways, too; otherwise he grows up too fast.

Experts agree that in adolescence, peers influence behavior more than parents, but they also agree that during the same time parents influence attitudes more than peers. Clearly, behaviors come and go, but attitudes are for the long term, and it's the quality of the relationships that determines just how much influence we have over and with our teenagers in the development of these long-term attitudes. But influencing long-term attitudes is an enormous challenge. Part of this is because whenever we are with them we are looking to the future, to the men and women they are becoming. We're constantly extrapolating current behaviors to future times. Teenagers, however, live fully in the present, moment to moment. This is why they always give you a strange look when you talk about patterns in their lives. "I'm seeing a growing pattern of irresponsibility in your behavior that worries me: late for school yesterday, missed homework two days ago, and you forgot to walk the dog today." This is gibberish to your teenager. For her, each example is an isolated event with its own explanation and with no relationship to the other incidents. They are just three distinct moments in time, nothing less, nothing more. Parents live in patterns, teenagers live in moments.

The responsibility for establishing a relationship with the emergent adult in your teenager rests squarely on your shoulders. Getting to know and appreciate this part of your teenager will take enormous amounts of creativity, patience, and faith. And it's worth every bit of the efforts involved.

Staying Connected to Your Teenager

The aim of this book is to give you solid, practical advice, ensconced in psychological and developmental research, on how to understand and how to improve the quality of your relationship with your teenager. Each chapter describes everyday openings and opportunities for connecting with and staying connected to your teenager. Each chapter also gives developmental understanding about how and why the approaches work. Throughout, you will learn different ways of relating to and connecting to your teenager. Moreover, while and after reading this book, your own creativity will lead you to discover more ways of connecting on your own—which I hope you will share with me. (Visit the Contact page at www.mikeriera.com.) As you read, you will come to have a much more accurate picture and understanding of your teenager during this enigmatic phase of life— and you are in for some surprises along the way.

By the conclusion of this book, you won't look at your teenager in the same way again. Instead, when you look over at her and she catches your eye and quickly turns away, as do you out of your self-consciousness, you will find yourself drawn to steal another glance. Now you will look for what she desperately wants you to know but can't tell you. Can't tell you because she doesn't have the words and because she doesn't want to feel like a child who depends on her mom and dad. Now, even though it takes time to read the subtleties between the lines, you will catch her unmistakable look that says: "Please stay connected to me no matter how hard I push. Please."

ONE

Late at Night

It was one of those nights when I kept tossing and turning, but sleep still eluded me. I finally gave up and went downstairs to have a snack and read a magazine, which is exactly what I was doing when my fifteen-year-old son walked in. It was 1:30 a.m., and he was bleary eyed from playing games on his computer. I thought he had gone to bed when he had arrived home "early" from the party, at midnight. Goes to show you how much I know.

"Watcha reading, Dad?"

"Not much." If I had learned anything from raising two teenagers, it was that even when they asked what I was up to they were never really interested in what I was doing. Then, pointing at my plate, I asked him, "Want some left-over pie? It's good."

"Sure . . . Dad, how do you know if you're ready for sex?"

I did my best not to choke on the piece of pie in my mouth. I swallowed and caught my breath, and then I remembered that the last time I had checked, my son didn't even have a girlfriend. I had twenty questions rolling around my head and even more ready-to-go lectures. Instead, I managed to stop myself. "Where's this coming from? Did you meet somebody?" Alright, we could have done without that second question.

"No, I didn't meet anybody. It's just that everyone seems to be doing it these days."

I knew that the old *If Johnny jumped off the cliff, would you jump too?* was way out of line, so I said nothing. I just looked back at my little boy—who clear-ly wasn't so little anymore.

After a moment I looked down at my remaining pie and noticed that I was playing with my food. Silence.

Then an amazing thing happened. John began to open up. He told me about how a few of his friends had girlfriends and he missed hanging out with these guys; about how he wanted a girlfriend, too, and was beginning to think something was wrong with him; about sex, and his curiosity about what it was like. He went on like this for ten minutes.

All I did was listen. Early in his monologue, I had realized that my job was to stay quiet and pay attention. To say the least, it was difficult. Finally, when he had finished his second piece of pie, he headed back to his video games as if we had just been talking about the weather. Now I was wide awake, and I knew that in a few moments my wife would be wide awake with me because there was no way I could go to sleep without waking her and talking this through.

At first pass the shocking pace and self-revelation in the above conversation almost makes it seem unbelievable. Believe it. But believe this story only because it occurs late at night, when teenagers act in some rather uncharacteristic ways, especially around their parents. That is, this kind of conversation could never take place when your teenager gets home from school, or at a Saturday brunch, or while cleaning up the dishes after dinner. No, what makes this story the stuff of real life is that it takes place late at night.

Adolescent Sleep

Adults and teenagers have very different sleep–wake cycles, and once you understand these differences you can use them to enhance your relationship with your teenager. Taking this approach to heart means checking your world (and sleep) at the door to cross over temporarily into your teenager's world of time and biological rhythms. Midnight and beyond is the time of deep conversation for most adolescents, even though for most of their parents it is the occasion of much-deserved REM sleep.

The average teenager needs just over nine hours of sleep every night, even though the average teenager gets just over six hours. Research shows that adolescents have a different circadian rhythm (sleep–wake cycle) than adults. This biological difference leaves them feeling awake later into the evening and, as a result, unable to fall asleep at the earlier bedtimes of childhood. Most teenagers don't get sleepy until around 11:00 p.m., which, of course, means they are dragging in the morning when the alarm rings at 6:30 a.m. (Falling asleep at 11:00 p.m. on the button and rising at 6:30 a.m. sharp still means only seven and one-half hours of sleep, or ninety minutes shy of what the average teenager requires.) Research conducted at the University of Minnesota indicated that over half the teenagers studied reported feeling most awake after 3:00 p.m. and that 20 percent claimed they fell asleep in school; this comes as no surprise given what time of night they fall asleep and what time in the morning they wake up. In another study, through Yale University's Center for Emotional Intelligence,[1] researchers asked teenagers to name the top five emotions they felt while at school. The top three emotions named were tired (39 percent), stressed (29 percent), and bored (26 percent). The irony here, however, is that "tired" is not an emotion, though it is most definitely a gateway for negative feelings. So, clearly, a shortage of sleep plays a major role in the moodiness of the average teenager.

The adult brain, on the other hand, releases the sleep-inducing chemical melatonin at around 7:00 p.m., and this is what makes us so drowsy just after dinner (leading some of us even to grab a catnap on the sofa under the guise of reading the newspaper, or, my favorite, meditating). This state ensures that we're in bed at a reasonable hour—if we're listening to our bodies—so that we are rested (or at least better rested) when the alarm sounds in the morning. Unfortunately, these different realities of teenage and adult sleep patterns only exacerbate the typical teenage mantra: "You just don't understand!"

> My sixteen-year-old daughter is so damn stubborn. For example, she never gets enough sleep and it's a major hassle to get her out of bed in the mornings. I swear, most of the time she seems to sleepwalk through breakfast and the ride to school, which worries me because she has been making noises lately about getting her driver's license.
>
> But no matter what I say, she won't go to bed earlier. I mean, if she just went to bed at 10:00 p.m., everything would work out better.

If you want to see a teenager in her natural sleep habitat, just visit any college dormitory. Midnight is the time of pizza munchies, group dancing in lounges, binge watching on Netflix, crisis counseling with friends, existential conversations about the meaning of life, and, occasionally, even some studying. Of course, college teenagers understand their sleep–wake rhythms and as a result avoid eight and nine o'clock classes at all costs. And, if escape from these courses is impossible, they supplement their early rising time with a two-hour late afternoon nap. (Or they find a note-taking buddy with whom they can alternate class attendance.) The point is that a built-in sleep debt is no longer a given once teenagers enter college—they can work with and around their environment to get the sleep they need. Not so in middle school and high school, where schedules require that students rise early in the morning and remain busy all day and into the evening. The teenager who lives this schedule can get enough rest only by going to bed and falling asleep by 9:30 p.m. at the latest, every night, which isn't likely or realistic.

All this means that, given the current configuration of most school districts, teenagers are unintentionally set up to accumulate some serious sleep debt, which in turn impinges on their moods, concentration, stress levels, and general ability to learn. Teenagers are more sleep deprived than any other population across the life span. Assuming a last-minute wake-up alarm of 7 a.m., let's look at how the typical sleep week goes for a high school sophomore:

Sunday Night.   She goes to bed at 10:00 p.m., but can't fall asleep until well after midnight because she isn't tired, in part because of her biological rhythm and in part because she stayed up until well past 1:00 a.m. on Friday and Saturday, and slept in as late as her parents allowed. *Minus three hours.*

Monday Night.   She begins her homework on time but gets distracted by texting and social media. Goes to bed at 11:00 p.m., but it takes her an hour of tossing and turning before she falls asleep. *Minus two hours.*

Tuesday Night.   She does her homework on time but has to counsel a friend who is having trouble with another friend. Then she has to check in with a couple of other friends to debrief. Goes to sleep at 12:30 a.m. *Minus two and one-half hours.*

Wednesday Night.   She starts her homework late because she is checking in with the friend who had a problem the night before. Then she feels lazy and surfs the Internet for a while before finally doing her homework. She quickly gets too tired to finish the homework but not tired enough to fall asleep. Goes to bed and sleep at midnight. *Minus two hours.*

Thursday Night.   She is anxious about the big test in school tomorrow— nervous because it's a test and overwhelmed because she didn't even finish the homework from the night before. She Skypes a friend to go over their study guide, but they end up talking an extra half hour about how stressed out they are over tomorrow's test and their lack of time to study. Goes to sleep at 1:00 a.m., but gets up an hour early for some extra cramming. *Minus four hours.*

At this point, our teenager has accrued a sleep debt of thirteen and one-half hours, and that's a conservative estimate. Worse yet, most sleep experts agree that for every hour of sleep debt we accrue we lose one point from our functional IQ. (Don't worry, getting caught up on your sleep brings you back to your base-level IQ.) This means that when teenagers have tests on Fridays (when most teachers give exams so they can correct them over the weekend and give them back to the students on Monday), most students are down at least thirteen points on their functional IQs. In short, Friday is the worst day of the week to test teenagers.

To complete the above scenario, most teenagers count on the weekends to reduce their sleep debt; on Saturday and Sunday mornings, they sleep in until noon and beyond, as well as grab naps whenever possible (usually when they are supposed to wash the car or rake the leaves). This drives parents crazy. In our society, sleeping late translates into sloth and lazy behavior, an attitude that will get our kids nowhere fast. One of all parents' top fears is that their teenager will never learn to push himself or put in an honest day's work. Ironic—for teenagers it's just about being tired, but for their parents it's about a good work ethic.

Using Their Sleep–Wake Cycle to Connect

The silver lining to the reality that society and biology seem to conspire against teenagers getting enough sleep is that the sleep debt gives you the perfect opportunity to connect with your teenager, for several reasons. First, they've had time to reflect on their day and to put it into perspective—to connect attitudes with behaviors, relationships with moods, big ideas with daily habits. In other words, they have things to say. Second, because it's the end of the day, their normally hypervigilant defenses are relaxed, and they're more apt to say things that they otherwise wouldn't discuss. Third, and again because of the late hour, there is less competition for their attention. No friends texting or dropping by. No critical choices to make about which party to go to later that evening. No agonizing decisions over what clothes to wear.

Teenagers open up most naturally late at night, and wise parents take advantage of this reality; an intrepid few even plan for these opportunities.

For the past couple of years, I've planned late-night "spontaneous" talks with my daughter. Every couple of months, on a Friday or Saturday night that she stays at home and watches TV, I say my usual "Good night" at 10:00 p.m. and head up to bed. Only on these nights I set an alarm for 1:00 a.m. When the alarm sounds, I hit snooze a few times before getting up and stumbling downstairs. It's at this point that I fudge the truth with my daughter—I swear, it's the only time.

"What are you doing up, Mom?"

"Insomnia, just couldn't sleep." Never mind those four snooze alarms.

I go into the kitchen and fix us each a cup of warm tea and a snack. Then I plop down on the sofa next to her and watch whatever is on the screen, hoping for some breaks or the end of a show; at this point, I knock on her door, so to speak: "So how are things with you?" Then I wait.

It's almost always the same: At first, she speaks haltingly, but then once she gets some momentum she more or less free associates in front of me. All I do is nod and give an occasional encouraging grunt or an expectant look.

I've learned more about her life during these talks than I have in all the family dinners we've shared during the past three years. The only rule I have for myself is never to interrupt her with my opinions, suggestions, warnings, and, above all else, lectures. Sure, when I'm back in bed a bit later, I'm often left sleepless (and experiencing real insomnia) and anxious over what she has told me, but at least I'm in the loop. Over the next few days, I usually manage to touch base on some of the highlights of those late-night talks with her—the things that kept me awake at night for days afterward.

Late at night is when your teenager is most reflective, so it's always worth your efforts to make yourself available when he is willing and able to catch you up on his world. It's just as important to learn how to stay receptive as an audience. This is not the time to lecture or have your needs met. That is, if you expect a late-night talk to quell your anxiety over the upcoming prom date, then you had better think again. This is the time for them to introduce you to their thinking process as well as to the young men and women they are becoming— the emergent adult in your teenager.

Parents often complain that their kids are too busy to talk with them. To some extent this is true, but, at the same time, this belief isn't exactly correct. The truth is that when they aren't too busy to talk with us, we aren't around, we're usually asleep. The parent who wants to connect with her teenager, therefore, does a certain amount of planning and strategizing to hang out and remain available late at night, when her teenager is most open to talking. But still some of the best moments happen spontaneously and because you trust your intuition.

My daughter was really upset from the moment she got home, but whenever I inquired about what was up, she gave me that evil teenage stare. I kept my distance: within reach if she needed me, but out of striking distance in case she wanted to vent on me. I had no idea what was bothering her, but she knew that I knew she was upset. I think she was a tiny bit grateful that I wasn't pushing her to open up, at least that is what I was telling myself.

Before turning in, I gently knocked on her door. "It's open."

"Hi, honey. I'm just going to bed and wanted to say good night." "Yeah. Good night."

"Okay, good night. Um, you seemed upset when you got home, anything I can help you with?"

"No. Well, maybe. Nah, I doubt it. It's just that . . ."

It was at this point that the daughter in the above scenario launched into a vivid description of what had transpired between her and her best friend at lunch that day. As the daughter told her story, the mom intuitively realized that her child had been replaying the event through her head ever since arriving home—the quality of her voice, the rapid pace of her speech, and her exasperated expressions had tipped her mom off. So after hearing the story, the mom waited to make sure her daughter was finished, then she asked a few simple questions. Before long, her daughter was opening up about all sorts of issues besides what had happened at lunch. Mom went to bed much later than anticipated that night, and she slept with a smile on her face. Sure, her daughter was dealing with some difficult decisions, but the connection between her and her daughter was intact. Here's what that mom had to say a few days later:

The next day, however, was a bit strange. By the light of day, we both realized that she had opened up with me much more than she had planned. There was an odd tension between us, actually from her to me—I felt great about the night before. Still, I could sense that for me it was some sort of test. If I pushed her to stay open or brought up all that she had said the night before, I was in for a rude shove. If, however, I could meet her glances, pick up on her nervousness, and give her the space she needed, our relationship was going to get stronger. Weird, as I realized this that next day, all I could think of was the woman at the gym who told me that after a hard workout, it's important to give yourself a day off to let the muscles recover and grow. That's what it felt like with my daughter.

This is worth reemphasizing: The day after opening up to you, your teenager will experience an emotional hangover—she's worried that she told you too much and is kicking herself for doing so. Expect this and plan for it. This means more than ever following her lead. In other words, don't rush in to tie up loose ends from the night before; let it all come together naturally over the next few days. Your silent presence reassures her that you are safe to open up to and that you believe in her. This approach lets your teenager know that you have confidence in her and in her ability to handle whatever it is that she is facing, and that you're always there for her.

Teenagers themselves might have another perspective on the effectiveness of these late-night conversations. This one came from a high school senior who was writing a story for the school paper on a talk I gave to parents at his school.

That stuff you said about late at night is really true, but not entirely for the reasons you cited. You see, every teenager knows that tired parents talk less and listen more, so when we open up to them late at night we know we've got their attention and that they are too tired to lecture.

Helping Your Teenager Cope

Given the foregoing scenario, if your teenager is like most of her peers, she is somewhat sleep deprived even when she is trying to get enough sleep. Here are a few tips to pass along for getting a better night's rest. (See Chapter 13, "Know Your Village," for recommendations about how to pass this information along effectively.)

- Establish a regular bedtime and regular rising time, and stick with it as best as you can. Even if you're not sleepy, go to bed at your chosen time and, even if you are tired, get up at the appointed hour.
- Avoid caffeine (coffee, soda, chocolate) from late afternoon through evening.
- Give yourself from thirty to sixty minutes of downtime before you go to sleep. Turn off the electronics for the night at the beginning of this downtime.
- Separate your work area from your sleep area—don't study on your bed. (Or at least clear off your bed and "hide" your books before you climb in.)
- Get regular exercise.
- Make sure the room is dark when you go to bed. Darkness seems to stimulate the release of melatonin, which helps you fall and stay asleep.
- If you can't fall asleep right away, learn to relax through either progressive relaxation or simple daydreaming. Resting while awake isn't as recuperative as sleep, but it's better than getting up and turning the computer back on.

Late at Night, Away from Home, and the Phone

Opening up late at night occurs in a few common locations: in the family room, the television playing quietly in the background; in the kitchen while making a snack; in your teenager's bedroom when he's settling down. But with teenagers, never expect the expected. In other words, expect your teenager to initiate these talks in and from unusual places. For example, when teenagers are away from home, this phenomenon does not come to an end, it simply adapts. Now the opening up occurs over the phone, text, or by FaceTime, and still late at night.

> The text alert jolted me out of deep sleep. Out of the corner of my eye, I read the clock: 1:27 a.m. This could only be bad news. "Hi, Mom. You asleep?"
>
> I texted back, "Uh, no, not really. At least not since your text. What's up?"
>
> "Not much. Feel like talking?"
>
> Two minutes later we were on the phone.
>
> "Hi. So how's camp?"
>
> "Okay, I guess."
>
> "What do you mean, 'you guess?'"
>
> "I knew I shouldn't have come back here. I'm so depressed and lonely. Can I come home?"
>
> "Let's hold off on that decision. Tell me more about what's going on at camp."

This mom told me that her daughter then went on for ten minutes straight without interruption. She spoke about how miserable she was; about how all her camp friends had changed for the worse; about how miserable she was; about how the kids were teasing her about her new hairstyle; about how miserable she was; about how she missed her mom, dad, and little brother; about how miserable she was; about how she shouldn't have come back to camp this year; about how miserable she was, except for this one new kid she had met who seemed kind of cool. By the end of the conversation, her daughter had turned herself around and was feeling optimistic about camp, even though her mom had not given her any advice. Mom simply let her daughter talk it through for herself. There are two critical points to glean from this last vignette about the combination of teenagers, late night, and phones: time-of-day depression and door handle revelations.

When they contact you late at night from wherever—summer camp, college, a cousin's house, travel abroad—you will usually first hear about all the depressing and worst parts of where they are and who they are with. They may even sound clinically depressed. But hang in there before you run off to your local pharmacist, as this is often a time-of-day depression. Or, as a graduate student in psychology once told me after I had inquired about her younger brother, who was three months into his freshman year at college and away from home for the first time:

> Zack's right on track, but it's taken the rest of us a lot of work to come to that conclusion. Over the last few months, we've all had some scary talks with

him—he's told us all that he is depressed and lonely. He doesn't feel that he fits in and he thinks that everyone around him is adjusting to college without a glitch, except him. And even though he is smart and has always been a good student, he still thinks everyone at school is smarter and more capable than he is. It got so bad that he was hinting around to my parents about coming home and dropping out. When I talked to him on the phone, I was sure that he was clinically depressed. He displayed all the symptoms: persistent sadness, hopelessness, lethargy, loss of interest in what had been pleasurable activities, insomnia, trouble concentrating, and lack of appetite. And it was going on for much longer than two weeks. Then a weird thing happened. One day, I texted and then called him in the middle of the day, when a meeting I was scheduled for was canceled. He sounded great, like the Zack of old. This made me suspicious, so I called my mom and dad. Sure enough, all our gut-wrenching conversations had occurred late at night with Zack, usually after 11:00 p.m. So for the next few days, we all called him at various times during the day, and sure enough he seemed his normal self to all of us. Zack wasn't depressed, he was homesick, which made perfect sense. In other words, he's a typical college freshman still adjusting to college, living away from home, and making new friends.

When teenagers are away from home and immersed in a new environment—camp, college, group travel—they are consumed throughout the day with adapting and fitting in: people, requirements, unspoken norms, eating habits, pace of life. They are too busy to think about home. But late at night, they stop adapting and start reflecting about home, especially about family and friends. Because of the hyperconsciousness and energy required to adapt to new surroundings, their new daily lives pale in comparison to their near mythical memories of life back home. In other words, they depress themselves. And when you talk with them only late at night, what you usually hear about is how difficult it is to adapt, how poorly they are managing, and how much they miss home.

This is not to say that some teenagers don't become clinically depressed during the first semester of college, and I would hate to hear that someone had mislabeled real depression as a time-of-day depression. Just take your time in jumping to the depression conclusion; with a bit of curiosity and creativity—calling at different times of day and checking in with the dormitory staff—you might pleasantly surprise yourself.

Door handle revelations are another matter entirely. In therapy, this phrase refers to clients who, as they are saying good-bye and reaching for the door, reveal some important information, just when it is too late to discuss it. *Oh yeah, I meant to tell you, my wife told me last night that she is sick of this separation and doesn't feel that anything is getting better. So we're getting divorced . . . See you next week.*

Sometimes after hanging out with your teenager in the kitchen late at night, or after saying good night and spending a few extra minutes in the dark talking, or at the end of a phone conversation when one of you has to go, don't be surprised by these door handle revelations. Then trust your instincts. Did he say this to get it out in the open even though he isn't ready to talk about it? Or was this an invitation to settle back in and get comfortable? Difficult to know. And, as always, it's a good idea to voice your process aloud, and then take your cues from your teenager. *I'm not sure what you want me to do with that—sit down and talk some more or give you some time and space to think about it some more.* A good general rule of thumb is to sit back down, don't ask any questions, and wait expectantly. He will either slip right back into it or gently shoo you away. If he gives you conflicting messages—telling you to go away as he pats the chair next to the bed—it's best to stay a bit longer.

But even if he does shoo you away, consider it good news. You passed the test. He revealed something to you that he knows stirred your anxiety, something he knows you have lots to say about, and you stayed present and silent. This means he can trust you with more down the road and that he can come back to you later on about what he has just unloaded. And he will.

One more thought about the phone or social media, and it's an obvious one: When you speak with someone on the phone, you are unable to see one another, which often makes it easier to open up about vulnerable topics over the phone than in person. Pragmatically, this means that if you have a big conversation with your teenager over the phone, he may not make the leap to the same kind of intimacy when he is eye to eye with you.

> We're a totally gadget-oriented family, so we have all the latest technology and personal devices. What's really strange is that both my teenagers, Melissa and Laurence, leave me the most personal and glorious messages on my cell phone voice mail. *Hi, Mom. Just calling to say hi. You know you're a great mom and I know I don't usually tell you that. Just wanted you to know. Talk to you later.* I've got at least half a dozen of their messages permanently saved. I listen to them when I get down on myself for being an impatient or combative mom. They help, a lot. The odd thing, though, is that when I see them after they leave a message like that, they act like they never left it; they never reference the message and they definitely don't go out of their way to treat me like the great mom they allude to in the messages.

Over the phone, teenagers are able to let go of most of the physical self-consciousness they feel, which allows them to speak more directly from their hearts. In these situations, the phone becomes a tool that puts them into a reflective mood. This is especially so with voice mail, as we all have a tendency to free associate when leaving messages for loved ones, often surprising even ourselves by what we say. The same is true for your teenager. Why?

Some experts suggest that a solid working definition of an adolescent is someone who can't tell you in any consistent way why she does the things she does. Think about this for a moment. Remember the last time you were perplexed by something that your teenager did or said? You probably responded to her behavior with the classic parent question: "Why did you do that?" Chances are (bordering on certainty) that your teenager shrugged and mumbled something like "I don't know."

What's a parent to do in a situation like this? Many throw their hands up in frustration and walk away, shaking their heads in astonishment. Others take the direct route: they lecture their kids on the importance of learning to make good decisions. Still others yell at their kids for not thinking and implore them to engage their brains before speaking the next time. And a small minority use these moments to try to teach their teenagers the value of introspection in the name of self-knowledge: *Take a few moments to see whether you can figure it out for yourself—then tell me what you come up with.* None of these responses is very effective, and all four of them, to varying degrees, undermine your connection with your teenager.

The reality is that the experts are right in this case—teenagers can't tell you in consistent ways why they do the things they do. Expecting a logical and well-reasoned response to the *Why* question is like trying to squeeze water from a rock. There is, however, a rational explanation for all of this. Along with their bodies, teenagers' brains are in the midst of huge growth spurts, specifically in the corpus callosum and the prefrontal lobes, the areas of the brain responsible for mature judgment and decision-making skills. Until the brain finishes this growth spurt, teenagers' impulses are way ahead of their abilities to control them. There is a solid organic explanation for the inability of teenagers to answer the *Why* question. Whenever any of us acts on our impulses, logic and rational thinking trail behind; this lag is the norm for most teenagers. With these growth spurts in the brain they do not possess the ability to control their impulses consistently.

Unfortunately, parents who do not appreciate this odd, but real, disparity between impulses and decision-making abilities often make the situation worse for teenagers. Imagine what it would feel like if you were organically unable to do a certain task, but the authority figures in your life demanded that you successfully complete the task. How would it feel if they further demeaned your efforts when you tried? The response to this type of interaction is humiliation.

And humiliation is hardly the foundation of a strong relationship between parent and teenager. But the specter of humiliation makes matters even worse. If you haven't already noticed, most teenagers are hyperdefensive; when attacked, rather than retreat in the face of potential humiliation, most take the opposite approach: they attack. This is the stuff of the all-too-common shouting matches between teenager and parent.

However, the parent who understands how brain growth can affect behavior is in a position to make a conscious choice to deepen her connection with her teenager instead of unintentionally pushing her teenager farther away. Sure, this parent still asks the *Why* question (what adult can stop herself?); but when no response is forthcoming, and her teenager looks perplexed, instead of walking away in disgust, or growing angry, or plowing forward with one in a series of lectures, she catches herself and pauses. She takes the lack of response in stride. Then, in her own words, she conveys, "Yeah, I remember what that was like. But don't worry, you'll start to make the connections more and more as you get older. Now what are we going to do about this mess?" Instead of feeling humiliated, this teenager now feels at least partly understood. Best of all, the connection between the two has grown stronger—or, at the very least, the connection is no worse off.

What's more, a sharp parent realizes that although her teenager cannot answer the *Why* question at the moment, she will have this knowledge down the road a bit, often as she prepares for sleep.

Allen, my eighth grader, was a total pain in the morning before he left for school. He was grumpy, whiney, and made fun of his little sister. That was the last straw, when he started picking on Liz.

"Allen, why are you acting like such a jerk? And stop picking on your sister!"

"I'm not a jerk, you are. Besides, I thought we weren't supposed to call each other names like jerk."

He had me on that one. We just stewed in silence for a few minutes before he grabbed his backpack and took off for school. We both managed a faint-hearted "See ya later," but nothing more.

We didn't talk about it at dinner that night, but as Allen was crawling into bed, I stopped by his room.

"Allen, I'm sorry I called you a jerk this morning. There was no need for that."

"That's okay, Mom. I was kind of acting like a jerk."

"Yeah, what was that all about?"

"I think I was nervous about the history test today. I stayed up late studying last night, but when I was getting dressed this morning I remembered that I had forgotten to study one whole section that was going to be on the test."

"Oh."

"I was kind of mad at myself, so I guess I took it out on you guys. Sorry."

"How did the test go?"

"Would have been better if I had studied that section, but not so bad."

All this is to say that a great deal more is going on beneath the surface of your teenager than meets your eye. This is just another example of why, when in doubt, it's usually best to sit tight, remain quiet, and bring it up later on, when he's in a naturally occurring reflective mood.

Haute Cuisine

A first cousin to the late-at-night phenomenon is what happens when you take your teenager to a fancy restaurant. When you can afford such an outing, most teenagers will reveal a wonderful side to themselves over a five-course gourmet meal. Make sure the restaurant is dressy and that your teenager is dressed up sufficiently and a bit self-consciously, just out of his element for the evening.

> We had talked about going to Chez Delicio for a couple of weeks beforehand. It was a special dinner to celebrate my son Enzo's upcoming graduation from high school. We all got dressed up: my husband and Enzo in suits, and me in an evening gown. It was sort of like our family prom. My son was so adorable; he wasn't sure how to order, or even which utensil to use, but he didn't want to ask. When his father leaned over as he was stressing over the correct fork and pointed to the outside one, his sigh of relief was audible.
>
> Through most of the evening, our conversation was a mix of current events, playful banter, and the upcoming NBA Championships, which, given the normal grunts and groans over the dinner table at home, was pleasurable and already worth the price of the evening. But then, just after ordering dessert, Enzo, without our prompting, began to express some of his feelings about graduating from high school: friends, teachers, regrets, memories. He even told us about some of his escapades, which were way outside of what we knew or suspected, or even wanted to know. I was dumbstruck. Then, after we got home, he went to his room, changed into his old sweats, and went back to his more typical style of communication—monosyllabic.

The haute cuisine approach is effective because of set and setting: teenagers are self-consciously out of their element in an environment where they are expected to act like adults. All this is implicit, and it takes time to sink in. Adjusting to these expectations in unfamiliar terrain is consuming, and it takes a while to settle in. Therefore, it's usually around the middle of dinner, or sometimes even on the ride home (when their defenses are down as they return to the comfort and familiarity of the family car), when they start to think and speak with you, their parents, like mature adults.

This phenomenon is also present when you visit your teenager in a new environment away from home, perhaps summer camp or college. One caveat, though: it's usually best to have this visit occur with your teenager alone, without any other friends around—his or yours. But as we'll see in later chapters, friends offer a different sort of opportunity to connect to your teenager's world. One practical point: Never expect much from these dinners if your teenager is hard-pressed for time, because then she will rush through dinner so that she can hook up with her buddies. Give yourselves plenty of time, and by all means put all personal devices on mute.

Connecting in Between

Transitions are hidden opportunities to connect with your teenagers because during these times they are more apt to reveal more of themselves, usually for the better. Typical transitions for reconnecting include holidays, the beginning of the school year, school vacations, the end of the school year, trips away from the family (from sleepovers to summer camp), graduations, leaving home for college, a first apartment.

> A week before his junior year, my son came down with a bad case of food poisoning. He was horribly sick for a couple of days, but recovered quickly thereafter. When he was almost fully recovered, he showed up in my bedroom early one morning—at a time when he is usually sound asleep—with a plate full of pancakes and a tall glass of orange juice.
>
> "Here, Mom, I made some breakfast for you."
>
> "Uh, thanks, I guess." This was not like him—the early hour or the breakfast in bed—but I just chalked it up to the food poisoning.
>
> "You're welcome. I just want to thank you for taking care of me these last few days. I'll never eat clams again! But I'm hungry and eating again, so I thought you might want some, too."
>
> I sat up and took the plate full of pancakes—there were more pancakes on that one plate than I eat in an entire year. Although they are my favorite breakfast food, he must have failed to notice that it takes only half a pancake to satisfy my taste buds, but I didn't want to hurt his feelings.

"Hmm. Good. Thanks." He was seated at the end of the bed, looking as if he had something on his mind. Then it hit me: School started in two days. "What are your thoughts about going back to school? You were away a lot this summer; do you think it'll be a little strange going back and seeing everyone again?"

Bull's-eye! He poured his heart out (and a few tears, too) until the sun came up. He was sitting on lots of stuff having to do with friends, academics ("Colleges really care about junior year grades!"), and family—his older sister had left for college while he was sick. It was a great heart-to-heart talk, a rarity in our relationship. And, as an added bonus, as soon as he began to talk, he failed to notice that I had put the pancakes down after only a bite or two.

H.A.L.T.

When it comes to the topic of stress, particularly as it relates to sleep, it's important that we arm our kids with information. I find that kids easily relate to the concept of H.A.L.T., which comes from the twelve-step groups. The acronym is used by recovering addicts as a self-assessment tool to help them avoid relapses into their addictions.

In the parlance of these twelve-step groups, the recovering addict never wants to let himself become too Hungry, too Angry, too Lonely, or too Tired. Any of these states leaves him vulnerable to the temptation to use again.

For teenagers, I translate H.A.L.T. into the quintessential stress buster. That is, whenever they are feeling stressed, they need to take a moment to reflect on the acronym, as most of the time it will give them an accurate diagnosis of where needless stress is coming from and what they can do to eliminate it.

- Your son might realize that, even though it's 4:00 p.m., he's eaten only a bagel all day, hence he must have something to eat at the first opportunity.
- Your daughter might begin to make the connection between staying up late to finish that English paper and her moodiness, hence she grabs a nap if possible, or at least plans to have a good night's sleep.
- Your son might understand that missing lunch with his friends was a bigger loss of companionship than he had imagined, so he stops what he is doing to check in with a friend.
- Your daughter might connect that fight she had with you on the ride to school with how frustrated she is with her drama teacher, so she might write about the fight in her journal or talk to a friend about it during study hall.

Seasoned parents understand that teenagers want to serve as masters of their own domain—this means that they don't need or want anybody to tell them why they are so moody or so irritating. Worse, if they don't think they can figure it out on their own, they'll pretend it isn't happening. (No, yelling at you isn't a sign that they are in a bad mood. Or complaining about "chicken again" doesn't mean they are angry about one thing or another.) That's the beauty of H.A.L.T.: it's a tool that assists them in figuring it out themselves; it's a narcissist's dream.

Self-understanding also points to a huge difference between adults and teenagers. If an adult realizes she is hungry, she'll eat something. Or if an adult acknowledges loneliness, he'll call a friend. Not so with teenagers. Just naming the cause of the stress is often enough to get them through that bout of stress. They feel so good about having figured it out that they don't need to do anything about it, at least at first. That's how powerful self-understanding is to a teenager.

By the way, H.A.L.T. is also a terrific tool for parents when interacting with their kids. That is, it encourages us to ask and answer two important and difficult questions: *Was there something tangible (H.A.L.T.) that got in the way of my handling that situation better?* And, *What can I do to take care of myself now to get ready for whatever is coming next?*

*   *   *

Remember, your teenager has a different rhythm to his day than you do. Therefore, even though it isn't convenient, it is well worth the effort that it takes to adapt your rhythms to match his, if even only for an evening every now and again. Those are the Saturday nights you'll remember for years and years—the ones you'll tell your grandchildren about. Those are also the nights that will help you get through all the other nights when it's an hour past curfew and you haven't heard a peep from your wayward teenager. It's all about balance. Just never let yourself forget that it is your connection with your teenager that will always lead him back home.

TWO

Narcissism 101

Adolescence is a narcissistic time of life, which is both natural and healthy. That is, although your teenager's self-absorption is disturbing to you, it's typical for the age. You need to come to grips with this reality. It's not going to change. No matter how much it bothers you, you need to learn how to work with this attitude to forge a deeper connection with your teenager. Also, as something to hold on to through these self-centered moments, remember that it is through this narcissism that they will develop genuine empathy and compassion. There is no shortcut.

The world of the average adolescent is rich in insight and complex connections; it's also full of ambiguity and mixed messages. Teenagers battle for a foothold of clarity amid this stream of conflicting thoughts and feelings. These are the struggles that they feel are unique to them, and they will not believe that you or anybody of your generation ever had to deal with such problems, let alone figure out issues of this magnitude. From your teenager's perspective, like it or not, the whole world is about her. Implicit in this worldview is that she is as opaque to you as your parents were to you, many years ago.

Living out their lives on this stage, the last kind of parent teenagers want is an expert—someone who knows all the answers even before the questions are formulated; someone who understands exactly what they are going through before they themselves know what they are thinking and feeling. If you accept their narcissism at face value, you also understand the inherent futility of trying to play the expert for your son or daughter. That is, because the nature of narcissistic thought is to believe that nobody else in the world is capable of the kinds of thoughts, feelings, insights, and perceptions that you experience regularly, you as a parent realize that during adolescence the door is closed to every type of know-it-all, especially parents. In short, they are sensitive to and suspicious of any adult who says or even implies *I know what you are going through.*

Remember that growth spurt in the brain that we talked about in the last chapter? This exaggerated sense of self is another ramification of that spurt, only now it plays out in dramatic fashion as teenagers move from the concrete, childlike thinking of childhood to the abstract, adultlike thinking of adolescence. That uneven growth spurt in the brain, in conjunction with inherent narcissism, is also why they will sometimes say and then defend something that you know they don't even believe. You just know they are defending it because they blurted it out and are too narcissistic to admit they were wrong. During these moments, use caution. Once they make the unrealistic statement, it's as if they had climbed a tree and then climbed out onto a flimsy limb. If you slowly disassemble their defenses, you essentially push them farther out on the limb while you meticulously saw off the limb. When they fall, you may get some perverse kick out of it; but they are humiliated and shamed, and these feelings creep into and undermine your connection with one another. When this happens, your best bet is to resist temptation. Look at them after they've made the unrealistic statement, shake your head, and then quietly walk away. This is akin to giving them the space and time to climb gracefully off the weak limb and back down the tree trunk to solid ground. Now they learn that you have their best interests at heart and they can trust you even when you don't know all the facts. This leaves their narcissism and brain development working for you and your connection with each other.

But before we explore further ramifications of teenage narcissism on your connection, let's get ourselves a dose of reality and a bit of humility along the way.

Do You Really Remember?

How many of you secretly harbor the fantasy that you actually do remember what life was like for you when you were a teenager? Be honest.

Sure, I joke around and cringe with my friends when I look at my high school yearbook. And, of course, I readily join in the refrain, "I would never go back to high school again!" But the truth is, for better or for worse, I can remember most of what happened to me in high school and the kinds of things I used to think about; it's just that it's too painful to bring back all those memories. But, yeah, I think my memories are pretty accurate.

Even though most adults don't say this aloud—especially to our own teenagers—deep down, most of us believe that we can remember what it was like when we were teenagers. On this topic, most of us are wrong. No matter how difficult it is to admit, we have been successful in blocking out much of what happened during our own adolescence. In addition, we have distorted much of what we were feeling and thinking, as well as how we remember the way others behaved toward us. In *The Seven Sins of Memory*, author Daniel L. Schacter[1] makes a pervasive case about the extent of our distorted memories when it comes to adolescence:

> We're all capable of distorting our pasts. Think back to your first year in high school and try to answer the following questions: Did your parents encourage you to be active in sports? Was religion helpful to you? Did you receive physical punishment as discipline? Northwestern University psychiatrist Daniel Offer and his collaborators put these and related questions to sixty-seven men in their late forties. Their answers are especially interesting because Offer had asked the same men the same question during freshman year in high school, thirty-four years earlier.
>
> The men's memories of their adolescent lives bore little relationship to what they had reported as high school freshmen. Fewer than 40 percent of the men recalled parental encouragement to be active in sports; some 60 percent had reported such encouragement as adolescents. Barely one-quarter recalled that religion was helpful, but nearly 70 percent had said that it was when they were adolescents. And though only one-third of the adults recalled receiving physical punishment decades earlier, as adolescents nearly 90 percent had answered the question affirmatively.

For now, the why of this phenomenon is not important, but that it exists is hugely relevant to you and your teenager. Perhaps the most important insight to derive from Offer's research is that in the areas he examined, the one that had the most anxiety (physical punishment as discipline) also had the most distortion. In a strange twist, this means that when we are adults, the adolescent memories that are the most unreliable are the ones concerning issues that made us the most anxious.

Sure, everyone remembers scoring the winning basket in the big game or getting the lead in the spring musical and performing in front of packed houses during senior year. But even these memories are open to distortion, or maybe it's just plain exaggeration. Over the years, that final shot you made to win the basketball game tends to get farther and farther from the basket and more and more opposing players swarmed over you as you took the shot. And over time, the crowd at the musical tends to swell in your memory, as do the thundering ovations afterward.

Memory distortion over time is natural, so don't deny the possibility, bordering on certainty, that you have some inaccurate memories about your own adolescence. More than ever this points us in the direction of curiosity over expertise—something discussed at length in Chapter 5, "Mastery over Compliance." In simple language, you don't know what your teenager is going through, and if you pretend otherwise you're headed for a crash into that proverbial wall that many teenagers build to keep their parents out.

Abstract Thinking

During adolescence, how teenagers think is at least as important as what they are thinking. This fact is essential to grasp. For teenagers, the conclusions they reach are not what fascinate them; their narcissism is captivated by the path their thinking led them down en route to reaching a conclusion. Abstract thinking allows them to think about their thinking, and for the average teenager this is an intoxicating phenomenon. But first some background on what's going on in the inner workings of the typical teenager's mind.

As we noted earlier, adolescence is a time of growth in the brain—specifically in the area of impulse control and decision-making abilities. At the same time, according to the observations and theories of Swiss psychologist Jean Piaget, adolescence represents a shift in thinking from concrete to abstract. That is, before adolescence, thinking is action and action is thinking. This type of thinking is no longer true for your teenager. She can be thinking a million disparate thoughts and sit as still as a church mouse. Once a person accomplishes abstract thinking, she is no longer limited by the physical environment around her. This is why teenagers are famous for their rich fantasy lives; for huge leaps in imagination; and yes, for unrealistic thinking. Adolescence is a time of heightened creativity. As adults, we work hard to learn how to think outside the box. Teenagers, on the other hand, regularly think outside the box, way outside the box, and the adults around them try to get them back into the box while simultaneously trying not to destroy their creativity in the name of order.

This shift to abstract thinking, however, does not happen during a discrete moment. Instead, it is a gradual process beginning sometime in middle school and not firmly in place until around the end of the freshman year. But rather than talk abstractly about abstract thinking, let's ground our discussion in two areas of heightened concern for most parents—conflict and the so-called big talks—all with an eye toward how to use the development of analytical thinking in your teenager to fortify the connection between the two of you.

Abstract Thinking and Conflict

When your teenager starts to become accustomed to the world of abstract thought, a new kind of argument begins to occur at home. During these conflicts, you come to realize, for maybe the first time, that your teenager is more perceptive than you had imagined. During these arguments, he pokes holes in your logic, disassembles assumptions, and points out your character flaws— usually in a less-than-graceful manner. At the same time, however, you grasp that, even though he is arguing vehemently, he doesn't seem all that attached to what he is saying. It's as if he were arguing just to argue, and that is often exactly what is happening.

To understand this phenomenon, think back to when he was five or six and just learning some new physical skill—drawing a certain kind of flower, kicking a soccer ball with his left foot, playing a song on the piano. As a child, he came to you and asked you to watch him show you this new skill he had developed. And you did so, with pride. You loved letting him show off his new abilities in front of you. For his part, he basked in your attention and positive feedback, and you reveled in his need to show you.

Fast-forward ten years, to when he is sixteen. Now instead of calling you out to the backyard to show off his mastery of the corner kick, he picks a fight with you at the dinner table. Nothing major, just some minor character flaw of yours or an opposite political view (a favorite of many teenagers). Suddenly you find yourself in a full-fledged debate over some issue you hadn't fully considered before this conversation, and your son is debating you as if the outcome might determine the course of humankind. Catch your breath. Although what he is saying is important, more often than not it's his best way of showing off to you. Only now he is showing off his new and more complex thinking abilities instead of some new physical skill he has just acquired. How else can he do this? Bring home a chemistry problem and solve it in front of you? Write a concise paragraph while you watch? No. The most frequent way—and the least vulnerable from their viewpoint—that teenagers let their parents know that they have made the shift into abstract thinking is by arguing. It's arguing in part for the sake of arguing, and to a greater degree to show off.

My son and I were on our way back home from dropping my husband off at the airport and we were listening to the radio. (It was my turn, so the radio was tuned to National Public Radio.) I'm not even sure of the topic, but suddenly he began to disagree with what the commentator was saying, so much so that he turned down the radio and looked to me to affirm his opinion. I cleared my throat and gently disagreed with him, as I'm sure he knew I would.

Well, you would have thought I had just trashed his friends. He grew indignant and debated me on the topic for the next twenty-five minutes. It was a much more engaging conversation than I had planned for, but engaging in that I was working hard to hold my own, and I'm not sure that I really did.

As we pulled into the driveway, we reached an awkward stop to the discussion. Neither of us was satisfied because we hadn't swayed the other person one bit, and I know I didn't feel that I had been that articulate in what I had to say—I imagined my son felt the same way, but I don't know for sure.

Then it hit me: He was showing off for me. So as we walked up to the back door, I stopped him and said, "You know I'm really impressed with the way you think and debate. You listened to what I had to say, looked for the flaws, and took them apart. You're a better listener than I thought, and more articulate, too. I'm impressed with the way you think." Then as I pushed past him to get in the house, I added, "Of course I disagree with just about everything you said, but still the complexity of your thinking is impressive."

He was stunned. At first his face lit up in a big smile, followed quickly by a look of consternation when he couldn't decide whether I had complimented or insulted him. I didn't stick around to find out.

Other Types of Good Conflict

As conflict often follows in the wake of a teenager, prudent parents learn early on to discern the different types of conflicts. That is, some conflict is good, even healthy. When, as in the story just told, your teenager argues as a means of showing off his newfound thinking skills or as a means of improving his ability to engage and debate, conflict is good. Your job is to understand the conflict for what it is—not take it personally—and to acknowledge his growing abilities, then move on.

When he argues because he is standing up for something he believes in, that is good, too. (For more on this, see Chapter 8, "Self-Esteem Through Integrity.") This is when you hear him out, state your own view, and hear him out again. You don't take his choice personally (it's his life), but you do take his willingness to stand up for what he believes in and let the chips fall where they may very personally—you've done a good job as a parent. In these instances, especially when it involves breaking an agreed-upon rule, he'll take his consequences without whining. This can happen when he's late for curfew because he made sure a friend got home safely, or when he skipped a class to console a friend. Yes, he broke his agreement, and yes he needs to handle the consequences, and yes you are proud of him for taking a stand that is important to him, and yes he still has to handle the consequences.

When she argues because she is overwhelmed, it might be good if you are razor sharp. That is, if you realize as the conflict begins that how she is carrying on is not like her, you stand a better chance of sidestepping the battle. This successful parry would include:

1. You withstand her initial onslaught without engaging her by going on a counterattack.
2. When she's done, you do nothing—neither defend yourself nor attack.
3. You make your process transparent by asking a question: *This doesn't seem like you, honey. There must be something else going on. Are you feeling overwhelmed somewhere in your life?*
4. You vacate the premises, leaving her to answer the question on her own.

In these instances, success hinges on discerning the different flavors of conflict with your teenager. That is, when the conflict isn't about trying to bully or manipulate you, you can make lots of headway toward strengthening and renewing the connection between the two of you. You do this by not engaging them at the level of conflict they bring to the table. You refuse to play the game. You also understand, at a deep level, that for the connection to grow stronger through conflict, you must move from *win–lose* thinking to *win–win* thinking, or at least to *no lose–no lose* thinking. In examples like these, your teenager will not thank you or appreciate everything you are doing. Your measured responses will, however, over time establish a trust in you from your daughter. She knows that you'll be there for her and that you accept her no matter who she is that day. This is the basis of a strong connection in any relationship.

Still, though, it is Pollyannaish to believe that every conflict is manageable without getting into it. The truth is, sometimes you do need to get into it with your teenager because sometimes she needs to know where you really stand on an issue. Sometimes she needs to see how you stand up for yourself. (This is frequently what happens when your teenager uses foul language with you. Often, she is subjected to this kind of treatment outside the home, and this is the best way she has of asking for help; it translates not to *Tell me how to deal with this*, but to *Show me how to deal with this.*)

In these situations, you simply do your best not to overreact. And then, after you've overreacted, you clean up what you've added to the mess. Conflict is never comforting, but depending on its flavor and your response, it can bring the two of you closer. And when you do blow it, even if just a little bit, always apologize.

In a 2009 experiment by Duke University professor Dan Ariely,[2] researchers hired an actor to interact with customers in a local coffee shop. The actor asked customers to find matching letters from several sheets of paper and promised each participant $5 for completing the task. Upon completion, he handed them a stack of singles and had them sign a receipt—and then he "mistakenly" overpaid them by $2, $3, or $4. The results were quite depressing: Only 45 percent of the participants returned or acknowledged the extra money.

In this case, however, Ariely was testing for what he called the "annoyance" factor. In a variation of the first experiment, the actor received a phone call from a friend about pizza in the middle of his conversation with the customer. The call lasted 15 seconds. At the conclusion of the phone call, he simply continued with his instructions to the customer. The focus of the experiment was to see if and to what extent rude treatment affected the honesty of the participants. Only 14 percent of the participants gave the extra money back, or a reduction in honesty by a whopping 31 percent!

In a final variation of the experiment, the actor, after receiving the phone call, offered a quick apology for the interruption and continued with his instructions. With this simple acknowledgement, the honesty jumped back up to 45 percent.[3]

The point of the apology is to invite back into the conversation the best self of your teenager—to reconnect before moving forward. Also, in any conflict with a teenager we usually share at least a small portion of the blame, so there is almost always room for a quick apology. By the way, this same strategy is equally successful with spouses. There is one final, positive aspect of conflict that is important to recognize, and it does not reveal itself easily. Sometimes, they need to get the better of you in an argument. They need to see and feel that they can influence your thinking. Think about it for a moment. Adolescence is about launching into adulthood, which means learning to think and stand up for oneself. But if mom and dad are 100 percent right all the time how do teenagers develop confidence in their own opinions, insights, and beliefs? And don't worry, there will be plenty of times where their thinking will cause you to reconsider, or at least expand your thinking.

Weird to admit it, but sometimes my son has some insightful thoughts in the midst of one of our arguments. Whether it is a rationale to stay out beyond curfew, how to fix something around our house, or what to do on a family night. At first I was in denial about it all, claiming my authority as a parent—

more like my dad than I care to admit—but then I realized how much it meant to him for me to acknowledge his point of view and to change my mind.

The bottom line is that although much of the conflict we experience with our teenagers is almost inevitable, sometimes that conflict is valuable to the emergent adult we are working to cultivate and celebrate.

Abstract Thinking and the Big Talks

Whenever we are under stress or pressure, we tend to regress. For example, think about the last time you had to speak in front of a group of people. Beforehand, if you're like most, you were probably regressed to some aspect of concrete thinking that left you doing the same mundane task over and over: folding and refolding your speech; checking the pleats in your pants; saying the first line of your speech over and over again; going to the bathroom every few minutes. This is anxiety manifested into something that is seemingly controllable. We do these kinds of concrete actions when we're nervous or under stress, in part because we can move out of the concrete thinking of these actions and into the world of abstract thinking at a moment's notice. In a way, this momentary shift back to concrete thinking and action allows us to catch our breath as we prepare for what is just around the corner. If for some reason we can't make that shift back and forth, well, that's called "choking" in the sports world and "stage fright" in the theater. Two possibilities we try to eradicate from our minds when in these situations.

For teenagers, the relationship between stress and regression is a bit different from what adults experience. As mentioned earlier, most teens are comfortable and conversant in the world of abstract thought by their sophomore year. Before they are securely settled into abstract thinking, however, they have still had many experiences with it along the way: in class, with friends, at home. During these times, for one reason or another, they have had access to abstract reasoning. This is wonderful. When you're around, this is when they see the big picture, make leaps of growth, and make perceptive insights. As we will see in Chapter 5, "Mastery over Compliance," one of the times and reasons teenagers gain access to higher thought is when they are with you and thinking about an area that is important to them. That is, they are intermittently able to tune into your abstract thinking and pull themselves along in your wake.

This is vital to remember when you have the so-called big talks—drugs, alcohol, sex, Internet use, violence, body image, driving, safety. That is, when they are with you and having one of these discussions (at least if you can get past the first few awkward moments), they can access their highest levels of thinking. This is when they can see and articulate the wisdom that every parent longs to hear: why it is best to wait until they are older to have sex, why drinking and drugs are bad for them, and the stupidity of drinking and driving, to name a few favorites.

For the sake of argument, let's suppose you have a wonderful conversation with your son about drug use. It would go something like this: You bring up the subject. He rolls his eyes. You persist and ask him to sit down. Your voice cracks, but you continue with your well-rehearsed first few paragraphs. You notice he seems to listen, almost in spite of himself. You ask a question. He grows fidgety. You stay quiet. He begins to talk. You listen. He asks a question. You respond. He continues talking, making all the wonderful connections you had yearned to hear him make. Later on, long after you have finished the conversation, you feel proud of yourself for having done such a great job as a parent and you reflect on all that transpired: about how he at first resisted the conversation but by the end was a full participant, even assuring you that he does not use drugs nor does he have plans to. It went better than you had hoped. And you go to bed assured that your son will not use drugs.

In the vernacular of this chapter, when you began the conversation, your son was in concrete thinking; and then over the course of that talk—with time, the topic, and your presence—he fully entered the world of abstract reasoning and stayed there throughout the duration of your discussion, most notably at the conclusion of the talk. This evolution to more mature thinking from the start of the talk to the end indeed confirms the confidence you have that your son will not try drugs in the near future.

Not so fast. Although your son may not want to use drugs, and may even think less of peers who do use them, he is still vulnerable to using drugs, despite the quality of your discussion and the thoughtfulness of his responses. This is where the limits of his abstract thinking abilities collide with the natural stress of adolescence. That is, the first few times he is confronted with the choice to use or not, and there are many of these times in every teenager's life—on an over-night field trip with the astronomy club, at a party trying to impress a romantic interest, at a friend's house—a momentary panic sets in. The need to make this choice naturally leads to a temporary regression in his thinking (which for an adolescent knocks him out of abstract thought and back into concrete thinking); then, because of the fragility of his abstract thinking abilities, he in all likelihood loses the ability to shift back into his abstract reasoning powers, at least during the moment of the critical decision. In other words, remember that great conversation you had about not using drugs? Well, as it stands, in the moment when he needs it most, he does not have access to that discussion. Once he regresses to concrete thinking, he loses most of what you two discussed when he had access to his abstract reasoning. Now, when he really needs to remember what he said and felt with you, he is at a loss. It is in moments like this that far too many teenagers say yes to activities they would otherwise not engage in.

> I was against drinking all through high school. I mean, I wasn't a goody-two-shoes or anything, I just thought it was stupid to go and get drunk every weekend. I had a few drinks now and again, but I never got drunk, and more often than not never even drank anything. I was also one of the peer mentors, and as a junior worked with a group of freshmen in social living class about choices in high school. You know, drugs, alcohol, sex, cars.
>
> Then, one night, I'm at this party at some guy's house. I went with a buddy of mine who disappeared as soon as we got there. Since I'm basically kind of shy, I was pretty uncomfortable. Then this girl I'm talking to asks me if I want to play a drinking game with her and some friends. Before I can even think about it, I hear myself saying, "Sure." A couple of hours later, I was wasted and having unprotected sex in the back of my car with this girl whose name I couldn't even remember. What a way to lose my virginity! Especially after everything I've told the freshmen all year—I basically ignored every piece of advice I believe in and gave them.

Teenagers mistakenly believe that they'll have plenty of warning before they are invited to use drugs or alcohol. Somehow, they imagine seeing these pressures riding in on the horizon and giving them plenty of time to get out of the way or to prepare themselves with the appropriate responses. They are wrong.

Your teenager's limited abstract reasoning abilities under stress mean that there is one more step you must add to your series of big talks—you have to go back to concrete thinking and concrete conversation before the conclusion of such discussions. When your teenager needs access to this talk, he in all likelihood is thinking concretely, so make sure all the insights from the abstract talk are translated back into concrete terms by the end of the conversation.

> Steven, it's great to know that you are clear about your stance on drug use. It makes me proud and relieved. But at the same time I'm wondering if you could help me just a bit more? Can you tell me five different ways you might say no to someone who offered drugs to you or pressured you to use?

At this point, no self-respecting teenager is going to jump to your rescue by reciting five ways of saying no. Instead, they'll go back to rolling their eyes. Be prepared.

I know, to you it seems that I'm treating you like a little kid, which you are not. But that's not so. The reality is that I need to hear your voice saying no a bunch of different ways, because in my head I'm going to make a recording of you saying all this. Then, when you're a little late for curfew or using the car on a weekend night, I can quell my nerves by playing the recording of you saying no in a bunch of different ways. This will reassure me, which in turn means I'll give you some more time before I come looking for you in the other car or call the police in desperation. So what do you say?

Most teenagers are more than happy to give you more than five ways of saying no at this point, and not just to stop you from calling the police at one minute past the curfew. Their motivation is much more than simple self-interest. It's in moments like this that they realize they can take care of you in more ways than they realized, and need to do so. In this instance, you are dependent on your child, which appeals to the emergent adult in your teenager. Not only that, but with the tables switched like this, her taking care of your needs strengthens the connection between the two of you. That is, she comes through for you during your moment of vulnerability, which in any relationship brings the two parties closer.

Perhaps the best developmental example I've seen of this shift back to concrete thinking around these big talks happened a couple of years ago when I was visiting a middle school in Connecticut. All the seventh graders had traced their hands onto construction paper and made cutouts of both hands. On the palms, they wrote the name of a substance they could imagine feeling pressured to try: cigarettes, alcohol, drugs. Then, on each finger, they wrote a different way to say no. The responses ranged from the direct to the silly to the creative: *No thanks, not tonight. No, I'm from another planet and alcohol makes me violent. No, I'm allergic to alcohol—it makes my skin break out in hives.* Best of all, these hands were all hung at eye level throughout the seventh-grade corridor, almost like an art gallery. When the kids walked down the hall, they looked from hand to hand and read all the different ways to say no, and thus loaded up their memory banks with the concrete responses they could imagine working for them. It was beautiful. I just hope the school took advantage of this project by inviting the parents into the school to peruse their children's artwork and to see, in their seventh-grader's words, what they needed from their parents on this all-important topic.

Learn to Think Like an Anthropologist

Anthropology is the study of human beings: their race, physical character, social relations, and culture. In this regard, if you've ever spent time with an anthropologist who was wearing her anthropology hat, you know how fascinating and interesting you feel when her focus is on you. That is, she will ask you all sorts of questions you have never before considered but that are essential to how you live your life and what you believe. These are the kinds of questions that linger for days and weeks, so that the next time you bump into this person—in line at the grocery store, at a soccer game, at church—you're liable to blurt out what's been mulling in the back of your head since the last time you spoke. *You know, I've been thinking about what you asked the last time we spoke, and . . .*

In this regard, parents of teenagers have a lot to learn from anthropologists. In essence, we need to learn to ask better and different questions, and then give our teenagers time to mull. Many of the questions we ask our kids are polite ways of asking for reports or executive summaries. *How was school? Did you finish your English paper on time? How did you do on the chemistry test? Did you win the basketball game? How much did you play? How many points did you score?* If your teenager is like most teenagers, then 90 percent of the time all you'll get is a one-word response to any of these queries: *Good. Yeah. Okay. Yeah. Some. A few.* Remember, from the teenagers' perspective, the less information they impart to their parents, the better. When in doubt, they stay vague, especially when it's the stuff of parental evaluations. And, perhaps surprisingly, most teenagers realize that this extends not only to incriminating information but to flattering facts, too. That is, they know that if they respond only in specifics when it makes them look good, you will notice this and push them even more to reveal the details when they are vague. So in the interests of self-preservation, privacy, and independence, most teenagers opt for ambiguity with their parents.

For parents, this means we need to ask better and different questions, and thinking more along the lines of an anthropologist is a good start. If you want to encourage your teenager to think, possibly even to respond, you need to think more about process and less about outcome. Business is based on outcome. Education is based on process, and when it comes to the connection between you and your teenager, education is the best game in town. If you take another look at the typical parent questions from the preceding paragraph, you will take only a moment to realize that they are all outcome-based questions that require nothing more than a one-sentence response at best. And for reasons noted already, you may not even get that. Although nothing is wrong with these questions (and please understand that I'm not suggesting we not hold kids to certain goals, achievements, and the like), they will seldom start the kinds of conversations you need to have with your teenager if you are going to have a strong connection to each other. Let's take some time, then, to look at how these process questions work across a range of activities and interests: academics, sports and performances, and school applications.

Academics

Imagine that you attended a talk about academics led by the principal or head at your teenager's school. Specifically, the evening was about what you could do to contribute to the scholastic life of your teenager. Now imagine that at the outset of this presentation, the person in charge said something along the following lines: *Actually, we have two different presentations tonight: one in Auditorium A and the other in Auditorium B. It's up to you to decide which one you want to attend. The talk in Auditorium A is for parents who want their kids to get all A's through school. The talk in Auditorium B is for parents who want their kids to learn to love learning. There is no time for questions, so please choose, either Auditorium A or Auditorium B.*

Where would you go? Although few, if any, parents would not want their children to earn all A's through school, most would still choose Auditorium B because parents understand that students who learn to love learning will, in intrinsic motivation, curiosity, and, later on, in job performance, surpass those who work only for grades. Not only that, but if kids do indeed come to love learning, they'll earn good grades, too. Therefore, sharp parents look to schools and teachers to instill a love of learning in their children.

Yet, even though most of us would choose Auditorium B, most of us act as if we had gone to Auditorium A. Think about it. Few of our conversations and questions address our kids' love of learning; instead, most of us simply ask for status reports. The parents who go to Auditorium B, and behave that way, understand the difference between process and outcome; they fall squarely on love of learning in how they talk to their teenagers about academics, school, and grades. They ask their kids questions that require their kids to investigate themselves and their learning process.

How did you do on the math test? is replaced, or at least supplemented, with *Was it a good test?* Most teenagers will give you a strange look when you first ask this last question, and then respond by telling you the grade they got on the test. It takes them a while to figure out what you're asking, that you haven't made a mistake. *No, not what grade you got, but was it a good test? You know, when a test is good, it forces you to learn more, to put together what you already know in new ways. A good test is one in which you learn something. So, was it a good test?*

Or, instead of just asking if she finished the paper or what grade she received, you ask about the process of writing the paper: *Where did you get stuck? How did you get through it? Did your ideas for the paper come in a flurry, or gradually, over time? Did you surprise yourself at all by what you wrote? How?* Now the focus is on the discovery that happens through the engagement of writing, not the mere opinion of a teacher. That is, you help your teenager form her own opinion of her writing through self-examination. But it's a self-examination that you guide her through, much as an anthropologist guides you through some of what she asks.

When you ask these types of questions, you need to be careful how you judge their relative effectiveness. That is, often your teenager will not have a response ready, but this is in no way a sign of a failed inquiry or a bad question. More often, it's the hallmark of an interesting question that has grabbed her attention; but given the inherent narcissism of this age, the question prevents her from saying so and from wrestling with the question in your company. But once you leave, or once she retreats to her room, that's when she'll tackle your query in earnest. Parents must therefore learn to give the question time to percolate before judging its effectiveness because the response might show up days later during a car ride or late-night conversation.

Athletics and Performances

When you pick up your teenager from a game, the approach discussed above is equally valuable and illuminative. Of course, you still ask the standard questions: *Who won? Did you play much? Did you play well?* In general, kids will talk much more about the game they have just finished than about their most recent paper or chemistry test. If they're talkative, stay quiet and listen; if not, try a few of the more anthropological questions. *When were you the most focused in today's game? How come?* Or, *When the referee made a bad call in the third quarter I watched you go from angry to calm; what was that all about?* (That's a key piece of this approach: observing carefully.) Or, *Seemed as if Chris got down on herself after that second goal got by her; what did you say to her to snap her out of it?* Or, *Even though you were down ten points with just under two minutes to go, you refused to give up. What were you saying to yourself?*

As with the academic questions, your teenager probably won't have a quick response to any of these questions. That's good, as it means she has to dig deeper into herself to find an answer.

Another way of understanding this line of questioning comes from Jerome Bruner,[4] who, when discussing writing, describes two types of plots that occur in a story: a plot of action and a plot of consciousness. The plot of action follows what occurs in the plot: who says what, where the action occurs, and what literally happens. The plot of consciousness, however, reflects what is going on in the various characters' heads: how they come to certain conclusions, what assumptions they are working from, and the internal emotions and dialogues they are having. The plot of consciousness is always the more engaging and insightful of the two, both when it comes to books and to your teenager. So thinking like an anthropologist means asking questions that tap into your teenager's plot of consciousness.

This anthropological approach is just as productive in areas of performance as it is with athletics. In a dramatic or musical production, the process and plot of consciousness are right on the surface; you just have to scratch a bit. *When the guitarist ended his solo earlier than expected, how did you manage to recover so well? What was it like to get that ovation when you and the other dancers came out for your final bow? Were you expecting it? Did any part of tonight's performance surprise you? Who surprised you by how well they did tonight?*

If nothing else, this line of questioning appeals directly to the narcissism in your teenager; so, even if these questions don't come naturally to you, your teenager will cut you slack. After all, you're asking your teenager about the most fascinating person in the world—at least in her eyes.

High School and College Applications

A few years ago, a high school teacher told me how she uses this approach when talking to seniors who are applying for college:

> If you want to engage a high school senior in a conversation, one of the worst questions to ask is *Where do you want to go to college next year?* Whenever confronted with this question, students' faces glaze over and their voices go flat and become a monotone. It's almost as if they had dissociated and put an old recording in place of any conscious connection or thought: *Well, I'm applying to State because it's nearby. And I'm applying to Ivy Institute because it's a great school, even though it's so far away. And I'm applying to . . .* It's almost the same patter for all kids. At first, these thoughts had meaning, but with time they have just come to fill the space as the kids go on automatic pilot and keep adults at a safe distance from their vulnerable feelings about going to college (and leaving high school, too).

Think about it from the teenager's perspective. If they tell you where they're applying and get their hopes up, then in six months when they hear from the same colleges, they'll need to share their disappointments and failures with you. Most teenagers avoid this kind of vulnerability.

Instead, I do the anthropological thing with them. I ask them what it's like to apply to college. What's the most difficult part? What's it like asking teachers for recommendations? What's it like to write the essay: Do you do it in one sitting? According to a timeline and plan? Do you consult your parents? Do you wait until the last minute? How are you at budgeting your time to complete all the applications, especially given your full schedule as a high school senior?

Recently, I met with a former student who had graduated from college the week before, and she instantly related to what the above teacher had to say about the typical questions a high school senior is asked about college. However, at the other end of her college career, she said the same phenomenon happens, only now it's under the heading of *So what are your career plans after college?* As I nodded and smiled to myself, she added, "That's why I have a fake plan. You know, what I tell people when they ask about my future plans just to get them to stop asking. Mine is about taking a year off and then going to law school or getting an MBA; my best friend's fake plan is about becoming a teacher. But the truth is, neither one of us has any idea what we are going to do."

Asking questions about process is always an effective approach with your teenager, no matter what the activity or subject. This line of questioning engages him, which in turn strengthens your connection. One warning, though: Use this approach to supplement the conversations you already have with your teenager, not to replace them; it's hard to talk and think that way all the time. That is, sometimes all he wants and needs to do is shoot the breeze without thinking too much.

Your Teenager's Friends, the Ones You Don't Like

Appreciating your teenager's narcissistic tendencies and the power of process questions allows parents to approach the topic of their teenager's friends in a new way; in particular, the friends that you don't like and that you feel are a bad influence on your teenager. We all know that once you tell your teenager that you don't like one of her friends, it's paramount to pushing her into a closer friendship. But, at the same time, not voicing your concerns and observations makes you feel that you are failing at your job of raising a healthy child. Fortunately, there is a middle ground, but first let's look at why trying to break up the friendship and doing nothing are both doomed to ultimate failure.

Because of her narcissism, as soon as you criticize her friend, she has to defend that person and prove you wrong. But it's more that she has to prove to herself that her initial opinion of this person as worthy of her friendship was correct. In her narcissism, she can't allow herself to recognize an error of judgment in something so important as friendship. In this regard, she is preserving her independence, too.

One day, I told Lester (fifteen at the time) that I didn't want him hanging out with Sean and Victor as much. I explained that they were a bad influence on him, that he could do better. Well, you would think I had insulted him. Within seconds, he was vehemently defending them, even to the point of saying things that I knew weren't true—that both were honor students and loyal to him.

It totally backfired, and for the next few months Lester, Sean, and Victor were inseparable. And whenever I came close to commenting on them or their behavior, Lester gave me a dirty look, cut me off, and went on to praise the virtues of his buddies. At one point, I realized it wasn't about Sean and Victor; it was about Lester and me, and who had the power. Or, at least, about which one of us was a better judge of character.

On the other hand, saying and doing nothing is not a sensible or viable alternative. Doing nothing is the equivalent of abdicating your responsibility, which never fortifies your connection to your teenager. Perhaps some parents can justify saying nothing on the grounds that their kids already know how they feel about their friends, but somehow that isn't quite good enough. Yes, your teenagers can read you like a book. And yes, they already know how you feel about their friends before you utter a word. But still, this is one of those times you must weigh in. Just make sure that you appreciate their narcissism when you do so.

When you comment on her friends, you inadvertently insult your daughter and her ability to choose friends, and it creates a disconnect. But because she is so focused on herself, keep your feedback directed toward her, not toward her friends. This strategy keeps you connected and represents your best chance of getting through to her.

> "You seem to have changed quite a bit in the last month, Sarah."
> "Really? Why do you say that?"
> "Well, you just don't seem yourself, not as happy and carefree as usual."
> "Really? Guess that's life."
> "Maybe. You just don't seem to enjoy things the way you used to: your friends; your brother, Geoff; even playing soccer. Not sure, but something seems to have changed in the last month."
> "Whatever."
> "Any pressure at school?"
> "No."
> "Anything at home bothering you?"
> "No. What is this, Twenty Questions?"
> "No, just trying to figure out what's different. I know some of your friendships have shifted, but that shouldn't matter because friends should bring out the best in you, right?"

"Yeah."

"I don't know, you've just changed somehow. Can't put my finger on it, though."

It's frustrating not to come right out and say it, but if you just line up the dots and let your teenager connect them on her own time, you are both better off. When she connects the dots, it's now her doing and her insight, so she is free to act on her improved judgment—better yet, she'll openly share this new and improved judgment with you. *Stephanie is different from me, more than I had realized at first. I just haven't felt that I could be myself around her, so we're not as close as we used to be.* (Just hold your tongue; one *I told you so* will undermine everything.) But again, as with the anthropological questions, it takes time for her to connect the dots, sometimes months. Be patient. If you can hang in there, you will win on both counts: You have real input and you stay connected. Better yet, your daughter wins on both counts, too: she makes better friends and she stays connected to you.

*   *   *

In many ways, it all comes down to what Nobel laureate Isidor Isaac Rabi's mother used to ask him each day when he came home from school: "Did you ask any good questions today?" This is something to bear in mind when you spend time with your teenager, and also at the end of the day when you're looking into the mirror and assessing how well you're doing in your role as a parent.

THREE

Give Up on Lectures and Advice

There is probably no more unsettling realization for the parents of teenagers than coming to grips with the reality that all your hard-earned advice, wisdom, and life lessons are falling on deaf ears. Much to your chagrin, your teenagers seem to want no part of what you have to offer. Even though, in your mind at least, you are different from how your parents were when you were a teenager; in that regard, you believe you have lots of useful information to offer.

Most parents, however, don't take the refusal of their advice so easily. Despite our teenagers' protestations, we continue to offer our advice and lecture them, even if we're sure they aren't listening. We can't stop ourselves. We don't know what else to do, and the idea of doing nothing and sitting powerless on the sidelines isn't an option. Of course, the impulse to "help" is good as long as we learn to use this energy in a slightly different and more indirect route. A much more effective route.

In Chapter 2, we looked at the inherent narcissism of adolescents (which definitely contributes to their ignoring our sage wisdom), and in this chapter we'll see why a regular patter of lectures and advice falls on deaf ears. First, let's take a hard look at the first cousin of adolescent narcissism: the push for independence.

Independence

A hallmark of teenagers is the need to establish their independence as they forge a stable identity for themselves. A tall order for any age—and one that most adults have yet to fulfill—yet teenagers think they can and must fulfill this quest, and usually in a semester's time. Few engage in this quest in an orderly manner. As in many other areas of their lives, teenagers are apt to exaggerate and push too hard in their insistence upon independence, especially with their parents. This is because the best way they know of to establish a sense of independence is to push away the people they have been dependent upon for so long: mom and dad.

This stage is never graceful or elegant, and it is frequently punctuated with many mixed messages—the sort of "go away and come here" double communications that teenagers are famous for and that drive their parents crazy.

> He's like a two-headed monster, and each time we interact, I have to figure out which head is speaking, and fast! One part of him demands to be treated like an independent adult at every turn. Buying clothes for him turns into an argument in which he accuses me of trying to control him. Me, I was just trying to do a nice thing by buying him a new pair of jeans; but for him, you would think I was trying to micromanage his every move.
>
> Then an hour later he wants to know if I'll wash his uniform for his game later that day. And, of course, if I try to connect the dots for him between the mixed messages—wanting near total independence and needing me to take care of his laundry—he looks at me as if I were from another planet and simply says, "Mom, I don't want another lecture. I just want to know if you are going to wash my uniform or not."

In staying connected to your teenager, you need to understand how this need for independence shows itself at different times and how to recognize it for what it is—normal, healthy adolescent development. You also need to know how it permanently changes some of the ways you used to communicate with your teenager, lectures and advice topping the list. But don't give up hope, when some lines of communication become tangled because of independence issues, other lines, in fact, are opening.

Lectures

Most of us fondly remember when our teenagers were children, when they listened to our character and teaching lectures—or at least politely pretended to listen. Even though they were in trouble for some misbehavior, they still paid attention to what you had to say. Those teaching moments were as important to you as they were to them. We knew that our words were making a difference in our kids' lives.

When it comes to your kids as teenagers, you need to realize that most of what you have to lecture them about they've heard from you before, in earlier lectures. This isn't to say you shouldn't lecture your kids; it's just not the best approach all the time. There are times, however, when their transgressions are especially frightening, and they need to hear and understand the heat of what you're feeling.

> I'll never forget the look on my dad's face when he figured out that my sister and I were going to have a party at the house on the weekend that he and my mom were going away. He was as angry as I've ever seen him, but at the same time as sad as I've ever seen him. It's one of the only times I can remember him yelling at me. He was furious. I don't even remember what he said, and I guess it didn't really matter. But what got to me was the hurt behind it all. It was as if he were seeing a part of me that he didn't want to have to see—a part of me that utterly disappointed him. It was awful. I just broke into tears. I never want him to look at me like that again.

Interactions like this are memorable for parents and teenagers alike as long as they aren't the everyday mode of communicating. This is when, for parents, the boy who cried wolf takes on new meaning. If at every misstep you yell, lecture, or pontificate, your teenager will come to see you as the parent who cried wolf, which is a profound loss for both of you. Now you've lost your ability to make a difference on the really big decisions. When everything is treated as vital and crucial, then in your teenager's mind nothing is vital or crucial.

Taken to the extreme, this constant lecturing takes on an almost comical twist. Listen to one counselor's experience of working with a family whose dad was the quintessential lecturer:

> I'll never forget the first counseling meeting I had with one family—the mom and the dad, their sixteen-year-old son and thirteen-year-old daughter. When I asked everyone why they were there, the mom and dad talked about the breakdown in communications between them and their teenaged children. The kids said they were there because their parents had made them come.
>
> We were getting nowhere fast, so after a few minutes I asked the parents to step into the waiting room while I talked to the kids. With the mom and dad out of the room, I asked the children whether there was anything they wanted to share with me. Silence, followed by some uncomfortable fidgeting. After a few more equally unsuccessful attempts, we sat in silence for a few moments. Then, out of the blue, I asked: "Does your dad lecture you much?"
>
> The sixteen-year-old twitched, and his sister leaned forward.
>
> "I ask because he seems like the kind of guy who would. At least, that's what I got from meeting with you as a family for the first twenty minutes."

Then the girl said to her brother, "Should we tell him?"

"No."

"Should you tell me what?"

"I'm going to tell him." Her brother moaned. "My dad is the king of lecturers. He's a professor, what do you expect? Anyway, Todd [her brother] and I are so bored by the same old lectures that one day we numbered them. So now when he goes into lecture mode, we say either to one another or to ourselves, 'Dad started with number five today, he'll probably shift to number eight after that and finish with number two as a closer.'"

I was shocked, but then I smiled. "How well do you know his lectures? Think you could replicate one of them for me?"

Both of them were now on board, and in unison they said, "Sure." To make a long story short, they spoke a couple of sample lectures into a tape recorder for me. Then we brought their mom and dad back into the consulting room. I figured I had enough rapport with the parents for what I did next. Fortunately, I was right. I had the parents sit down while we played the tape of their teenagers reciting their father's lectures.

About two minutes into the first one, the dad raised his hand, leaned forward, and softly said, "I've heard enough. I get the point. It's just that I don't know what else to do when you guys misbehave. Guess I'm just scared is all."

From there we had lots to talk about. The family began to work together to come up with alternatives to the dad's lectures and for everyone to brainstorm more productive ways for both parents to have input and influence with their teenagers.

Lectures are not very effective for improving your connection to your teenager. The next time you shift into this mode with your teenager, watch him closely. You'll see all the signs of someone dissociating from the moment: eyes fixed in space and glazed over, fidgeting (or the opposite, complete stillness), and a slack jaw. In these moments, most teenagers either get angry or check out to another time and place, usually away from the person delivering the lecture. When you notice this happening with your teenager, your best bet is to stop talking. You are going nowhere fast. Better to cut your losses then and there and hope for a fresh start the next time around.

Teenagers have a way of making sane parents intermittently insane. This is why we often resort to lectures—it's the civilized alternative to hitting our kids. In those cases—when lecturing helps you cool down—lecture away. Physical force with your teenager will only sever whatever connection and influence you have in his life. During the rest of the time, however, consider some of the alternatives to lecturing spelled out later in this chapter, as well as in Chapters 8 and 13.

Advice

Given the inherent narcissism of adolescents and their drive to establish independence, it's easy to see why your advice is no longer solicited or appreciated. Remember a few years ago, when he solicited your advice on a range of subjects: how to fix the flat tire on his bike, how to stand up for himself when friends tease one another, when to practice the piano? Now, during adolescence, when the stakes have risen and your advice is more valuable than ever, he has turned a deaf ear.

Take a moment to consider how the drive toward independence influences your teenager's openness to your advice. Every time he asks your advice (and every teenager does seek the advice of his parents, at least a few times, during adolescence) he is undercutting his own independence. That is, at a time in life when autonomy is most important, he is setting himself up to remain dependent on you (on your advice and greater wisdom), the same person he is trying to persuade to see him as independent. Talk about a Catch-22! That's why one moment he is earnest in seeking your advice, and the next he is frustrated and feels compelled to reject whatever you have to offer. For him, each rebuff restores his temporarily lost sense of independence, which was in jeopardy when he sought out your input in the first place.

> I know it must drive my mom nuts, but I can't help myself. When I ask for her advice, I really want to hear what she has to say. I never ask lightly; it's usually only after I've been confused and stuck for a while. So by the time I ask, I really need the advice. But it never fails—as soon as she opens her mouth, I feel as if I were nine years old again, which I hate! I immediately stop listening and begin to point out to her how her advice is all wrong. If she insists on continuing to offer input, or defends what she has already said, I get angry with her for trying to run my life.
>
> I know, it's crazy, and I sort of say that to myself as I walk away and curse her under my breath. It's just that I can't help myself.

It's strange, but just because your daughter rejects your advice does not mean that she ignores it. Once she hears what you have to say and rejects it—either by pointing out what is wrong with what you have to say or by allowing herself to feel insulted by your wanting to control her life—she is free to discover the usefulness of your advice on her own down the road. Yes, the suggestion you made about how to deliver that difficult feedback to her friend was rejected out of hand. But then, two weeks later, she might stumble upon that same idea and attribute it to herself. Now the idea serves her growing autonomy in the world, not her regressed dependence on you. That is, she thinks it is her idea. So when she tells you how she resolved the problem, don't you dare try to reclaim credit for the idea. Instead, smile and nod your head—a lot. Let her show off her independence to you and to take the credit. She will not get a big head from all this, and, best of all, the connection between the two of you will grow stronger and deeper.

The bottom line is that when your teenager asks your advice, beware. If you freely give it, expect initial rejection, which, ironically, frees her up to make use of your advice later on. If you hold it back unreasonably, then she'll feel abandoned; so tread lightly, because abandonment is the last feeling you want to instill in your teenager. Your best bet is to ask her questions about what she has done so far. Get her talking. Then at the end of that, if she is still around, give her the advice she asked for. Just be concise.

There is, however, the exception to the rule; this occurs when your teenager solicits your advice, listens, and then makes use of your wisdom. This does happen occasionally, but the emotions that accompany what seems like the most natural and pleasant of interchanges between parent and teenager are toxic. Reflecting for a moment on the central role of their burgeoning independence helps to clarify the emotional undercurrent that happens when your teenager listens to and follows through on your advice.

He asks you about some problem that has him befuddled. He seems sincere in his request, and, as luck would have it, this is an area where you have quite a bit of experience. You pause and he remains attentive, so you go ahead and give your advice. He seems, in his own adolescent-indifferent way, to hang on to your every word. He doesn't interrupt or contradict you as you speak, and when you have finished he sort of nods to you and walks away. You're confused. Did he really listen or was he being polite? At that moment, there is no way to tell for certain.

The next day, you inquire about the problem he was having. *How's it going with Rickie? Did you take my advice?* Your son is back to his old self, because his responses are of the one- or two-word variety. *Okay. Yeah.* He worked it out with Rickie. He actually took your advice! *Well, how did it work? Are you guys still friends or what?* Not only are his responses clipped, but, no matter how excited you get, his emotional response is rigidly flat. *You must be happy, aren't you? Glad to see you are still friends.* At this point, you realize the conversation is over, because either he walks away or he somehow gives you the cold shoulder.

Now you are confused. Why isn't he happy and thanking you for the advice? Over the next few hours, though, you will not have the time to ponder these questions because your son is busy picking a fight with you over some innocuous matter: He's sloppy while washing the car and accidentally lets the water spray through the screens into your bedroom; he's unnecessarily abrupt and rough with his younger sister and she's complaining to you about him; he ponders his next snack way too long and with the refrigerator door wide open. He gets your goat and makes you react to one thing or another. Once you do respond—and usually not in a calm, collected way—the scene quickly deteriorates as he alternates between grumbling, defending, attacking, and whining. He's acting like a spoiled little child, and just when you expected his gratitude for helping him resolve a tense issue with his close friend Rickie. At this point, the interaction usually ends with parent and teenager going in opposite directions and mumbling about the other under their breath.

Believe it or not, this is a normal reaction after a teenager has taken and successfully used your advice. What's going on is that by soliciting and following your advice, he has made himself unduly dependent on you at a time of life when independence is sacred. The best way he knows to recover from this momentary lapse is to exaggerate his sense of independence, and picking a fight with you and holding his ground (whether he is right or wrong) is the classic way for a teenager to do this. At the end of the fight, his sense of independence has been restored. Sure, there is a cost—some confusion on your part and perhaps a few bad feelings—but that's all secondary to his independence. Plus, to add insult to injury, he expects that you know the fight was nothing personal. At least, that's how he takes it, which is why an hour later, while you're still stewing over the argument, your teenager has moved on without a backward glance.

When you do find you have given advice to a teenager who wants it and needs it, here's one practical idea to keep in mind: Expect the exaggerated reclamation of independence through some sort of argument like that described above. Then when it happens, try as much as you can to see what it's all about—independence—so that you don't take it personally. If you can keep your equilibrium through this, then your connection with your teenager grows enormously. He learns that he can count on you to understand what he can't say and doesn't yet understand himself.

Advice about Advice

I like the following suggestion offered by the mom of three teenagers:

> My rule on advice giving is to make my kids ask three times before I make any suggestions. If they have the perseverance to ask three times, I figure they are serious—I'm right about 50 percent of the time.

When your teenager asks your advice, remind yourself that what she really wants is not your wisdom, but your presence. (See Chapter 5, "Mastery over Compliance," for more on this.) She just doesn't know how to ask for this more subtle form of support, which is why she asks for something that is more familiar: advice. It's the best she can do.

Fortunately, the best you can do is better and subtler than what they bring to the table. Here are a few ideas to keep in mind the next time your teenager asks for your advice:

1. Whatever the issue, acknowledge that it's a difficult topic. Even if the situation is one that you see clear through, you need to slow down and realize that from her perspective it is a difficult and complex problem, otherwise she wouldn't ask for your input. *Hm. This is a tricky question, I can see why it's got you confused.* If you don't validate the difficulty of what she is asking, you risk infantilizing her and enraging her at the same time. *Oh, this is easy! Can't believe you couldn't figure it out for yourself; what are you, six years old?* At least that is what it will feel like to her if you fail to recognize that, for her, this is a real conundrum.

2. Find out what she has already tried. Count on her having already spoken to friends, possibly even a few other adults, before she came to you. *How have you tried to deal with it so far? What has been helpful to this point? Who else have you talked to about this?*

3. Listen. Listen some more. Let there be silence; you don't have to rush to fill the void. This is when your teenager will feel safe to explore the problem with your support. Often no words are spoken, just silent support given. She'll make some progress during this time. Sometimes her progress will astonish and confuse you. *Oh, I see it now. Thanks, Dad!* More often than not, she'll come close to clarity but land just short of it. *I'm still not sure what to do, but it feels like there is something I can do. I just can't put my finger on it. I'll just give it some more time.*

4. Now, if she's still hanging around, you get to play the historian of her successes. This is a fun job. It's also a role that will at first confuse your daughter, but it will soon help her to solve whatever problem she has brought to you. Remind her of other times in her life when she was just as stuck in some other problem but eventually landed on a solution that worked. *I'm not sure how you'll figure this one out, but you will. Remember that time in sixth grade when you had that falling out with your best friend, Samantha? Somehow you got through that one and you're still good friends today. Or that time last year when you got so mad at that coach? And this year*

you had him write you a letter of reference for the summer camp job. Kids, like adults, in the throes of a problem are experts on the problem at the exact time they need to become experts on the solution. Therefore, part of our job is to remind them of their expertise in solving problems. That's what will help them get through whatever difficulty they're experiencing. And when you assist them in this way, you strengthen your connection to one another, too. That is, after a conversation like this, which leaves her with a smile on her face and reflecting—maybe for the first time—on how she got through some difficult situations from the past, she is in a much better position to resolve whatever is at hand.

Parent Intuition

When kids become teenagers, too many parents mysteriously stop trusting their own intuition. That is, five years ago, when your daughter was nine years old and had a guilty look on her face, you would confront her with your intuition without hesitation. *What's going on here? You look fidgety and guilty. You can't even look me in the eye. What did you do wrong?* At this point, your daughter would either 'fess up to the wrongdoing or sulk away in a huff. Either way, you both win. You stood your ground as a parent and she learned that her parents care enough about her to hold the limits even when they aren't sure exactly just what limits they are holding. You see, even when she doesn't confess to you, your calling her on her behavior (even without proof) says to her that you are noticing her behavior and aren't afraid to comment and step in. For most kids, this is enough to persuade them to stop that behavior.

These days, there are experts of all sorts, but none of them knows your child better than you. Wise parents consult experts whenever possible but seldom follow their advice blindly. Instead, they filter the advice through their own knowledge and expertise of their sons and daughters, then they decide on the appropriate action.

That trust in your intuition, however, wanes as your child grows older and eventually enters adolescence. When your son is fourteen and has that same look on his face (the look that he had as a child who was up to no good), rather than confronting him with what your intuition is saying—that something is amiss—many parents instead walk away and look for proof of wrongdoing. Instead of acting like parents, we act like detectives or district attorneys, neither of which is very helpful to our teenagers. Throughout your teenager's adolescence, it pays to remember the words of former defense secretary Donald

Rumsfeld, which, even though said in a very different context, are even more appropriate when it comes to intuition and your teenager: "The absence of evidence is not evidence of absence."

One of the by-products of less faith in our intuition is that we are more vulnerable to our fears, which in turn causes us to lecture more, negotiate less, argue more, and laugh less, all of which creates further distance between ourselves and our teenagers. Without our intuition, we're left at the mercy of the media; and I've rarely, if ever, seen a teenager in the mainstream media who resembles any of the over twenty thousand teenagers I've worked with during my career. Instead, we see stereotypes foisted one on top of another, a spectacle that leaves us quaking in our boots when our teenager enters the room with a blue streak in her hair, or with two inches of his underwear extending beyond the waistband of his jeans. When we don't trust our intuition, we begin to view our own kids through the dominant stereotypes presented in the media.

This all goes right back to what that father said (earlier in this chapter) about lecturing because he wasn't sure what else to do. Listening to and trusting your intuition is one of those something else to do's. It's also what keeps you connected to your teenager despite all the negative stereotypes floating around.

For our teenagers' sakes and for our relationships with our teenagers, we need to give more mind to our intuition.

Give Back the Problem

Once you begin to understand the nuances of your teenager's rush toward independence, and when you are able to cut back on your lectures and advice-giving habits, your teenager will surprise, shock, and infuriate you by going against the grain of all that we've discussed thus far. In essence, she comes to you with a problem and insists that you solve it for her, but there's a catch—there's only one right answer, and she already knows it. And she will do everything in her power—bullying, whining, crying, screaming, cajoling, teasing, threatening—to make you come to the same conclusion.

"Hey, Mom," says fifteen-year-old Tiffany as she walks into the kitchen. "There is this great party tonight that I want to go to, okay?"

"You know the ground rules: parents home, no alcohol, and give me the number."

"No problem, it's just that it starts after the play is over tonight. So can I stay out until two?"

"Two in the morning?! That's ninety minutes past your curfew."

"I know, but it's a special party. Besides everyone is going, even the freshmen parents are letting their kids go."

"Well, I don't know, it's awfully late. How come you didn't ask me about this before the day of the party?"

"I wasn't sure I wanted to go, but now I'm sure. So can I go?"

"Where is the party?"

"It's at Jason's. And yes, his parents will be home, and you know they would never serve alcohol. So can I go?"

"It's a cast party, right? So that means seniors and juniors will be there too?"

"If they're in the cast, they'll be there, Mom."

"I don't know, honey. It's an older crowd and it's awfully late. Let me think about it."

"Mom! It's tonight, not next week. Everyone is going. Please."

"Maybe. I don't know. Let me talk to your dad first."

"But he won't be home until after I leave for the play. Mom, don't do this to me. Are you trying to ruin my life?"

"Stop that kind of talk, you know that's not true. I want what is best for you."

"Then let me go. I swear, if you knew how good a kid I am compared to most of the kids in my school, you would let me go in a second. Maybe I should be more like everyone else."

This kind of discussion seldom ends amicably. In essence, teenagers are experts at handing over some of their problems to us and then rejecting all our solutions, at least until we land on the one they wanted from the beginning.

Those who have ever found themselves in a similar situation—read, most parents—understand that it's a trap. If you insist that it's just too late, no matter that it's a special occasion, you'll get that disgusted look from your daughter along with either the silent treatment or the full-blown histrionics for which teenagers are famous. Moments later, you'll notice a nagging feeling in your gut; you'll worry that the next time a special opportunity like this comes around (and it will), she may not trust you enough to ask your permission: She'll come home early, hang out in her room until you go to bed, and then sneak out of her bedroom window to go to that special event that she never asked you about. Then the refrain *But everyone else's parents are letting them go!* comes to mind and you wonder whether you are really that much out of touch with teenagers in general and your daughter in particular. (Of course, if you were able to pursue just who *everybody* is, she's got several names ready-at-hand—and she's just as quick to distract you from mentioning the names of those whose parents have already said no.)

On the other hand, there are parents who will say yes to the special request and momentarily bask in the admiration of their teenager. But that admiration is all too quickly replaced with a look of shock on her face because you actually said yes; next, the limitless look of anything goes crosses her face and simultaneously turns that nagging twinge you've been feeling in your belly into a full-blown ulcer. You've been snookered, you know it, and you feel it's too late to take back the permission you've just granted. Even if she hasn't actually slipped one past you, you realize that you gave in much too easily. You should have made her work harder. At bottom though, you now realize that all the nervousness she carried with her when asking for permission has been transferred to you. Now you can't sit still and you know you'll stay wide awake until she is safely home from the cast party.

Whenever you are confronted with these not-so-innocent requests for permission, your best bet is to give the problem back to your teenager. She wants a special privilege, so let her do the work. This means holding off entirely on saying yes or no:

> I'm willing to consider letting you stay out the extra ninety minutes past curfew, but how are you going to make it work for me? We have a 12:30 a.m. curfew for reasons, mainly having to do with your safety and your age. If we were to say yes, what special steps would you take to ensure your safety? And what would you do to assure us that you wouldn't get in over your head? If we say yes to your idea, how are you going to make us feel like responsible parents when you're still out at 1:30 a.m.?

In the short run, this will drive your teenager crazy. *Uh, okay, was that a yes or a no?* This, however, is not a bad thing, as research is clear that kids who learn how to delay gratification and to stay comfortable with ambiguity do the best later in life. And make no doubt about it, this response forces your teenager to take some time to think about what she is asking, which means both delayed gratification and living with some doubt. Also, after you respond a few times like this to these special requests, your teenager will come to you with such requests having already anticipated your questions and armed with a variety of proposed solutions. She will have internalized what you need before you have to ask, which is a testament to your connection with one another.

The point here is that when you insist that your teenager take responsibility when she comes to you with requests outside the norm, you teach her how to work with and through anxiety—an invaluable ability at any age.

> When I was a little kid, third grade through about sixth grade, my mom met me at home every day after school with a sandwich and glass of milk. But every once in a while, before I went to school, she would tell me that she had

something to do that afternoon—usually a doctor's or dentist's appointment—and wouldn't be at home when I got home after school. At first, she left me a sandwich and glass of milk on the top shelf of the refrigerator. Then, after a few times of doing this, she left the bread and peanut butter on the table for me to make my own sandwich. Then, by sixth grade, she didn't leave anything out for me; instead she just reminded me in the morning to make a snack for myself.

When she first started doing this, she would always arrive home while I was finishing my sandwich. But over time, she was away longer and longer, until eventually I had finished my snack and written her a note telling her whose house I was going to.

At least, that's what I thought. It was years later, after I had graduated from college and after she had passed away from a sudden illness, that a neighbor told me the true story. She never had any appointments to keep her away from home after school; that was all fabricated for my benefit. Instead, on one of these days, she parked the car a block away and had coffee with the neighbor directly across the street from us. And during coffee, she tracked my every move throughout the house. She was teaching me to manage my anxiety and take care of myself all while I was under her watchful eye.

Although our job is not to solve our teenagers' problems for them, it is not to abandon them, either. Putting them in charge of managing (or at least considering) our anxiety (and theirs) is a start to letting them flex their decision-making muscles while staying connected to us. Yes, sometimes we still say no to their requests, but only after giving them a fair hearing. Over the long haul, their knowing that you are listening and are willing to consider what they have to say is a powerful message. This deepens the connection. In the short run, however, it will do little to diminish their disappointment and frustration at not persuading you to acquiesce to that particular special request; but take heart, you're not alone—it's part of the terrain of raising a teenager.

Limits, Consistency, and Fairness

According to parenting experts, limits and consistency are the hallmarks of families who raise healthy children. The idea is that kids need the structure that comes from consistency in which to feel secure and from which to grow into healthy adults. Although limits and consistency are important, we also need to stay realistic. Is anyone really good at this without becoming uncompromisingly rigid? Teenagers are masters at making special requests during your most vulnerable and disorganized moments. You're on the phone and in the midst of an argument with your mother. You get a text from your spouse that the debit card is no longer working. You're certain there is something wrong with the scale because you've eaten nothing all day and there is no way you could have gained two pounds since you woke up. At these moments, consistency is a distant fantasy; teenagers know this and wait until these times to ask for those exceptions to the rules.

The only way to maintain strict limits and consistency is to remain rigid and embrace the old school mantra: *The rule is the rule.* The problem with this philosophy is that although it's simple and straightforward, it's not an effective way in which to raise a thoughtful and responsible teenager. In many respects, parents who exercise rigidly consistent limits give away their authority in the name of the rules. *I would love to let you go to that party, but it's against the rules we agreed to and if we are inconsistent on this one, it'll come back to haunt us over and over again.* From your teenager's view, you are now nothing more than a cop enforcing the law. Therefore, when it comes to your teenager, you're always better off thinking of fairness rather than maintaining rigid notions of consistency and limits. Your teenager knows the difference.

When you make decisions based on fairness (and by fair, I mean what is fair for a teenager, and your teenager in particular) your teenager learns to trust you. She gets to know what you consider fair and so bases her requests on how well she understands your views. For her, it's well worth the time needed to consider her requests from your perspective: What will worry you? How can she respond to that worry? That is, she engages her creativity in working with you to see the fairness of her requests. When she can count only on rigid adherence to rules, she engages her creativity in manipulating and tricking you. This is when kids live two lives: the one in which they tell their parents what they want to hear and the one in which they do as they please once they are out of their parents' sight. Rigidity leads to a disconnect between parents and teenagers. On the other hand, a flexible sense of fairness is the underpinning to a strong connection.

*   *   *

Once your children reach adolescence, they no longer hang on to your every word nor eagerly request your advice; this is disconcerting at first and sad for a long time afterward. It's also the only way they can grow up. They need to push their independence and to make some mistakes of their own. One mistake parents make is when they take too personally some of their teenager's pushing away behaviors and not personally enough their indirect requests for reconnecting.

FOUR

The Car

As usual, Mick and his baseball buddies, Skylar and Jorge, were late. I can't wait for him to get his license because I'm sick and tired of this thankless job of abused and neglected chauffeur. I know coach always ends practice at 5:15 p.m., so why can't they get out of the locker room by 5:45 p.m., as we agreed they would?

"Hey, Mom."

"Hi, Mick. Skylar. Jorge. How was practice?"

"Good, I guess." Sure, we've got the suburban minivan, but why do they all have to sit in the back seats? I remember that when I was a kid, we used to fight for that front seat—"I got shotgun!"

"Hey, Mick," said Jorge, "think Sternstein will pitch for Tech tomorrow? I hear the pro scouts were at his last game."

Skylar jumped in. "Pro scouts, really! Man, I played with him in Little League, he ain't that good."

I tuned out. The chances of my Mick's attracting that kind of attention were nil; he was lucky to get in a few innings here and there. Blah. Blah. Blah.

As my thoughts drifted to work and what we would have for dinner, I heard their voices change—not louder or softer, just different.

"Jorge, you gonna ask Julie to the dance?"

"I don't know. I'm not sure. I mean, she's only a freshman."

The boys had my attention now. And because they were all seniors, I silently concurred with Jorge—Julie was too young.

"What about you, Mick, are you and Rita still going to go?"

Rita? Who the heck was Rita? And when was this dance? I felt myself involuntarily slowing down as my ears perked up.

Carpools

Driving the car with your teenager and a few of his friends is one of the best places to catch up on what's going on in his life. This is when you learn about future and past parties; about arguments with teachers and coaches; about major term papers due the next day; and yes, about budding romances, too. But if you are not alert to the vast potential of car rides, you may miss this opportunity. That is, it takes a little patience and a lot of discipline to get the most out of these backseat conversations.

At first, your teenager and her friends get into the car, pile into the backseat, and jabber on about nothing. All you know for sure is that they are loud and energetic. (And, of course, oblivious to your presence other than as driver.) Usually, after a few minutes, someone will utter the test phrase or comment—something that will challenge your integrity: You'll feel it as a shiver from the base of your spine to the crown of your head. *Did you see* . . . You now have a split-second decision to make—to say something or to remain silent. Be liberal here. Unless it is something that is grossly offensive, let it pass—which will be about 95 percent of the time if you're like most parents. Now the conversation gets interesting and the eavesdropping is juicy. Now they'll talk about all the interesting things happening in their lives—the ones they don't normally share with you—and they'll act as if you weren't there and can't hear what they are saying. When this happens, a second interesting phenomenon occurs: You become a model driver. You stop for a full two seconds at all stop signs; you drive the speed limit, or just below; you stop at yellow lights, even a few green ones, too. You want to make this moment last.

Your job now, more than ever, is to drive well and stay quiet. This is your teenager's way of catching you up on some of the details of her life. Don't ruin the moment by asking lots of questions. Let her friends ask the questions and make the points. You just listen and take it all in.

Of course, after you have dropped off the last of her friends, the big moment arrives. As she climbs into the front seat, you think, *What next?* Every cell in your body will scream out and tell you to ask her follow-up questions: *I didn't know Jocelyn is having a party this weekend. Who is Steven, and when am I going to meet him?* Restrain yourself. Your job now is to have a two-second, nonverbal conversation with your daughter. As you glance her way, your eyes open wide. Your expression tells her: *I heard every word you guys said and I think we need to talk, or at least you need to tell me more.* If you can stay quiet instead of panicking, you will see a different sort of expression flash across her face, a much more relaxed look that says: *I know you heard everything we talked about, and I know you're cool enough not to interrogate me over the details.* Then she will look away. Again, restrain yourself. Do a double take if you need to, but when you do look back to your daughter, do so with an expression that says: *You're right.* Then turn your attention forward and attend to the details of driving. If you're really in the moment, you will notice, just out of the corner of your eye, that as your head turns forward your daughter's left hand simultaneously reaches out to turn up the volume on the radio, or more likely, back to her cell phone. This movement signals the end of your two-second, nonverbal conversation.

Properly understood, this behavior on the part of your teenager is elegant and brilliant. In one car ride, she has managed to update you on some of the more pertinent details of her life without having to answer twenty questions about the details. Or, from another perspective, you now know enough about what is happening in her life so that if something goes wrong—her best friend starts dating the guy she had planned to ask to the dance, she isn't invited to the party this weekend, her teacher won't let her make up the test she missed because of an away volleyball game—she can count on you for support. That is, when she is in her room crying and you ask what is wrong, she'll tell you because you have enough background information to make sense of the bits and pieces of information she'll throw your way: *Jeff is going out with Leila.* Now she counts on you to remember what was said during that car ride so that you can put two and two together and realize that Jeff was the guy she had a crush on. And Leila was her best friend. In other words, your daughter is in a crisis.

Imagine you had not overheard that conversation in the car; now when you enter her room and ask why she is crying, instead of letting you support her there's a good chance she'll either turn her head away in dismissal or attack you for asking the question. The reason is that without the background information you can't possibly understand what she is going through, and she doesn't have the energy or patience to catch you up on the history of the crisis during the crisis. In short, she is angry with you for not understanding what she never told you.

Savvy parents recognize the carpool as the opportunity it really is: the chance for your teenager to update you safely on the vulnerable areas of his life on the long shot that things will go haywire and he'll need your support. Put another way, driving the carpool and staying quiet as he discusses his life allows you, when the crisis hits, to transform yourself into the caring, compassionate, and good parent your son needs. During these car rides, your teenager tosses you gems; it's up to you to catch them and to recognize their value in strengthening your relationship with each other.

Dinner and a Drive

We hear a great deal about the value of eating dinner together as a family. Family dinners are still important when your kids become adolescents, but the way they are important changes. Seldom is the dinner table the site of meaningful information exchange and value clarification, as it was several years ago when your child was still in grade school. Given that the average family dinner at home involving a teenager lasts around ten minutes, it makes no sense to expect life-changing conversations to occur during this time. Yet, although the meaning of the family dinner has changed, its overall importance is unwavering. Researchers have shown that until around age eleven or twelve, when you ask kids whom they would talk to if they had a problem, most list, in order: parents, teachers, friends.

However, once children enter adolescence, the list reverses itself: friends, teachers, parents. This means that your teenager talks about all the juicy stuff at school, on the phone, at work, and on the playing fields, but not at the dinner table—and usually not within earshot of his mom and dad. During adolescence, dinner becomes the bridge that leads to bigger conversations later on, long after the dishes have been cleared. Dinner is the time for small talk. It's the time to make eye contact and check in with one another. It's the time to crack a joke or two and laugh. It's the time to reconfigure logistics for later that night or the next day. These exchanges build the bridge of communication between parents and teenagers. It is over this bridge that they travel late at night, on a car ride together, and at other times when they need to talk. (Though if you have more than one child, once the teenager excuses herself, the dinner conversation often slides back to the big stuff.) Make no mistake about it, without the check-in time that dinner provides—you know, when you ask her about her day and she does her best to give up as little information as possible—these other breakthrough conversations will not happen. There is a direct correlation between the small talk of dinner and the big talks that happen away from the dining room table.

Once Sylvia entered high school, we had this weird little ritual that was unspoken until years later when she was home from college one summer. Our family dinners were always scattered because she was the oldest of four, but as an adolescent she more often than not was leaving the table before having even settled in. I don't think she ever lasted more than ten minutes. I chose not to fight this behavior; rather, I just used dinner to sort of get a gestalt of my daughter: *How was her mood? Was she losing weight? Did she seem okay?* But every once in a while, after dinner I would make some excuse to go for a car ride with her to the local convenience store or for an ice cream cone. Often, bordering on always, we got into great conversations on those rides—the same kinds of talks we used to have at dinner, the ones I missed so much. Now we still had them, but we just had to make special arrangements is all. Though I am delighted to say that since she entered college, dinner conversation—when she's around—is better than ever.

I hear similar stories from parents every year. For some, it's the car ride after dinner, but not always. For others, it's the walk around the block, shooting baskets in the driveway, doing dishes together, a cup of hot chocolate, or tea in the backyard. It's different from one family to the next. The constant is that it occurs after dinner, in the transition times between dinner and personal time.

Family Car Trips

Besides the carpool, there are other times in the car that are just as valuable. In fact, the car can, with a little creativity and courage, become the transformational vehicle for making lemonade out of lemons.

It was Sunday evening and we were on our way back from Lake Tahoe to our home in San Francisco, normally a trip of just over four hours. But during the winter on Sunday afternoons, the trip can take up to six hours, depending on weather and traffic. This was definitely one of those longer trips. At first, my wife, my sixteen-year-old daughter, and I were cranky and moody with one another. It wasn't pleasant. Then my wife decided to play a podcast of some pop psychologist talking about teenagers. My daughter groaned on cue. But once my wife makes a decision, she is tough to stop.

I had never heard the guy before, but I have to admit that after a few minutes he had me hooked. He was making sense. A moment later, my daughter spoke: "Wow! How does he know that?"

This was my wife's big play. She hit pause and asked, "Know what?"

"How I think. I mean, how teenagers think. It's like he's describing exactly what I do in my room after school—flop on the bed, listen to music, review my day, text my friends, check all my social media—only now I understand why. He's right, I'm just checking in with my friends to make sure everything is okay."

She went on like this for a few miles, making all sorts of connections to her life. I felt as if I were listening to her speak into her diary. When she finally stopped, neither my wife nor I said anything; my wife simply hit the play button. About ten minutes later, my daughter shook her head: "He's crazy, that's not how kids get together anymore, it's much more random than that."

Again, my wife hit the pause button. "Has he got it all wrong or just part of it?"

"Most of it. You see, most kids . . ."

Near the end of my daughter's monologue about how teenagers get together as couples and as random sexual partners, my wife and I exchanged a look that said, *This is incredible stuff we're hearing and scary as all get-out.*

The podcast was only forty-five minutes long, but with my daughter's commentary it took us the better part of three hours to listen to it all. What a ride! My wife and I felt honored that our daughter had opened up with all this stuff that she normally never talks about with us. More important, I think my daughter felt proud that she could describe her life, and teenage life in general, so well.

And when we got home and out of the car, there was an unspoken agreement between us and our daughter that there was to be no direct follow-up to the conversation we had just had. Back to normal, but with a difference.

I've heard similar stories from lots of parents. Usually the impetus for the conversation is some sort of self-help audio or a talk radio show, and this unknown person somehow puts parents and teenagers on the same side. Together they are the audience, but while riding in a car they are free to disagree, support, and generally talk among themselves. Parents and teenagers are equals during this time. And smart parents make sure their teenagers are more than equal. That is, they defer to their teenagers' ideas as long as it keeps them talking and opening up. Then, as their teenagers build some momentum, they ask questions they've been holding on to for the past few months. Sometimes, they even gently debate with their teenagers.

During these exchanges, if you keep your teenager and his views as your focus, you will see him rise to the occasion. Suddenly he becomes more articulate, more thoughtful, and more mature; in short, he is exactly the kind of person you have been working so hard to raise. He is the expert; he surprises not only you but also himself with all that he has to say.

As one would expect, most of these open and honest conversations between parent and teenager that occur in the car also happen at night. It's a great one-two combination. Best of all, when your teenager is opening up this way, you won't even need coffee to stay alert behind the wheel.

Often during workshops with parents and teenagers, I break the audience into groups of five or seven parents and two or three teenagers—the only organizing criteria is that nobody in the same group is related. Then I give them topics or questions to discuss. No matter where I do this, the results are always the same. Within minutes, parents and teenagers are leaning into the circle speaking to one another and, more important, listening to one another. At the end of the evening, parents are astonished by how articulate the teenagers in their various groups have been. Within minutes, they put the rest of it together. Because their own teenager is more alike than different from all the other teen-agers at the event, it only makes sense that their teenager is every bit as articulate as those in their groups earlier that evening. Sure enough, on the way to the parking lot, they get that feedback from the adults who were in the groups with their teenagers. *Your son is so well spoken and thoughtful. You should be proud.*

From the adolescent perspective, it's similar and different. For them, the shock is having spent time with adults who hung on to their every word. That is, most teenagers don't expect adults to listen to them, nor have they had such an experience—at least, not past the typical twenty questions: *What time are you going to be home? Who will be there?* What surprises them is that once they are comfortable with how much attention the adults in the group are giving them, they realize how much they have to say. They actually impress themselves, which is, of course, right in line with the narcissistic nature of adolescence.

One-on-One in the Car

If you think back to the relationship shift that occurs when your child enters adolescence, from manager to consultant, then the basic configuration of a car takes on added significance. When you and your teenager are riding in the car, you are sitting side by side, which is the perfect configuration for a consulting relationship—not ahead and not behind, but next to each other. For them, it's also the easiest physical position from which to open up and express themselves. In my years of counseling kids in middle schools and high schools, I learned early on never to sit directly across from them. Instead, I always sat just off center, away from their direct gaze. In effect, I gave them the space straight ahead of them to stare off into. Often, when speaking candidly with me or when putting together disparate pieces of information into a new insight about themselves, they would look off into the space in front of them, speak their thoughts aloud, and then turn their eyes in my direction for my reaction, comment, or question. This configuration naturally occurs when your teenager is riding in the passenger seat of the family car while you drive.

Riding in the car with her mom or dad gives your teenager the space ahead of herself to stare into. If she wants eye contact, she can initiate it; otherwise, she's content to sit beside you and to talk. Pragmatically, sitting side by side also encourages your teenager to free associate more easily (think of the Freudian therapists who sit behind their patients to ensure their clients greatest access to their unconscious thoughts), which is exactly what you want. The nature of free association is that the normal defenses are bypassed or dropped. Without this type of defenses-down, free-associative thought, there is no way to catch up on your teenager's life—at least, not in any meaningful way.

I guess my dad was smarter than I thought. All through high school, he used to insist that I accompany him on his once-a-month trips to the Berkshires (about an hour's drive) to check in on the cottage by the lake that our family owned. He would wake me early on the appointed Sunday morning, plop me in the passenger seat, and drive. I slept. When we got there, he did his checking, which was nothing more than a quick walk around. Then he bought me breakfast at the same diner; in fact, I ordered scrambled eggs and toast each time. (Thirty years later, I still order the same meal when he and I go out to breakfast.)

Over breakfast, we read the paper and chatted about the news and sports; then we got back in the car and drove home. Always in the last thirty minutes of the drive, I found myself talking to him about something that was happening in my life, something I had never expected to talk to him about. To his credit, he just listened. He never lectured or gave advice, he just listened. Then when we got home, he would thank me for accompanying him (as if I had been given a choice) and we would go about our business . . . Now, as I raise my own teenager, I know why he waited until I had graduated from high school before he sold that cottage.

The Driver's License

If you are like most parents, when your teenager begins taking the steps toward getting a driver's license, you will experience intermittent waves of anxiety and excitement. (Conversely, if you live in an urban area and your teenager is not interested in the driver's license due to mass transit and ride sharing, you may feel the disappointment of your teen missing a ritual into adulthood.) You will have anxiety over the prospect of your child driving a car; after all, driving accidents are the leading cause of death among American youth. For example, teenage drivers—16 to 19—are three times more likely to be in a fatal crash than drivers 20 and older. You will also notice some excitement over your newfound freedom from having to play chauffeur on twenty-four-hour call. But just below the surface of these two dominant emotions, most parents will detect a small current of grief. And this grief is twofold.

There is no greater signifier of your teenager's independence than her driver's license. Once she has her license, she no longer needs you as much as she used to. Furthermore, you have less control than ever over where she goes and with whom she goes. It's scary. All this says that you need to do your work about your teenager's driver's license long before she goes to the Department of Motor Vehicles for her driving test.

At the same time, her getting her license means less time spent with you, less opportunity each week to connect. This is when parents suddenly realize how many of their best conversations happened in the car.

> I took it for granted that Cy and I had a good relationship. Maybe because I was a single mom and he was an only child, but for some reason we had always enjoyed good communication throughout his childhood and into adolescence. But it was when he got his license that I realized how much time we spent together in the car talking. At home, we were too busy living our lives; but in the car, that's where we talked.
>
> Strange, now that he's driving, I know less about what he's up to than ever before, and not because of any conscious choice on either of our parts. More than that, I miss him—hanging out and especially laughing together on some of those rides.

And:

> Sheila has been counting the days until she gets her license for the past two years. It's been kind of a family joke: "How many more days, Sheila?" And she always knew. She worked hard at part-time and summer jobs so that, after getting her license and driving safely without any tickets or accidents for six months, we allowed her to buy herself a used car.
>
> But just last week the radiator sprung a leak and it took a couple of weeks for her to earn the money to have the repairs done. During that time, we reverted to old patterns, and I was again the designated chauffeur. It was wonderful. I had forgotten just how much I used to learn about my daughter by listening to her and her friends chatter and gossip in the backseat. It was great to catch up like that again; so much so that I'm thinking of slipping the mechanic another $100 to keep the car an extra week!

Of course, the time it takes to learn to drive and to get the driver's license offers yet another wonderful opportunity to connect with your teenager. In this context, he more than ever wants a close relationship with you so that you will teach him to drive, support him in getting his license, and let him use the car afterward. Make use of these temporary and very real motivations. These are the times when he will open up to you, as much to let you in and hear your input as to show you how mature he is and, therefore, how capable he is of driving the family car responsibly.

Take What Your Teenager Gives You

Savvy parents recognize the motivations of their teenager to earn her driver's license and have access to the family car months, sometimes years, before she is eligible for her license. Preparing for the license is a prime opportunity to practice giving the problem back to your teenager and sharing your anxiety:

> Once we realized that Sheri was counting the days until she was eligible to drive, we decided to make it work for all of us. We told her that for her to learn to drive and to get her license, she first needed to sit down with us and talk it through. We wanted to address some of our concerns and some of her concerns as we created a plan that worked for all of us. Sheri was a little disap-pointed when we told her this because she had been hoping just to sail through and get her license as if it were no big deal. Though at the same time, I think (I hope) she was a bit relieved, too.

Given most teenagers' propensity for looking for the easiest way around an obstacle, it's no surprise that most display surprise, even shock, when you seem hesitant or mention concern over their driving. Don't take it personally. At the same time, don't believe it, either. Most teenagers, underneath that veneer of self-confidence, are anxious about learning to drive. Many, though not the majority, are open with their parents about this, and some even choose not to get their license as soon as they are eligible. So if your teenager is one of the admitted minority that isn't itching to get behind the wheel of the car, don't worry, he's still a normal teenager.

Many teenagers, even though inwardly anxious about learning to drive and getting a license, seldom share this with their parents. From their perspective, showing vulnerability invites parents to conclude that their teenagers are not yet ready to drive. That is, acknowledging doubt is tantamount to courting defeat, at least in the average sixteen-year-old's mind.

The cornerstone of a deep connection is that your teenager feels safe showing doubt and vulnerability with you. When she trusts that you understand these uncomfortable feelings are part and parcel of the complex myriad of emotions that we label as confidence, she will voice her doubts more easily; this, in turn, gives her more confidence in her ability to learn to drive successfully. And if that isn't a recipe for a close connection, I don't know what is. That is, if you have someone in your life with whom after talking about your fears, doubts, and anxieties, you feel stronger and more connected than before you shared, you quickly come to count this person as a trusted ally—exactly the role every parent wants for herself. Your job is to court this type of relationship with your teenager:

> "We know that you're looking forward to getting your license in another eight months. Over time, this means lots of details to address, from passing the written test to learning to drive to getting insurance. But before all this kicks in, we want to talk with you about what you're thinking and feeling about driving."

At this point, don't expect much other than a shrug of his shoulders and a response of *Not much.* Hold your mud. Ask again, only now because you know he is motivated to get his license you can let him know the kind of response you're looking for. (This is the adolescent version of the colder/warmer hide-and-seek game: colder, colder, warmer, warm, really warm, on fire, etc.)

> "Statistically, one out of three teenagers and other new drivers have an accident during their first year of driving. And since we know you don't want to be one of these statistics, we're wondering what kinds of doubts you have about driving. I mean, it's responsible to consider the consequences and let them scare you a little. It's a hallmark of mature people. So does anything about driving make you nervous?"

Besides the confused expression on your teenager's face, you can expect one of two responses: Either he'll launch into the doubts he has been having, or he'll ask, in his own way, for more time to consider the question. "Geez, there's a bunch of stuff I'm thinking about, but I gotta go right now. Can we talk about it tomorrow?"

Count on an interesting conversation in the next few days. Hear him out, and prompt him when appropriate: *How do you imagine your anger about the stuff that happens every day—getting cut off, a bad day at school, and your anger with us, too—will affect your driving? Do certain roads worry you more than others? Will your friends support your driving responsibly?*

After this kind of conversation, it's time to ask him to take care of you as you support him in getting his license. That is, given all the foregoing, and given your anxiety over the possibility that he might be hurt in an accident, how can he learn to drive and get his license in a way that makes you feel responsible as parents? (Note that I did not say *comfortable*. When your teenager is getting his license, there is no way to feel totally comfortable; therefore, *responsible* will have to suffice.) From here, you move backward in time. Start with a point in the future when he has his license and is a responsible and experienced driver, then move backward until the present, noting all the growth points along the way. Somehow, conversations with teenagers always take on a different tone when you move backward from a time when they are responsible and have what they want. This lets them know that they will get there and that you believe in them, but right now you both just need to figure out how this is going to happen.

In getting the driver's license, one of the biggest questions is just exactly how your teenager will learn to drive the car. But before volunteering yourself (or your spouse), ask yourself whether you are really the right person to teach her to drive. If so, it can become a substantial piece of a solid connection between the two of you. If you're not the best person to teach her to drive, then acknowledge this, find the right person, and stay involved.

> Neither my husband nor I have the temperament to teach Sarah to drive, but we wanted to be part of her learning. We posed this to her, and without missing a beat she suggested my brother, Ed, who lives on the other side of town. He's her favorite uncle and he was honored to teach Sarah to drive. The only caveat has been that either my husband or I accompany them: I'll drive Sarah over to Ed's and hop in the back seat while they drive. The only rule is that I keep my mouth shut!
>
> I love it, and Sarah even seems fine with it. I know she's nervous about driving and welcomes my support, especially when it's not accompanied by my anxiety. And Ed is a terrific teacher, so I can relax about that.
>
> Of course, she's still learning to drive with an official instructor in her driving course, but we all agreed it was best to have extra practice, especially in front of her dad and me so that we could see her progress with our own eyes.

Don't fool yourself in this regard, either. If you're not suited to teaching her how to drive, admit it. To do otherwise can do permanent harm to your relationship with your teenager:

> Learning to drive nearly destroyed my relationship with my parents. My dad insisted that he would be the one to teach me to drive, and that we had to drive for at least twenty hours together before I could take the test. Let me

tell you, my father is a terrible driving teacher. Before I even had the keys in the ignition, he was correcting me. *You should adjust the seat and fasten your seat belts before you start the car. But who said anything about starting the car?* I was just putting the keys in the ignition to free my hands to adjust the seat and buckle up! He was nonstop talk, always correcting me on something or another. I was nervous enough, but he just made me worse. But that wasn't even the worst part. After that first time driving together, he bailed whenever I asked him to drive with me: *Not now, honey. I've got to finish some work today. How about tomorrow?* But the next day, he always had another excuse. I even tried scheduling times to drive, but he always canceled. I was furious with him for flaking on me, but no matter what I said he insisted on being the one to teach me to drive. My mom was useless. She just said it was between my father and me. There was nothing I could do, which is why it took me until the middle of senior year to get my license.

Your job is to help make it possible for them to learn to drive, not get in their way at every turn.

When your teenager is learning to drive, he is most apt to talk with you in a more real and a more engaging manner than either of you are accustomed to, especially if you are the one doing the teaching. Stay on the alert for the connection opportunities that occur right after some practice driving. His vulnerability in learning to drive combined with your role as teacher sets up a level of communication and honesty between the two of you that will carry over into the time immediately afterward. If you play your cards properly, this is when he will catch you off guard and suddenly open up about some other aspect of his life. Plan for this. Stay available after driving sessions, and, whenever possible, don't schedule a driving session too close to any other commitment—yours or your teenager's. Enjoy the afterglow and debriefing that naturally occur after times of shared vulnerability and of working together toward a common goal. In a similar vein, athletes and performers enjoy rehashing the big moments of games and productions long after they are over—many, many years later for some of us. Do the same with your teenager after your shared driving experiences.

At the same time make sure that you have the right attitude and are the right person to teach your teenager how to drive. Some of the best parents in the world are some of the worst driving instructors. Just be honest with yourself.

I was definitely the designated driving instructor in our home. My husband who is a great driver was both too nonchalant and too emotionally charged to teach either of our children how to drive. I must say I did pretty well with both kids. One of the best things we did was institute a "What gets said in the car stays in the car" agreement. We would lose our tempers periodically or I would express shock at how he could drive so close to the edge of the road, but no matter what we would pinky shake before leaving the car and agree to leave in the car all the emotional baggage that comes from learning/teaching to drive.

The Family Car: Your Teenager's First Apartment

For parents with a teenager who drives, this section makes for uncomfortable reading. Yet knowing the lay of the land helps.

Monday through Friday the family car is simply a means of transportation: how you and others in your family travel from point A to point B. For your teenager, this all changes on the weekends, and it is important that you appreciate the change. On any given Friday or Saturday evening, the car is transformed into your teenager's first apartment. It just happens to have wheels.

It was early in the afternoon and I was in the kitchen cleaning up after lunch. As soon as I saw Jason, I knew he wanted something from me. "Mom, can I use the car tonight? And, yes, I already asked Dad and he said it's fine with him if it's okay with you. Can I use it?"

"What time are you going to be home?"

"By sunrise, I promise. Regular time, of course, before one."

"Who are you going out with?"

"The usual suspects: Tim, Mychal, and Griffin. And no, we won't be drinking. And yes, if by some strange twist of the gods I did have something to drink, I would never drive. Yes, I know I can call you for a ride no matter what, but no, I won't need to call."

I smiled and relaxed, quite a bit. He was a smart kid—smart aleck, too—and he was definitely saying all the right things. "You're pretty sure of yourself, aren't you?"

"Just know the routine, that's all."

"That makes me feel better. Sure, you can use the car. Just remember to leave some gas in the tank."

"Thanks, Mom. You're the greatest! No, really, I mean it."

"Stop with the brownie points; just be careful."

Jason had a new bounce to his step as he headed toward the kitchen door.

"Oh, one more question: Where are you guys going?"

"Not sure. Maybe a party or a movie."

"Which one, party or movie?"

"I don't know."

"When will you know?"

"When we get there."

From here, these kinds of conversations normally deteriorate quickly. The more you press for "when" and "where," the more evasive and vague your teenager becomes in his responses. Although none of this is comforting, it is normal. For your teenager, it's not about where he and his friends are going, it's about their going together. They have committed to one another for the evening, and your teenager is their host. In the car, his car (at least for the night), everyone is free to speak his mind (no need to watch language or be polite). They can listen to whatever music strikes them (remember those songs you don't let him play at home?). They can act like little kids in the car, climbing across seats, unbuckling one another's seat belts. Best of all for your teenager, he is their toastmaster. In essence, it's his dinner party; it just happens that the dining room is the family car, and the table and chairs are the front and back seats.

On a night like this, your teenager and his buddies spend much of the evening in the car hanging out with one another and looking for something to do. Essentially, they're on the lookout for other apartments on wheels. In this way, they find out what is happening of interest on that night by being out and about. On a typical Friday or Saturday evening, there are all these apartments on wheels driving around town looking for one another; and they can't tell you where they are going because they don't know themselves, yet.

As I said at the outset of this section, this is the reality, and it's an uncomfortable one for parents. Yet knowing it allows you to keep your connection with your teenager as you negotiate the terms of driving. That is, giving the problem back to him will usually win the day, and the night, too.

*   *   *

The car is an integral part of most teenagers' lives, whether they choose to get their licenses or not. Smart parents understand this reality and work with it to improve the connection they have with their teenager by recognizing that sitting together in the car, whether they are sitting side by side or front and back, is a natural setting for the new relationship of parent as consultant. The intensity of face-to-face contact is diminished, which allows for more flow in conversation. Never be surprised by what is said in the car, whether it be on a short trip to the grocery store, on a long journey for summer vacation, or in a typical Tuesday carpool. Big moments happen during transitions, which means rides in the car—by definition always a transition—present a myriad of opportunities.

FIVE

Mastery over Compliance

We stay connected with our teenagers as they pursue their independence not by trying to make them compliant to our wishes but by staying focused on their developing mastery in and over their lives. Our job is to help them become experts on themselves and discover what they want for themselves. This is definitely not top-down parenting, but neither is it laissez-faire parenting. Instead, this approach recognizes that healthy teenagers need to struggle with and for their autonomy; when parents recognize and embrace this developmental reality, the relationship is able to sidestep many of the struggles associated with stereotypical teenage rebellion. Issues of independence and dependence, viewed through the goal of mastery, become a continuum rather than a dichotomy.

"Zones of Proximal Development"

Lev Semenovich Vygotsky, a Russian psychologist who lived in the first half of the twentieth century, examined how social interaction plays a role in cognitive development, and it is here that parents play a vital but often overlooked role. All parents like to believe that they play an important role in their children's development—the old nature versus nurture argument—and Vygotsky's ideas actually give us something to hang our hats on.

According to Vygotsky, there are certain times in people's lives when they are open to specific kinds of learning; he called these times zones of proximal development. He believed that during these times, social interaction was necessary to maximize potential development, and that this social interaction could either take the form of collaboration or guidance. Furthermore, he believed that all development shows up first in social interaction and second as an ability in the individual. Suddenly, John Donne's poem "No Man Is an Island" takes on new meaning. From Vygotsky's perspective, without collaboration and guidance, individuals miss out on specific types of learning available to them only at certain times in their development.

We can extrapolate from the work of Vygotsky to make some important insights about our teenagers and our relationships with them. According to Vygotsky, individuals accomplish more in learning new abilities when in social interaction than they can alone. Furthermore, they make the most gains when that interaction is with someone more knowledgeable in that particular area.

The most obvious example of environments predicated on these types of interactions are schools, where teachers and students operate side by side and interact constantly. (Please note that by interaction I mean the reciprocal action or influence that occurs between students and teachers. Sometimes this is active, as when the teacher is calling on the student; and many other times, although not active, it is still present—the student is working quietly at her desk doing her history homework as her teacher goes from student to student, checking on individual progress and answering questions.)

In the name of gaining insight into the role that parents and other adults play in teenager's learning, follow me as we play with Vygotsky's ideas a bit; we'll see how his theories help explain some of the mysteries of the everyday classroom. After that, we'll apply these understandings to the parent–teenager connection.

Imagine the typical day in a ninth-grade math class. For the sake of clarity, let's further imagine that a student's knowledge of math is measurable in discrete units—one student has 26 units of math knowledge and another has 31 units—and that these units are measured before the course begins, as well as before, during, and after each class. Now consider the teacher, whose math knowledge hovers around 272 units, much higher than any of her students, which is why she is the teacher. Now let's focus on the student who enters class with 26 units of math knowledge. (See Graph 1.)

Once class begins, and once the students start doing the work and discussing the ideas with their teacher (not a guarantee every day in every classroom), they experience an increase in their number of math units. To the untrained eye, it looks as if they had added these units to their overall total of math units. That is, when participating in class, the average student's math level goes up 5 units just from the interaction with the teacher. Therefore, the student who enters class with 26 units of math knowledge is, by the end of the period, operating

Graph 1: Student Goes to Class and Sits Down as Teacher Arrives

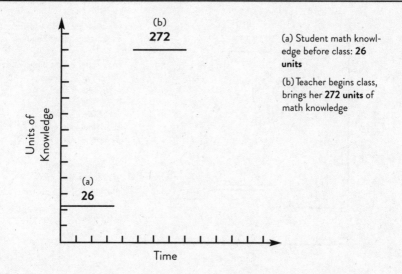

(b)
272

(a)
26

Units of Knowledge

Time

(a) Student math knowledge before class: **26 units**

(b) Teacher begins class, brings her **272 units** of math knowledge

Graph 2: Student and Teacher in the Midst of Class

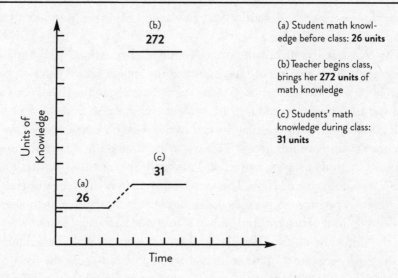

(b)
272

(c)
31

(a)
26

Units of Knowledge

Time

(a) Student math knowledge before class: **26 units**

(b) Teacher begins class, brings her **272 units** of math knowledge

(c) Students' math knowledge during class: **31 units**

with another 5 units, or 31 units of math knowledge. This is education and learning at work. (See Graph 2.)

However, and this is a huge *however*, once class ends and the teacher is no longer present, the students' math knowledge drops on average 2 to 3 units—that is 2 to 3 units better than they began class with, but lower by the same amount than they ended class with. This is the inherent messiness of education

Graph 3: Students at the Conclusion of Class

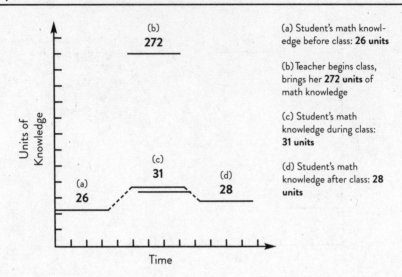

(a) Student's math knowledge before class: **26 units**

(b) Teacher begins class, brings her **272 units** of math knowledge

(c) Student's math knowledge during class: **31 units**

(d) Student's math knowledge after class: **28 units**

at play—two steps forward, one step back; or, in this scenario, five steps forward, two or three steps back. Regardless, progress is still being made and that's what is important. (See Graph 3.)

This dynamic is a nightmare for beginning teachers, who, because students have over the fifty minutes of class increased their math knowledge by 5 units, assign homework based on those 5 extra units of understanding. That is, to complete the homework successfully, the students need access to those 5 units of math knowledge that they had at the end of the class. Of course, as we have just seen, they don't have this access. This is why beginning teachers are constantly frustrated by students' pleas of *Honest, I tried to do the homework! I couldn't understand it, no matter how hard I tried.* Then, to the chagrin of both the new teacher and the student, when the teacher asks the student to attempt one of the homework problems in front of her, the student is able to complete the problem successfully. Was the student lying? No. Was the teacher wrong in basing her assessment of the student's proficiency on what he had accomplished in class the day before? No. Neither party is wrong. Instead, both student and teacher have missed the value of the student–teacher relationship in action. That is, when the teacher is standing by him, the student is able to gain back access to some of the math units he had gained at the end of class the previous day, and that is usually just enough for him to succeed at the homework problem in question. (See Graph 4.)

This is the social and transitory nature of knowledge. Now, to take the math class example even further, imagine it's the day of a math test. During the test,

Graph 4: Students and Teacher the Next Day

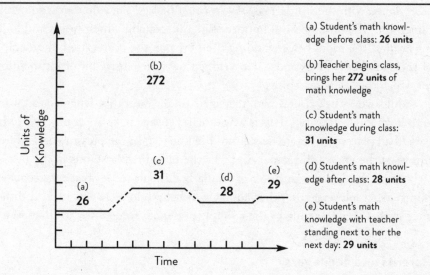

(a) Student's math knowledge before class: **26 units**

(b) Teacher begins class, brings her **272 units** of math knowledge

(c) Student's math knowledge during class: **31 units**

(d) Student's math knowledge after class: **28 units**

(e) Student's math knowledge with teacher standing next to her the next day: **29 units**

the teacher notices a strange phenomenon that occurs regularly. When a student gets stuck on a problem that is almost within his grasp, he contorts his face in an attempt to remember what he has studied, looks away in a quiet search, looks back at the problem with mounting frustration, looks away again, looks directly at the teacher, looks away briefly, and then turns his gaze back to the paper with excitement, for he has now found the answer he was searching for. Experienced teachers know this behavior all too well.

It's a strange one indeed, and a bit disconcerting at first, I must admit. Initially, I thought students had a question for me when they looked at me like this; but whenever I met their gaze and raised my eyebrows in the customary *Can I help you?* they would stare right through me. It was as if I had reached out to shake someone's hand, but that person did not reciprocate and instead left me feeling a bit foolish, my hand hanging in the air. But soon I realized the students were somehow using me to help them remember something or other that we had studied in class. These days, I just smile back at them, and barely a student has ever noticed. Unfortunately, it does mean I can't use test time to work independently because I have to make myself available for this kind of nonverbal interaction with my students every few minutes or so.

In fact, at one school I know of, the biology teacher used his intuitive understanding of this dynamic to his students' advantage during Advanced Placement tests. The rules of the test prohibit the AP teacher from being in the room while the test is being given, so he has done the next best thing: Each year he constructs an altar to himself, with flowers, and a huge photo of his smiling face framed with the words *You Know a Lot of Biology!* I'm sure that if someone filmed the AP exam, he would notice students scratching their heads and looking around the room before landing their eyes on the poster-sized photograph of their teacher, and seconds later writing down the elusive bit of information for which they were searching.

Adults who work closely with teenagers understand this dynamic and work with it whenever possible. This is why coaches always make eye contact with the basketball player just before he steps to the line to take the pressure-packed free throws at the end of the game. And why the play director stands in the line of sight of her lead actress during a particularly difficult scene. Teachers, coaches, ministers, employers, and other adults who believe in teenagers make a difference in that teenager's life by their simple presence. Sometimes, it's that easy.

Parents and Teenagers

Believe it or not, your presence, much like a teacher's, elevates your teenager's intelligence and abilities in various areas, and it's most important in interpersonal and intrapersonal decision-making skills. Teenagers have greater access to their own thoughts and problem-solving skills when they enjoy your presence. This is a very specific type of presence: when you aren't lecturing, peppering them with questions, accusing them of some wrongdoing, expressing disappointment in something they did or did not do, or praising them in the name of self-esteem; in other words, when you are silently connected to your teenager through your presence.

The other day, just like most days, I was waiting in the kitchen for my daughter when she got home from school. And as usual, she mumbled a hello, grabbed something to eat, and headed for her room. Rather than take this behavior personally—her need to be away from me and not to tell me about her day—I made use of this time. As soon as I heard the door close, I set about doing some chores. I prepped the meatloaf for dinner, I took out the trash, and then I set to vacuuming the living room carpet. It was in the midst of vacuuming that I could feel my daughter's presence. I looked over my shoulder, and sure enough she was standing in the living room doorway sort of staring at me and sort of spacing out. I stopped what I was doing, turned off the vacuum, and asked, "Can I help you, honey? You okay?"

She sort of just shook her head quickly, as if she was just coming to her senses and kind of surprised to find herself standing in the living room with her mom. "Oh, nothing. I was just thinking, that's all." Then, almost as an after-thought, or perhaps just to make sense of what she was doing for herself, or maybe even just to save face, she asked, "When's dinner?"

"In about twenty minutes, at six." I didn't add, though I thought it, just like every other night.

Then she nodded and headed back to her room.

For several days I didn't know what to make of that event, but I couldn't shake that look she had on her face: staring at me and spacing out at the same time. It was familiar. Then I remembered, that's exactly the look she used to get on her face when as a child she sought me out for support, assurance, or advice. I got it; this is her new way of getting my support and advice—somehow I help her gain entry to a better, wiser part of herself, but only so long as I'm not trying to help her. If that's not the ultimate parenting paradox, then I don't know what is!

Teenagers are sometimes unbelievably subtle in how they use you for their own good. Most parents would burst with pride if they only knew. When your daughter makes fleeting eye contact right before she takes the big penalty kick in the soccer game, she is counting on your gazing back in a way that says, *Relax, honey, you'll do fine.* When it's your son's turn to sing his solo in the class musical, he looks right at you seconds before because he is depending on your confidence in him to transfer over to him instantly and replace the nervous pit in his stomach. When your daughter leaves the house with her handsome new boyfriend, she pauses as if to say, *I'll be fine; you did well.* She now needs your look back that says, *We know* (which, of course, doesn't mean there aren't lots of things you need to say and do before this new date arrives to pick up your daughter!). When your son says good-bye to you in the parking lot at his college orientation for freshman year, he assuredly needs your hugs and love, but he also needs that look from you that says, *You'll make it. It may be hard at first, even a bit lonely, but you'll do fine.*

It takes keen-eyed parents to learn to read between the lines of what their teenager is saying and not saying. Once parents learn to do this, however, they rest easier and are able to do it more often for their teenager. A wondrous cycle evolves, and the connection between teenager and parent grows at every turn.

For a moment, remember the times your teenager presented you with a vulnerable part of herself—she was needy but dared not ask for your attention; he angered you and was worried you were pushing him away but didn't know how to reconnect; she was under stress and regressed before a daunting task and needed you to give her the assurances that she couldn't let herself ask you for. Now think about how you responded. Chances are that if you were successful in reading the signs and supporting your teenager, you did so with a minimum of fanfare and a minimum of words. This is when a gentle pat on the back, a spontaneous "I love you," or the knowing look says it all. This is when less is more.

Friends

Peer pressure gets a bad rap when it comes to teenagers. Admit it, as soon as you hear the phrase you think of all its negative aspects and the behaviors stereotypically associated with peer pressure: smoking cigarettes, having sex, driving recklessly, taking drugs, drinking alcohol, cheating in class. It's not a pretty picture. But when you apply the ideas of Vygotsky to peer pressure, you have an entirely different view. Because social interaction maximizes cognitive development, it stands to reason that the positive interaction of friends serves this same goal. Friends can learn bad habits from one another, but they can just as easily learn good habits, too, which, believe it or not, is more often what happens.

Every day, teenagers learn the value and difficulty of maintaining the qualities of respect, empathy, support, delayed gratification, loyalty, self-sacrifice, honesty, and love in their relationships with one another. This stuff is the fabric of their friendships. In other words, teenagers regularly push one another to better themselves. Whether it is as part of a team, in a community service project, during a performance, or just hanging out on a Saturday night, they look for the best in one another and bring it out. Not all the time, but much more often than you might imagine.

> I think my parents have watched too much TV. They think me and my friends are like the teenagers they see on television, which is insulting. I like spending time with my friends because (and I know this sounds selfish) I like myself more when I'm with them than when I'm with anybody else, including my family. (Sorry.) Sure, sometimes we do stupid things, but then we have to do real smart things to get ourselves out of the situations we've put ourselves in. This is how I learn to live my life: in the moment.

This learning and personal development occurs in good friendships and even the so-called bad friendships. Yes, your teenager will occasionally suffer a lapse in judgment in some of the friends that she chooses. This does not mean, however, that in these relationships she doesn't learn some of the same values and qualities you have been emphasizing all along—compassion, empathy, setting limits, giving hard feedback. Sometimes we all have to learn the hard way—which is especially true if you are between the ages of thirteen and nineteen.

Levels of Relationship

When I work with groups of teenagers, we often discuss different levels of communication. As adolescents are often fond of progressions and hierarchies, I share with them the following five-level model of communication with friends:

1. B.S. Level. In short, bus stop conversation—what you would talk about while waiting for the bus. This is where you discuss topics and subjects that are not that important to you, things like the latest baseball scores, a recent movie, the weather.

2. Gossip Level. This is the juicy stuff, the details, rumors, and exaggerated stories of other people's lives. Usually this type of sharing is based on a kind of self-esteem through disparagement. *By the time we're done poking holes in this person's life, we'll feel pretty good about ourselves!* Exchanging gossip also gives us the illusion of intimacy. Though once you realize that when you're not present, you are in all likelihood the subject of gossip—something seventh-grade girls and boys painfully discover—the falseness of that intimacy is all too apparent. Even though we know we shouldn't gossip, we still do, mainly because, in its own way, it is fun. In the end, however, no worthwhile relationship is founded solely on gossip.

3. Ideas and Opinions Level. These discussions happen only when there is some trust between the parties. At the very least, you need to listen to one another, even if it's just to debate. But this level really points to discourse beyond debate, to when you are sharing some of your more intimate and vulnerable beliefs. This may include religion, family, career, life's meaning. This level is the sharing of ideas and beliefs that leave us feeling vulnerable, and then recognizing and taking care of that same vulnerability in the person with whom we are speaking.

4. Emotions and Feelings Level. At this level, we are secure in sharing and exploring our emotions with another. This is when we may spontaneously well up with tears or laugh aloud. We tend to the other person's well-being and trust that he or she will do the same for us. Sometimes, it's just an airing of our pent-up emotions, and sometimes it's moving forward and through some emotionally stuck place.

5. Self Level. At this level, words are almost unnecessary; presence is more important. This is when you go for a walk with a friend, barely converse, and have a great time. And part of that great time was in sharing the space with that person. I remember one college freshman who summed up this experience quite well:

> You know how when you're normally driving around with someone you have the radio on and you're talking about all sorts of things, right? Well, this last level is when you're riding in the car with a friend with the radio either off or on real low and you're not talking that much to one another. But most important, you're totally comfortable with the silence. The silence makes you feel even more comfortable, and somehow closer, too.

Teenagers quickly understand that the most rewarding and valuable friendships go in and out of all five levels. Good friends skip from the space of quiet self to the level of B.S. (bus stop) in seconds, and then back again. The ability to express yourself in your full range of thoughts and feelings in the presence of friends is what makes them so special. We all, teenagers and adults alike, look for these qualities in our relationships and friendships with others.

Listening, Listening, and More Listening

Once you understand the different levels of relationships, you can see just how important your listening habits are when it comes to your children, and especially to your teenagers. It's that last level, Self, where you maximize your influence on your teenagers and your connection with them, at least in how much they can use you for their own well-being.

Most of us were born with the ability to hear, but listening is different. Listening is a skill that is open for improvement in all of us. At its deepest levels, when a speaker feels fully listened to, it allows her to open up to herself and to explore parts of herself that she ordinarily wouldn't even perceive. The noted psychologist Carl Rogers took the idea of listening further than anyone else in the profession. He believed that deep listening was the cornerstone, in fact the only thing that mattered, in effective therapy.

In typical conversation with peers, most of us listen until what the other person says sets off an association in our heads: a question, a story of our own. Then we politely wait until the speaker pauses before we ask our question or share our story. This is how conversations move back and forth through the levels of communication and the exchange of information.

I'm sure many readers who consider themselves good listeners are feeling pretty virtuous right about now. But not so fast. There's bad news, too. When it comes to your teenager, no matter what you think, he probably does not consider you a good listener. Sorry, but at least that's what they say when asked. When I speak with teenagers, I often ask them what they wish their parents did better. Across the country, at public and private schools, in urban, suburban, and rural environments, the answer is the same: *I wish my parents listened better.* Even if you are a terrific listener with your coworkers, your spouse, and even your younger children, most parents falter when it comes to their teenagers. The good news is that there is a clear reason for this slip in listening skills, which, when understood, makes room for dramatic improvement.

When your teenager is talking to you she is testing you, whether or not she realizes it. She starts out by telling you things that are easy to hear—successes in the classroom, with friends, on the field, onstage—and you do a terrific job of listening and following her lead. Then she shifts into the subjects that are somewhat ambiguous and more difficult to talk about—a disagreement with a teacher, a concern over a friend, a new guy she likes and is sort of seeing. Rather than present you with neat little reports of events, she instead haltingly unfolds a mystery with no clear way through it. This is when the listening stops, because as a parent you immediately see and hear all the potential for trouble no matter what your daughter does—let alone the consternation you feel over her even being friends with that guy, or taking that class, or going on that date. Therefore, you feel compelled to intervene. To tell her what to do. To chastise her for getting into this predicament in the first place. To change the subject to avoid the anxiety. In fact, you may find yourself intervening before you have ever made the conscious decision to say anything. The reason for this is simple: You love your teenager. You love her so much that you don't want any harm to come to her, ever. So literally without thinking, you do everything you can to protect and save your teenager—yell, scold, lecture, debate. Unfortunately, none of these strategies works for you, your daughter, or your relationship with each other.

It's easy to listen when the person you are conversing with is telling you positive and resolved things. It's another matter when what she is talking about is messy, anxious, and unresolved. At times like this, most of us feel our own anxiety, and sometimes we even act on it. We try to make everything okay. *Don't worry, it'll be fine.* We shift attention back to ourselves. *That reminds me of when . . .* We try to solve her problem. *Oh, that happened to a friend of mine, all you need to do is . . .* This is why learning to listen when what is being discussed is uncomfortable or stressful is the brunt of good therapist training—and it takes lots of time and practice to improve in this regard. However, it's in moments like this, when whatever your teenager is talking about is making you uncomfortable or anxious, that she needs you to listen more than ever. If you can listen during these times, you both help your teenager solve her problems and strengthen your connection with her.

Practical Listening

When your teenagers were kids, some relative or perhaps even your child's pediatrician passed on to you the age-old wisdom of counting to ten before saying no to your children. This practice leaves your kids feeling listened to and gives you some reflection time to consider whether no is indeed what you want to say. That is, maybe there is no reason to have your five-year-old stay buckled in his car seat while you and he wait for your wife who has run into the convenience store for a half-gallon of milk. Your kids feel listened to and you have the opportunity to think anew about the situation at hand rather than to respond reactively. When your child reaches adolescence, this practice of counting to ten before saying no needs an upgrade.

Now instead of counting to ten before saying no, you need to count to ten before saying anything! That is, when whatever they are saying activates your anxiety, that's when you need to stay quiet and expectant for ten seconds, which gets you a passing grade on the test your teenager is putting you through. *Will you listen even when the stakes go up and make you nervous?* Your counting to ten slowly and staying silent gives her the time to realize that you are respecting her independence (you aren't brushing her aside), that it is a tough situation (you don't have an easy answer), that you believe in her (the expectant look on your face and in your demeanor), that you won't try to control her (you're not lecturing her), and that you won't abandon her (you're still there). In other words, a lot happens in those ten seconds of quiet. (By the way, as a practical matter, you can't rush from one to ten as a six-year-old does in a game of hide-and-seek; you have to take your time. I suggest one-Mississippi, two-Mississippi, three . . .)

I took to heart the idea of counting to ten whenever my teenage son made me anxious by what he was saying to me, or, more often, by what he was implying. It was hard. At around seven or eight, an ulcer seemed to be forming in my stomach and I could feel the beginnings of what I could only imagine was a migraine. But just before I hit ten, everything shifted. Suddenly, I was calm and my breathing was back to normal. I took a deep breath and looked at my son. He was watching, and as soon as our eyes met he shifted his gaze and began talking again. Only this time, it was different. He seemed more sincere and more trusting of me. He began to tell me what he had already tried to do to resolve his problem, which frightened me—but I said nothing, I just nodded. Then he explained why each previous attempt had failed, which surprised me because he was more insightful, reflective, and mature than I had expected. Then he told me what he was thinking of doing, which made me proud—because it is pretty much what I would have done. In the end, all I had to do was support him in what he had already determined to do.

Sometimes, just staying vigilant about your listening will actually come full circle over a short amount of time. Here is one parent's story worth remembering when you're tempted to intervene:

At my twelfth-grade son's school, the counselor was offering a six-week course on becoming more authentic parents—I like that kind of stuff, so I signed up. We did lots of journal writing and each week had a couple of our own homework assignments to complete. One week our assignment was to listen to our teenager for five minutes straight—no interruptions, no advice, no lectures, no swapping stories. Just pay full attention to our teenager for five minutes.

As usual, I forgot about the assignment until the day before class met. Fortunately, it was a holiday so there was plenty of time to get in my five minutes. But just as I was thinking this, I heard a crash in my son's room, followed by a string of words that I'm sure he had never learned from his father or me. When I walked into his room, Larry was sitting on the floor with tears rolling down his cheeks.

"I'll never get my college applications done on time."

"What do you mean? You told me they were all almost done."

"Well, they're not. And they're due in four days."

At this point, when I was ready to get on my high told-you-so horse, I remembered this week's assignment—to listen for five minutes. What the hell, why not? At first it was really difficult just to listen to him whine, but after only a couple of minutes it got easy—because I was doing an assignment, I had no other obligations and no other role. I just had to listen. I got into it. In fact, for most of that day, I helped him with his applications and for the most part all I did was listen and take my cues from him. And I could tell that he was grooving on this, which was great because the last couple of months had been tough between us.

A few days later, he had all his applications lined up on the kitchen table—he was showing off for us and looking for last-minute corrections.

"Hey, Mom, the applications want to know your profession. What should I put, teacher?"

A few years ago, I would have said yes; but now with four kids—Larry is the oldest—I'm comfortable with my decision to stop teaching and be a full-time mom. "No. Just put that I'm a mom."

He looked surprised, but then I saw a twinkle in his eyes. "Sure." A few minutes later, I sauntered over to see what he had written. Next to Mother's Profession he had written "World's Greatest Mom."

Then I felt his arm around me as he said, "Thanks for helping me with my applications, Mom, and everything else, too. Most of all, thanks for not getting angry at me the other day when I was so behind."

Emotional Intelligence

Emotional intelligence entered the mainstream as a concept with the publication of Daniel Goleman's 1995 book, *Emotional Intelligence: Why It Can Matter More Than IQ*. He defines *emotional intelligence* as "the ability to monitor one's own and others' emotions, to discriminate among them, and to use the information to guide one's thinking and actions."[1] In essence, it's the ability to understand your own emotions and motivations as well as the emotions and motivations of others.

Without a doubt, raising emotionally intelligent teenagers is the goal of most parents; and, as in many other areas, it all begins with the connection between you and your teenager. That is, from birth onward, your child has an emotional connection to you that is the beginning of emotional intelligence. It's the birth of empathy in your child. As children enter and proceed through adolescence, their emotional intelligence must grow accordingly. Yes, teenagers are famous for their emotional ups and downs, but this is not the same as emotional intelligence.

The hallmark of an emotionally intelligent teenager is that she can identify a myriad of complex and subtle feelings within herself and others. Furthermore, she can understand these emotions well enough to discern motivations, which in turn gives her more influence over her own emotional life. Kids with this aptitude are able to differentiate between anger, sadness, frustration, rage, guilt, shame, and a host of other feelings. They gather information from these feelings about the meaning behind them and, most important, discern how to move through them and not get stuck.

Teenagers learn emotional intelligence from their parents when their parents engage in two separate activities. The first is when they reflect back what they are seeing in their teenager. This simply means verbalizing what you are seeing on his face. *You seem sad today, honey. Is there anything wrong?* Or, *You seem* to be on edge; is something bugging you? Or, *You have that guilty look on your face—anything you want to tell me?* Seldom will this type of query lead to an in-depth conversation with your teenager. These questions will, however, help your teenager learn to recognize certain emotional states within herself—that is, by your identifying them. This is just how they learned to talk when they were toddlers. They pointed at the dog and you said *dog*. They touched the ice cube and you said *cold*. It's the same with your teenager, only now it's an internal language, the language of emotions.

Sometimes this means coming up with playful ways that help your kids learn to read your emotions.

> In our house we each have a little flat rock—on one side is painted a happy face, on the other a sad, sort of angry face. Each morning when we come down for breakfast we each find our rock and turn it so that it reflects our mood that morning—good or bad. In this way we know what to expect from one another, as well as learn what these different moods look like on each other's faces.

Some teenagers I know took this game one step further. The kids developed code words for the moods their parents were in. A reference to shampoo meant a good mood—ask for favors—but a reference to conditioner meant beware.

The second activity in which you teach your kids emotional intelligence is when you are transparent and verbal about your emotions. That is, when after nearly crashing into a car that was making an illegal turn, you say, "Wow! That was scary. But that guy was such a jerk, just look at him. But just look at my hands, they're shaking. I've got to pull over for a minute and calm down."

We do this in conversation with them, too, when we make our process transparent. *I'm really annoyed that you haven't done your homework yet, but I'm also worried that you're overwhelmed by your classes, and more than anything I'm concerned that you seem sad, that you're not as happy as you were a year ago. I wish I knew how to help.*

Emotional intelligence comes from feeling and from meaningful connections with people, and you are a primary person in your teenager's world, no matter what. It's not about resolving every situation down to the final detail. It's about moving forward in a manner that expands your teenager's access to and understanding of his emotional life.

There is a wonderful app, *The Mood Meter*, developed by Yale's Center for Emotional Intelligence that is terrific in helping users identify their various emotions and to create and follow strategies for changing these emotions when they are not optimal for the task at hand. Download and familiarize yourself with how to best use it, and then casually show it to your teenager. Most teens are quick to take an interest in this app. It's available at http://moodmeterapp .com.

> I've been playing with the Mood Meter for a couple of weeks now, and just showed it to my daughter a couple of days ago. She's gone crazy for it—even has turned on a few of her friends. So now she is the expert, suggesting different songs and images to help me shift from one mood to another. Also, as we become more nuanced in naming our different emotions I've noticed that our disagreements have been a bit less intense, softer and more reflective somehow.

The *Boss* Game

A game that I often recommend to families with teenagers is called *Boss*. This game encourages families to have fun with one another and to see the world through each other's eyes. Best of all, family members discover sides of each other that have gone untouched for too long. Parents, in particular, often have a glimpse of their teenager displaying some level of mastery that catches them by surprise.

Boss is a simple game with simple rules. Pick a block of time, usually two hours or more, then divide that by the number of people playing—that's the amount of time each person has. It's ideal when the whole family can play together, but if they can't, make do with those you have. If you have two hours and four people are playing, each person is allotted thirty minutes. Each player then draws a straw, or by some other random process picks one of the four blocks of time—first half-hour, second half-hour, third half-hour, or fourth half-hour. During your block of time, you are the boss and in charge of what you do as a group. These are the only two guidelines: you can't pick an activity that goes against someone's morals or that endangers anyone's health; and when you are not the boss, you must enthusiastically go along with whatever activity the boss has chosen.

> I ended up with the first, forty-five minute block. I chose a family hike in the recreation area near our house. It was wonderful, primarily because everyone, according to the rules of the game, was in a great mood. Lots of laughter, joking, and general fun. But then it was Nan's turn (our fifteen-year-old daughter). She took us up to her room and announced that we were all going to write in our diaries for the entire block, which we did. It was strange at first, but after

a while we were all writing away, looking up every once in a while at each other, but then quickly returning to our own writing. I was bored after about ten minutes, but I stuck with it and stayed cheerful, too. When Nan announced that time was up, I was on a roll and started to object; that is, until I remembered that it was my son's turn.

Ken (thirteen years old) took us into the basement and proceeded to play his electric guitar for his "adoring fans." That's right, he had us play his groupies. Although it was way too loud for me, I must admit that by the end I could see how much he loved playing music; and not only that, I realized that he was turning into a handsome young man with lots of stage presence. At the conclusion of his block, my wife stepped in and announced that we were all marching up to the kitchen where we were going to prepare dinner while she oversaw our work. She had us make bruschetta, Caesar salad, crab cakes, corn on the cob, and ice cream sundaes for dessert. Ironically, she worked harder than any of us by just trying to keep up with our questions and our general bumbling—at least for me, but my daughter and son were much better than I was. And we actually spent lots of that time laughing with each other, at each other, and at ourselves. Best of all, when her block ended, dinner was ready and we all shared a wonderful feast. Of course, minutes after dinner was over, Nan was on the phone with a friend and Ken was heading out the back door to meet some buddies. Nonetheless, my wife and I hung out at the dining room table drinking an extra glass of wine and basking in one another's company.

The point of playing *Boss* together is that it brings fun, curiosity, and connection back into the family. Yes, it's pretty contrived at the beginning, but once you get into it, most people have wonderful things to report about playing the game together as a family.

To Track or Not to Track

Given that just about every teenager owns some sort of cellular device it also means that parents have the ability to track their teenager's whereabouts with a high degree of accuracy. Thus the question: Should you track or not? And if you decide to track, do you tell your teenager or not?

For me this question is akin to drug testing your teenager on a regular basis. I'm against it. So let me diverge for a moment and then come back to the question of tracking your child's whereabouts.

Although some will argue that regular drug testing supports your teenager's ability to say no—and this is true—it unfortunately also undermines the connection between you and your teenager. That is, you are basically telling them that you do not trust them or their judgment. And no matter how you frame the issue, all they hear is that you do not trust them.

> Yeah, my parents have been drug testing me every couple of weeks since eighth grade. At first it was like, "Whatever." And maybe deep inside I was relieved because it made it easier to say no to people. But now that I'm in eleventh grade I feel like the regular testing holds me back. I don't get to make the decision so in a weird way I don't know if I can really trust myself. And if I can't make my own decisions around this how can I make my own decisions around other choices in my life? I mean I'll be on my own at college in just a couple of years and they're definitely not drug testing me in college. Hell, I'll go to college as far away as possible to avoid that.

It was Mark Twain who coined the wise adage "Good judgment comes from experience, and experience comes from bad judgment." Although I'm definitely not advocating drug use, I am advocating letting teenagers wrestle with and strengthen their decision-making abilities. That is, within limits, let them make some bad decisions. For instance, on the topic of drug testing, it gets in the way of their growing autonomy to drug test teenagers who have never had a problem with drugs. Conversely, for those who have had a problem—been caught at home or school—it makes sense to drug test for a limited period of time to help them get their feet back under them and to learn from their poor decisions. This is a form of failure analysis within the temporary safety of the drug testing.

> My mom found my stash at the beginning of ninth grade. She and my dad went ballistic—way more than I ever expected. Right away I promised to never use again, though I'm not sure I really meant it. Long story short, they said they were going to make me take a drug test every week for the next four months, and if I was clean that entire time we would stop the tests. They also required me to see a counselor every week. I hated both ideas but didn't have much choice. At first I just went through the motions, but after a few weeks it became clear that a lot of my identity was built around getting stoned— what I did on weekends, my friends, how I handled stress, and how I made or avoided making decisions. My use had sort of snuck up on me. Anyway, by the end of the four months I had grown up quite a bit so when the drug testing stopped I was stronger and could easily say no when offered. And who I was hanging around with and how I viewed my future had also both changed for the better.

In my mind, the same goes for tracking your teenager's whereabouts. If they have lied to you about their whereabouts then use the tracking for a set amount of time. In addition, ask yourselves and them why they don't trust you. That is, if they profess certainty that you will say no to their request you need to look in the mirror and ask yourselves if their assessment is correct. That is, sometimes there is a disconnect when teenagers think their parents will say no to a request that is a stretch from the normal ground rules, like where they go with their friends on a weekend evening. If this is the case, they will frequently lie about their whereabouts. If, however, you would be open to their requests and they are not trusting you with making a considered decision—and sharing some of the risk—then they are shortchanging the relationship. Clearing this up will, of course, deepen the connection between parent and teenager.

> Just one more question: Now that we know you lied about where you were last night I am wondering why you just didn't ask us for permission? You keep asking us to trust you, which I get. And you need to understand that you have to trust us as well. In this case, you should have trusted us to hear you out and possibly even agree to your request. As it is, you never gave us that chance.

So, in the end, just because you can track their whereabouts does not mean that you should. In general, it's a great idea to balance what technology is capable of with whether or not it's a good idea. And, in this context, whether it deepens or undermines the connection between your teenager and you.

Passwords to Code

One of the best tools any parent can give a young child is a family password, usually a word that the child has chosen. This is the word that protects the child from the predators in the world. We teach our kids that if someone they don't know tries to talk to them, invites them to go for a ride, says their mom or dad wants them to let this person give them a ride home, then this person must also know the family password. In essence, nonfamily members can learn the password only from a family member. If someone outside the family knows the word, then that person can be trusted. If that person doesn't know the word, your child says that his mommy and daddy won't let him do anything without first hearing the password. And then your child can do whatever it takes to get away: be rude, yell, run, scream, walk away.

This is a great idea with young children, but it changes when your kids enter adolescence. Now you move from the family password to the family code phrase.

By the time your kids are teenagers, they know the right thing to do in just about any circumstance (see Chapter 8, "Self-Esteem Through Integrity"). However, this does not mean they always do what they know is the right thing.

Sometimes this is because of a yearning for a new experience; sometimes to fit in with a new group of friends; sometimes because they are bored; and sometimes because they don't have the strength to say no. When they fail to do the right thing because of this last reason—they don't have the internal strength to say no—this is exactly where the family code phrase comes to the rescue. In any situation that requires teenagers to take two big steps forward in responsibility when they are capable of only one step forward, the family code phrase helps you to meet them halfway.

Like the password, the code phrase is something that your teenager is familiar with and it's a phrase known only to family members. The simpler the better. The names of nonexistent relatives is a favorite of mine: Aunt Rose, Uncle Mickey. This is how it works: As soon as your teenager utters this phrase while in conversation with you, your job is simple: to say no to whatever she is asking. Then, no matter how much of a struggle she puts up, hold your ground. Let her have the full range of her abilities to argue with you and to make a scene if necessary. It's worth it, and here's why.

The point of the code phrase is that it's a means for your teenager to say to you *There's something going on here that I don't want to be a part of, but it's too big a leap for me to take to get out of it now. I need your help. Please say no to what I ask and then let me make a fuss so that I can save face in front of my friends. Please!* Instantly, you know that your teenager is in over his head, that he needs your help, that he is clear about the help that he needs, and that whatever follows is not meant personally.

It was around 11:00 p.m. on a Saturday night when Carmen called. She had gone out earlier that night with her friends Julie and Sandy and wasn't due home for at least another hour.

"Hi, Mom. I'm over at Sandy's and I'm wondering if I can spend the night? We're just hanging around watching movies and talking. And yes, Sandy's mom is home."

A good sign when she could answer my questions before I had asked them. I congratulated myself and said, "Sure. Sounds fine. Will you need a ride home in the morning?"

"Oh, Mom. I meant to tell you before I left, but Uncle Mickey called today and said he wanted you to call him back. Sorry."

I was stunned. We had talked about this moment, but somehow I had never imagined it happening. "Uncle Mickey? Did I hear you correctly?"

"I'm sorry. You're right. I should have left you a note."

As I wondered what could possibly be going on for her to use the code phrase, I said, "Well, in that case you need to come home. How about I come get you in fifteen minutes?"

"Mom! You've got to be kidding! Why can't I spend the night?"

Momentarily stunned by this apparently mixed message—using the code phrase and getting angry with me—I then realized she was playing to her friends, who were probably within earshot of our conversation.

"Are Julie and Sandy standing right there and listening?" I asked.

"Of course. It's fine with Sandy's mom if I stay, so why won't you let me?"

"Carmen, if it helps, you have my permission this one time to swear at me. Just this once."

"Stop being an asshole, Mom!"

"I'm not sure what's going on over there, but I'll be out front in fifteen minutes."

As she hung up the phone, I'm pretty sure I heard her take full advantage of the situation by spewing out a few more curse words.

When she came out of Sandy's front door, she sent me a look full of anxiety. I knew we were still in role. She got into the passenger seat, crossed her arms, and stared straight ahead. I put the car in gear and drove away.

After we had driven down the block and out of sight, I asked, "Are you okay, Carmen?" She just nodded. "I'm not sure what was going on at Sandy's, but I sure am proud of you for getting yourself out of there."

"It was terrible—they were both talking about sneaking out at night to go to some party with some boys they just met yesterday! No way I was going, but I didn't want them to think I was a goody-two-shoes, either. Thanks for coming and getting me, Mom."

Much later that night, after staying up with Carmen and talking some more, I lay awake in my bed: Should I call Sandy's parents? Carmen had done the right thing in a tough situation, and now I had a similar choice to make.

This mom did a wonderful job of meeting her daughter halfway, and so did her daughter by meeting her mom at the same place. But doing so is never a free ride, as we see how the mom was left holding the anxiety far into the night, long after her daughter had fallen asleep. And this is just one more reason why parenting a teenager is the toughest job you'll ever have.

*   *   *

Your teenager counts on your quiet presence and deep confidence in her more than she can or will ever tell you. And when you see this for yourself, it becomes easier and easier to listen to her more deeply and to reassure her more concisely, which in turn deepens the connection between the two of you.

SIX

The Sexes Are Different, and This Is Good News!

Most of us would mark the box next to Men if the SAT question read "Teenagers are to adults as _____ are to women." Then we would smile, because, although sometimes reluctant to admit it, we all know the confusing feelings that accompany our best efforts to understand the opposite gender and adolescents. The proverbial gender gap and generation gap live and thrive, side by side.

At the same time, when it comes to stereotypes around gender (and teenagers, too), I'll stand at the head of the line in opposition. I'm not a proponent of stereotypes of any ilk. Still, though, there are certain gender-based behavior and personality predispositions that are important to understand and consider. That is, although I'm not a believer in gender-based clichés, it is irresponsible to not acknowledge the general gender differences that occur during adolescence, even as we look with fresh eyes at our own teenagers. We have to understand the stereotypes and then push ourselves to look past them to see our teenagers for who they are, which is much more than any simplistic gender convention. But first, we need to consider just how the sexes are different, and it helps to begin with some relevant theories and research that have emerged in recent years. We'll apply these same ideas later in the chapter.

What the Experts Say

Nancy Chodorow, PhD, is a scholar who has focused much of her interdisciplinary attention on the origins of gender differences, what she calls "preoedipal development."[1] Because the mother is female, Chodorow hypothesizes that boys and girls must and do develop differently. Girls, because they are physically like their mothers, feel a natural and powerful connection that forms an underlying dynamic for females: nurturing relationships. As a result of this instant "we are the same" connection with their mothers, girls tend to prioritize relationships and relationship skills over developing a strong sense of self.

Boys, according to Chodorow, because they are physically different from their mothers, experience an early pull toward autonomy, specifically in needing to reject their mother's world so that they can gain acceptance into the masculine world—a world different from that of their moms. Because they have had to reject their mothers due to their physical differences, boys have developed a strong sense of self through attention on accomplishment and competition, but at the expense of relationship skills. That is, boys feel the need to search out and to prove themselves to "be a man."

Chodorow's work lines up nicely with Carol Gilligan's research into the different moral development of males and females.[2] In many ways, Gilligan picks up where Chodorow left off: She defines male and female morality as somewhat different because it is based on the differences between males and females that stem from the preoedipal phase of development. In short, she distinguishes how males focus more on individuals and basic rights whereas females focus more on the responsibilities they have for others. For Gilligan, Male = respecting individual rights; Female = meeting responsibilities to others. She calls the male mode "justice orientation" and the female mode "responsibility orientation."

According to the theory, as children grow up, these differences play out with females being more focused on connections to others and males on separation as individuals. Gilligan frequently cites how boys and girls handle disagreement differently as an example of the relative importance of connection and separation. Boys actively resolve the situation and tend to do whatever it takes to reach some sort of resolution, even if it means hurt feelings along the way. Girls tend to stop whatever they are doing when relationships are threatened; rather than push through for resolution, their priority is on preserving the connections. This is also why girls are more apt to share their emotions with others—it furthers the connection—and boys are more apt to keep their emotional lives private—it preserves autonomy and separation.

I consider myself a staunch feminist and for years (all before giving birth to a boy and a girl) I believed and even preached that there were no differences between boys and girls. I believed that all the differences between the genders are imposed by society and well-meaning adults who consciously and unconsciously sculpt males and females into the existing stereotypes. As a result, I believed that, given a truly neutral environment, boys would play with dolls as often as girls, just as girls would play with toy soldiers and model airplanes as often as boys. Well, with a five-year-old boy and a three-year-old girl at home, I'm here to say that I was wrong! There are huge differences between boys and girls. Despite my best efforts, I can't tear my daughter away from Barbie nor my son away from his action figures. My daughter will sit still and play by herself; my son can't sit still for a minute and is constantly banging into things. And these differences have been apparent since birth. Now I'm convinced boys and girls are different, yet I'm hopeful that we can learn lots from each other, too.

But even beyond these differences are the societal stereotypes and assumptions we bring to bear on how we see and treat the sexes differently. Lawrence J. Cohen, author of *Playful Parenting*,[3] describes research that he refers to as "The Tabletop Experiments." In one of these studies, researchers watched a baby at play—dressed only in a diaper and young enough so that the gender was indecipherable. Then the researchers told one group of subjects that the infant was a boy and the other that the infant was a girl. The fascinating part is how differently the subjects responded, depending on whether they were led to believe they were watching a male or female infant.

When observers thought they were seeing a girl, they responded much more quickly to her cries and engaged with her more often. If they thought the baby was a boy, they left him alone longer with his cries and encouraged him to explore the environment as well as his own motor activity.

In another of these experiments, subjects were shown a video of a nine-month-old baby at play. Again, the gender of the infant was indecipherable and half the subjects were told the infant was a girl and the other half that the infant was a boy. The big difference between the two groups occurred when on the video a jack-in-the-box sprang up and made the infant cry. Subjects who thought the infant was female thought her tears meant that she was afraid. When they thought the infant was a boy, they attributed the tears to anger. From these experiments we can draw a couple of conclusions about how we generally see boys and girls as different and, as a result, how what we believe boys and girls need from us is different. We tend to give girls more comfort than we give boys; and boys receive more encouragement to explore than girls. The big cost of these unconscious assumptions is that girls often aren't encouraged enough to actively explore the world around them, and boys are overlooked when they experience vulnerable emotions such as fear or sadness.

One of the leading authorities and authors on the differences between boys and girls is Michael Gurian, and from his work a couple of points are worth making that pertain to becoming and staying connected to your teenager. First, compared to females, research shows that males are better with spatial relationships, abstract thought, and in general are more task oriented. Females, on the other hand, have the edge when it comes to memory and their ability to take in greater quantities of sensory information and to process it more thoroughly. As a result, although males are more goal oriented than females, if they are thwarted in the accomplishment of that goal, they have fewer resources at their disposal to overcome the obstacles that are blocking them.

Second, as the parents of a teenage boy and a teenage girl already know, males and females handle emotions differently. Gurian points to brain differences for an explanation:

> The female brain processes more emotive stimulants, through more senses, and more completely than does the male. It also verbalizes emotive information quickly. Boys can sometimes take hours to process emotively (and manage the same information as girls). This lesser emotive ability makes males more emotionally fragile than we tend to think.[4]

This has some practical and important ramifications to grasp. First, because girls are efficient at processing their emotions and are generally more open with their emotional ups and downs, they look more emotionally vulnerable than boys. In actuality, their up-front approach to addressing unpleasant emotions is healthier and makes them somewhat more resilient than boys in this area. Second, because boys don't look as emotionally vulnerable, we are more likely to miss or overlook a boy in emotional distress. This is kind of like the adage about the difference between extroverts and introverts: If you want to know what an extrovert is thinking, stay quiet and listen; if you want to know what an introvert is thinking, you need to ask and wait. Only now, instead of thinking, we mean feeling, and instead of extroverts and introverts we mean males and females.

Gurian points out some differences between boys and girls during adolescence, two of which are pertinent to the task of maintaining a strong connection to your teenager:

1. According to one study, 69 percent of high school males suggest "fighting" as the best way to resolve conflict; 69 percent of their female counterparts suggest "walking away or talking things out" as the best way to resolve conflict. (This finding falls right in line with Gilligan's earlier observations of how males and females respond to disagreement.)
2. In high school, male bullies still enjoy popularity among their peers and female bullies are among the less popular girls.

From the Ivory Towers of Academia to Your Home

Obviously, the scope of this book limits how much can be written on the differences between males and females. Therefore, to help you form and maintain a strong connection with your teenager, consider the following questions and allow them to guide you in making use of gender differences as you work to stay connected to your teenager, male or female. This reflection will help you to identify some of the gender assumptions you carry around, and, more important, to see your teenager with fresh eyes:

1. When you think of girls, what words or phrases come to mind?
2. When you think of boys, what words or phrases come to mind?
3. How would each of your parents have answered questions one and two when they were your age and raising you?
4. How do your responses to questions one and two compare to how you see yourself as a male or female?
5. How do your responses to questions one and two compare to how you see your teenager?
6. Now, most important, where and how do you and your teenager not fit the lists you generated in questions one and two?

Keep your responses to these questions in mind as you read the rest of this chapter because they will help you clarify some of the dynamics of your relationship with your teenager as well as assist you in identifying some hidden resources for a better connection between the two of you.

Parent and Teenager by Gender

Bearing in mind the foregoing theories, research, and ideas, let's take a look at how some of these gender differences play out in the various permutations of parent–teenager relationships: mother–daughter, father–daughter, mother–son, father–son. In particular, we'll pay attention to how gender affects your relationship with your teenager in the main task of adolescence: creating a stable identity based on increased autonomy.

Mothers and Daughters: Fire Meets Fire. Without a doubt this is the most intense of all relationships, sparks alternately flying around and threatening to blaze the surroundings and then coming to rest in the intimate warmth of a glowing campfire. Until adolescence, the mother–daughter relationship is one of general warmth and closeness. Sure, there are the occasional blowups, but most resolve themselves with heartfelt apologies from both sides, and lots of hugs. In the younger years, daughters freely profess their love and admiration of their mothers. *When I grow up I want to be like you, Mommy. We can always work things out because we listen to each other, right?*

But during adolescence, when the teenage daughter is faced with the task of differentiating herself, the mother–daughter relationship becomes one of alternating intimacy and hate, both marked with an intensity that only teenagers can bring to a relationship and bring out in their parents.

> My daughter and I are either best friends or worst enemies. There is no in-between. Sometimes she confides in me as an ally. Sometimes she wants to hang out with me—well, mostly when I offer to take her shopping. Sometimes we even discuss her future in civilized and intimate ways. But at other times, we can't even be in the same room without insulting each other—yes, I admit it, sometimes I'm just as bad as she is, maybe even worse. The worst part is that everything can be fine between us when I make some tiny suggestion to her— *Why don't you do your homework now? Your other shoes would look better with those pants*—that sets her off. She accuses me of trying to control her when I make these innocuous suggestions. But at other times she seeks me out for a wardrobe consultation and hangs on my every word. It's nutty.

Teenage girls want both their freedom from and their connection to their moms, but they are just not sure how to navigate the terrain and as a result give lots of mixed messages. When teenage daughters are exercising their autonomy in their attempts to construct a differentiated self, they push their moms away. Author John Gray believes that because girls overcomplied with their mothers during childhood, there is a certain rebound effect away from their mothers in adolescence: "To develop a sense of self, adolescent girls feel a greater need to fight, defy, or rebel against their mother's control."[5] But given the female inclination toward relationships and connection, moms are not going to take these pushes passively. Just when their daughters need independence, their moms need connection. This is the old Mars–Venus dynamic at play, but instead of the males needing space and the females pursuing, the daughters are pushing away and the moms are pursuing.

On the other hand, when daughters are looking for connection, they typically turn to their mothers. When the mom is available, these are some of the most treasured and intimate moments between mothers and daughters; they just don't last all that long.

There is one additional variable that is too huge to overlook here which, when in place, plays havoc with the mother–daughter relationship during adolescence: The two M's, menstruation and menopause. During a teenage girl's adolescence, marked by her beginning to menstruate, many moms are going through their own set of physical and hormonal changes in the form of menopause. At the very least, these two sets of hormones and physical changes happening in the same relative time frame in the same home is a recipe for interpersonal inconsistency and strife, to put it mildly.

> It seemed that there was only a week or two between when I experienced my first hot flashes and my daughter had her first period. And for me, menopause was the whole deal: hot flashes, irritability, mood swings, even the ringing in the ears (tinnitus). With my daughter going through all her mood swings and physical changes from menstruation, we were like two alley cats trapped in a tight space. Talk about a cruel joke by Mother Nature! It wasn't until later in her adolescence that we connected in any consistent way—it was that big of a deal for us.

The dangerous dynamic here is that mothers, in their attempts to keep the relationship alive and healthy, might smother their daughters. Mothers have to learn to stay close while also giving their daughters the space in which to claim their independence. Look back to how you responded to question three in the preceding section—how your parents would have described the differences between boys and girls. If your parents bought into the prevailing gender stereotypes of their day, the danger is that as a teenage daughter you were never able to declare your autonomy while staying connected to your mom. That is, you either had to stage an outright revolt, possibly even running away from home, or you had to sacrifice yourself for your mother's lack of ability to differentiate herself from you. If either of these dynamics applies to you, you need to appreciate the power of your past to make sure you don't do the same with your daughter, or, in an attempt to correct the misdeeds of your mother, the opposite.

Mothers and Sons: Fire Meets Rock.   This relationship, in stereotypical form, is dominated by a mom's need to connect and her son's need to differentiate himself, often at his mother's expense. Most sons simply don't communicate that well with their moms, at least in their moms' words.

> My son and daughter are so different. I mean, foremost they are both teenagers, and that definitely dominates the scene at home. But with my daughter, when I can finally get through all her teenage angst, we really talk. We laugh, cry, and just enjoy hanging out in moments like this. Time seems to rush by when we're in synch like this. But with my son, even when we are in synch he doesn't have much to tell me. It's like he is in his own world and I can't penetrate it.

Of course, teenage boys have a different perspective on the mother–son relationship:

> My mom is, like, constantly in my face—it's like she wants to know everything I do and think. And she can't take a hint. She doesn't realize that when I go into my room after school, close the door, and turn on the stereo I don't want to talk. No, she knocks on my door every day and wants to hear all about school. It's just crazy—I wish she could just give me some space. I don't hate her, but I do hate how she sometimes barely gives me enough room to breathe.

Sons are struggling for autonomy and identity, which means that on some level they will reject their mothers as a primitive form of "not-me" and discern for themselves just who they are and what it means to be male. This is particularly so during early adolescence, when boys are going through or have just gone through puberty. At no time in his life does a boy feel more unlike his mother than now as he grapples with the physical and hormonal changes associated with puberty. Worse, from his perspective at least, even if he did want to talk about these changes, it would not be with a female, especially his mother.

The good news, however, is that once boys have put enough distance between the two of you, have adapted to puberty, and have established themselves somewhat as individuals, they are open to bringing you back into the fold. And who better in the world to help them grapple with two of the perennial issues of adolescence: intimacy and the opposite sex.

> Will and I had a tough stretch for a couple of years, when he was thirteen and fourteen years old. It seemed that no matter what I said, he either disagreed or just tuned me out and walked away. It was aggravating. But somehow we got through it, and now things are good between us. I give him more space than I prefer, but he opens up to me more than I ever expected—especially compared to those first couple of years during adolescence.
>
> It all shifted after his first girlfriend broke up with him. When I walked by his door, I saw him sitting in his room with a depressed look on his face. I stopped and returned for two reasons: the look on his face and the open door, which was a first. (I took the open door as a handwritten invitation to talk.)
>
> "What's up, Will? You seem down."
>
> "I just don't get it, Mom. Why did Sherry break up with me?" I sat down on the edge of the bed. He made room for me.
>
> "At first she liked me because I wasn't like other guys: I'm sensitive, I listen, and I talk to her about my feelings." I began to swoon on the bed. Was this

really my son? "But now those are the exact reasons she breaks up with me. She says I'm too serious when all she wants is a casual relationship. She even said I should try being more like other guys."

That I managed a response was a minor miracle. "Really?"

"Mom, you're a girl. What do women want in men?"

That sure took me by surprise, but it's also the kind of question I had always wanted him to ask. Not that I had an answer, but exploring the question with my son is the stuff families are made of, at least in my mind.

When they are with their moms, teenage sons sometimes are able to let down their guard. For many teenagers, searching for identity initially includes buying into the gender stereotypes, especially for boys. As a result, in front of peers they play the male role, staying tough and in charge on the outside, but away from peers, especially when with their moms, they drop their guard.

I remember watching my son, Peter, play on the school soccer team during his freshman year and noticing how rough the game was being played. The referees were letting a lot go and the players were getting pretty aggressive with one another. But neither of the coaches said anything, nor did any of the players. It was almost an unspoken ethos to not complain. Anything to avoid the moniker of sissy, or even worse. At least, that's what I imagined.

Peter sat through the postgame meeting, said good-bye to his friends, and eventually found his way to me as I waited for him in the parking lot. He looked just as he did on the field, kind of stoic, but in a sad way.

"Tough game today."

"Yeah."

"Seemed kind of rough, too."

"Mom, I don't want to play soccer anymore." This from a kid who had lived and breathed the sport for the past six years. His room looks like a shrine to World Cup Soccer.

"Where's this coming from?"

"It's just no fun anymore. I don't like it."

"This have anything to do with how rough the game was today?" Nothing. I waited some more, heard him sniff, and out of the corner of my eye saw his left hand wipe away a tear from his cheek. "You okay, Peter?"

It was too late, he was falling apart. I pulled over and comforted him while he had a huge cry—the way he cried when he was six or seven years old. He was scared, confused, angry, embarrassed, and, above all else, emotionally hurt from how rough soccer had become. And he was at a threshold, either to ignore his feelings and continue to play soccer to be "tough" in the only way he knew or to acknowledge his emotions and get away from soccer. Fortunately, after some conversation, he realized there were other options available to him, and that there are many kinds of tough, including playing a rough sport and having feelings.

It's often with their moms that boys risk emotional vulnerability. That's why it's so important for moms in particular to give them some of the space they need, but not too much. It's also why differences between the genders are good. In this example, the mom's greater access to feelings and emotions makes it safe for her son to explore and express feelings that are typically difficult for an adolescent boy to acknowledge.

When fire meets the rock, neither overwhelms the other. Instead, the fire warms the rock, but it takes time. And when that happens, they are able to coexist—the rock stays warm and the fire knows the rock will emit its heat long after the fire has been extinguished.

Fathers and Sons: Rock Meets Rock.   On the outside, this relationship often presents itself as the most peaceful, but is that because of a mutual respect or an accepted disconnect? Fathers and sons intuitively understand the need for independence and identity through a respect of the basic rights of individuals. For sons, this respect is created through accomplishment in a chosen area: academics, social, sports, drama, music, church. And fathers allow them the space for this and offer their support, too. But seldom is this support addressed directly. The quintessential father-son relationship is played out side by side, engaged in activity. And what is not said is often as important as what is.

"So you really think you're ready for a full-time job this summer?"

"Yeah. Otherwise, I'll just sit around all day, which is boring. Besides, I could use the money."

"What kind of work you thinking of?"

"Doesn't matter. Maybe something physical that will keep me in shape for football when school starts."

"Don't suppose you would want to work in my office? I could talk to my boss."

"Nah. Would hate being indoors all summer. Thanks anyway."

"We could talk to your Uncle Stan, he's the foreman of a construction crew downtown. If he's hiring summer help, I'm sure he would consider you."

"Cool."

"We can call him when we get home if you like."

"Thanks, Dad."

A great deal about the father–son relationship is implicit, especially during adolescence. The danger here, though, is that boys miss out on their dads just when they need them, when they struggle with what it is to be male. That is, out of respect for independence, fathers can erroneously give their sons too much room. And like mothers with daughters, fathers must examine the gender biases of their own childhoods. Which assumptions and biases are you prepped to pass on to your son? The point is that if you want to pass on a different and more liberating set of gender expectations, you need to take an active role in making it happen, otherwise it'll never occur.

My father was the classic male of his day. He worked sixty hours a week so that my mom didn't have to work, even though we barely ever saw him. And when he was home, he stayed to himself, and definitely never opened up to us. Although I love my dad, I vowed to be different with my kids, especially my son. Even though it's difficult, I go out of my way to talk about my emotions with him, something my dad never did with me. It's awkward for both my son and me, but it's getting better. I just want him to realize that being male doesn't mean not having feelings.

Fathers and Daughters: Rock Meets Fire. In all parent–child relationships, the level of engagement and trust, at least as reported by children and teenagers, diminishes by about the same amount across the board when children become teenagers, except, that is, for fathers and daughters. This relationship experiences a greater drop in closeness than all the others, by nearly double.

Stop and consider the players involved and this only makes sense. Stereotypical fathers are most at home with the dynamics of independence, autonomy, and justice, which means these are the filters through which they interpret most behavior. Thus, when their teenage daughters push them away—as they need to do to assert their autonomy—fathers take this literally and personally, which leads them to back off. (Consider this in juxtaposition to mothers, who, when pushed away by their daughters, refuse to go and instead only push back harder—thus the intensity and volatility of that relationship, but also the connection.) Fathers, through their orientation toward accomplishment and independence, believe they are giving their daughters the space that they are demanding. Their daughters, however, feel that their fathers abandon them when they need them most.

The differences between the genders hit me in the face the other night. Jessica, my fifteen-year-old daughter, was upset and on the verge of tears about something. Whatever it was, she was so stressed that when I asked her if she was okay she said no. Then she proceeded to tell me why, or at least a thumbnail version. "I found out that Chelsea and Monique are going to a party tomorrow night that they told me they weren't going to. They're ditching me!" I couldn't follow much of what came next, but I got the gist of the situation.

"Well, it sounds like they're not really your friends."

"Dad! We've been best friends since, like, the third grade. How can you say that?"

Rather than defend what had just gotten me in trouble with Jess, I tried a new tack. "Any chance it's just a misunderstanding? Are you sure they are leaving you out?"

"Of course I'm sure. They lied to me."

"Maybe you can call them and tell them what you've heard—maybe they have an explanation. I'm sure there's some sort of explanation."

"Dad, you're impossible. Don't you get it? They're ditching me."

Next thing I knew she was closing the door to her room, which she had just entered, leaving me in the hall by myself and scratching my head. That's when my wife came by.

"Everything okay with Jess?"

"Not really. She thinks her friends ditched her and I think I only made things worse."

"Hmm, mind if I have a try?"

"Be my guest, but don't get your hopes up."

Thirty minutes later, Jess and my wife came downstairs with their arms around each other's shoulders. Jess's eyes were red from tears, but she had a gentle smile on her face.

"Everything okay, you two?"

My wife replied, "Sure, we're just going to make a couple of fruit smoothies; want one?"

"C'mon, Dad, we make them better than you can get at the store. Right, Mom?"

Later that night, when I was alone with my wife, I asked her what had happened. What had she said to get Jess to open up and to snap out of her angry depression? She just smiled and said, "Not much really, I just said that she must feel awful given what her friends had done. At that she just broke into tears and hugged me the way she did when she was a little kid. Honest, I didn't say much. After that, all I did was reassure her that she would be fine, no matter what Chelsea and Monique did."

With her connection to her friends in jeopardy, what Jessica needed was to reconnect with her parents. Her mom offered that reconnection by acknowledging the suffering and opening the door for an emotional connection. Her dad had unintentionally closed the door on that reconnection by focusing on problem solving and fairness without ever touching upon the underlying emotions.

On top of all this, there is one more issue that fathers seldom confront directly: their daughters' emerging sexuality. As their daughters grow into young women, something that no father can miss, most dads aren't sure what to do, so most take the safe way out and step back, giving their daughters even more room. That is, the hugging, hand-holding, and general touching that typifies many father–daughter relationships before puberty are now punctuated by a distinct lack of physical contact. Worse, in retrospect at least, many fathers realize that one of the primary ways they connected with their daughters before puberty was through physical play and spontaneous physical gestures of affection. But, suddenly, all the connection that occurred through physical contact disappears, which is something that is alternately confusing and liberating to their daughters. They see their fathers withdraw from them without understanding why. And for someone driven by relationships (females), this development is tough to reconcile.

> It was so strange after I hit puberty. I was totally uncomfortable with my body and the fact that I was all of a sudden having a period every month and that my boobs were growing out of control; all this made me neurotic about myself. And my dad didn't help. It's like he just removed himself from me. He kept himself at a distance, as if I had cooties or something. I hated it and hated him for how he was treating me.

But, on the other hand:

> Ever since I reached puberty, I can't stand it when my dad wants to hug me or put his arm around me. It's just too weird. And whenever I bristle if he reaches out to me like I'm some little kid, he gets that hurt puppy dog look on his face, which only makes everything worse!

The big hurdle for fathers to get over is to learn how to make an emotional connection not heavily dependent on physical contact. Or as John Gray says: "To bond with his daughter, a father needs to put in time asking informed questions and to practice listening without always offering advice."[6]

Single Parents.*   In general, this book does not address issues unique to family structures: single parents, grandparents raising grandchildren, coparenting, stepparenting, same-sex parents, divorced parents—because the strategies and understandings required to become and stay connected to your teenager do not change significantly under these different configurations. (Though, and to be clear on this, any type of single parenting is exponentially more difficult on the parent.) Gender difference is the exception.

Understanding the role of gender casts sharp relief on one of the intrinsic difficulties of single parents: providing your kids with access to adults of the opposite gender. Ideally, your teenager will find adults to connect with who are of the opposite gender—coaches, teachers, ministers, parent of a close friend, aunts, and uncles. If this does not happen naturally, it is a good idea for you to encourage these relationships, perhaps even to play a bit of the matchmaker. This might mean letting a teacher know that your son looks up to him and later on letting the teacher know that your son's father is no longer around. It might mean driving an extra twenty miles for your daughter's piano lessons because the piano teacher is an important woman in your daughter's life.

In situations of single parenting, it's important for the single parent to supplement wherever possible. At the same time, don't be overly perplexed if your teenager doesn't naturally connect with an adult of the opposite gender, because she will at some point during her adolescence. And like almost everything else, it'll happen in her time frame, not yours.

Same-Sex Parents.   As soon as you enter the gender fray, it's just a matter of time before the question of gay parents emerges. That is, aren't the kids of gay parents worse off because of their exposure to just one gender? The answer is an emphatic and simple no. In general, in all two-parent households there are certain roles that each partner plays, often broken down along stereotypical masculine and feminine lines. That is, one parent takes on the more typical behaviors and attitudes of the male and the other of the female. This means that one is more emotionally available and focused on connection, and the other is more focused on justice, rights, and achievement.

Even in same-sex relationships, this breakdown according to roles tends to happen, which means the teenager is exposed to the attitudes and behaviors of both genders even though the parents are of the same gender.

---

*By "single parent" in this instance, I mean when one parent has full responsibility for the child and the other parent does not play a role in raising that child. This is different from single parents who split custody of their children, as is often the case in divorce.

And, of course, similarly to single parents, encouraging connections to adults of the other gender is a good idea. But then again, the more connections your teenager has with adults outside the home, of both genders, the better off he or she is.

Natural Strengths and Weaknesses

In studying the qualities of successful business people, researchers have made a few unexpected discoveries. The top one on my list is that successful people tend to focus on building their strengths and avoiding their weaknesses, which is different from what many of us were taught as children. The idea then was to improve your weaknesses for better performance. But business leaders do the opposite, and with great success. In essence, they know themselves well enough to make sure they surround themselves with coworkers of different skill sets, which gives them even more freedom to run with their strengths.

To a large degree, the same is true for parents, at least in a couple of key areas: your natural strengths and the stages of parenting. We all know the areas in which we shine with our kids. For some, it is as the enthusiastic supporter who shows up to cheer on her kids at all sorts of events and performances. For others, it is as the comedic-teaser, giving one another good-natured ribbings. Some parents may be the quintessential listeners who let children speak their minds fully and then wait to let the next layer unfold. For yet others, it is in the doing of things together: cooking, hiking, swimming, drawing, reading. Or maybe a parent's strength is in the fine art of hanging out together, in the car, at the grocery store, late at night eating popcorn in front of the television. Or a parent may be effective as a teacher, helping him to learn how to sound out his first words, instructing her in how to change the car oil, showing her how to strike the nail with a hammer, without injuring herself.

In your daily life with your teenagers, it's important to find those moments for yourself, because when you are your most comfortable the likelihood that you'll connect with your teenager rises.

You also know where and when you are at your best outside the home. Part of what every parent wants to do is to incorporate, whenever possible, these areas into their parenting duties; this deepens the connection between you and your teenager. Your teenager sees you at your best and is able to discover parts of you that might not normally reveal themselves otherwise. In short, you need to find places and times in your family life when you naturally shine.

From the time I was a little kid, my dad used to drag me to his basketball practices—he was a coach at the local state college—and when I was a teenager I used to insist that he still take me. It was fun for me, in part because I loved to play basketball and in larger part because I got to see my dad in his world. He was a great coach. It was even cool to see how all these older guys—college players—respected him, and as a result they treated me well, too. His shine seemed to rub off onto me, at least in their eyes.

This is why, no matter what you might think about the safety issues involved, I loved what Dusty Baker did during the 2002 World Series when he invited all the players to have their kids in the dugout, where they acted as bat boys and girls and wore San Francisco Giants uniforms. It's also why a "Take Your Kids to Work Day" of any type is a great idea—your kids see parts of you that are normally just off to the side of their everyday lives with you.

This is a dynamic with which all parents are familiar. When our strengths overlap—and our weaknesses, too—this is what leads to flipping a coin to see who loses. *It's your turn to be the limit setter—get him bathed, in his pajamas, teeth brushed, and read to. Call me when you're ready for hugs and kisses.* At other times, these similarities lead to sparks between us. *You are too hard on her. Give her a break. She needs tenderness now, not tough love.* This is the grist for the mill of everyday parenting.

The other area in which to consider your natural strengths and weaknesses has to do with the different stages of parenting. Simply put, everyone is better with kids at certain ages than they are with kids at other ages. Some of you shine with infants and smash into brick walls with teenagers. Others never learn to decipher the meanings behind your infant's different ways of crying but instantaneously discern the difference in a fifteen-year-old's gait and its implicit meanings. Some of you shine with young school-age children, others with middle schoolers. This is natural. And because it's natural, you need to work with it, which means playing to your strengths and away from your weaknesses, though this isn't always possible.

I was a whiz with my kids when they began school. I was patient and great with them while they learned to read. I was a good baseball coach. Parenting came easily to me. But once they hit middle school, it seemed that everything I was so good at not only didn't work anymore but now made things worse. Telling my thirteen-year-old to choke up on the bat gets me the eye roll, but five years ago it got me the eyes like saucers that hung onto my every word.

All kids require the same general qualities from their parents: unconditional love, values that make sense, respect, listening. But how these translate through the different ages is another matter entirely. So, although parenting a seven-year-old may feel like second nature to you, it's important to know that down the road somewhere will come a time when you feel lost in the woods. This understanding gives you compassion for other parents as well as for yourself. More than that, it gives you hope whenever you are in one of your weaker periods.

This also means that we have hidden resources for how to connect with our teenagers: our pasts with them, and, in particular, those times when parenting was most natural to us. If we look back at those times, we'll easily remember what we did to connect with our kids. Then, with just a little imagination, we can update that method and bring it forward in time to the present so that we can make use of it with our teenagers.

Also:

My son and I used to make each other laugh like crazy when he was in pre-school. No matter what we did, it included laughter: getting him dressed in the morning, feeding him, taking him to the park. We shared the same sense of humor. But now as a teenager, it all seems so serious, and I miss the laughter. So on a whim, I began renting all these funny movies and turning up the volume really loud on the television. They're some of my favorites and they always crack me up. Well, to my surprise, not long into my Fun Fest my son began to join me. And together, we sit on that old sofa and crack up together. Right now, it's my best time with him.

Make sure to give yourself a healthy dose of compassion if upon reading this you've realized that your most natural and easiest stages of parenting are behind you. Then take a deep breath and see whether you can imagine once again some of those old ways you used to connect with your teenager, when he was a child. You may surprise both of you.

Body Image

For better or worse, eating disorders are a stable landmark in the terrain of today's teenagers, at least in the United States. This is different from when we were growing up. As parents, we cannot ignore this reality, and along with the Alcohol Talk, the Drug Talk, the Sex Talk, the Internet Use Talk, and the Driving Talk, we need to add the Body Image Talk to our repertoire. More than anything else, we need to let our teenagers know that we are aware of the pressures they face around this topic, and what they face is different according to gender.

Of teenagers suffering from anorexia and bulimia, roughly 90 percent are girls. (The bad news, however, is that eating disorders in boys are on the rise.) More important, despite what the average parent is led to believe through the media, not every or even most female adolescents suffer from an eating disorder. However, most girls, at some point, are tempted by the allure of an eating disorder, or what I call flirting with eating disorders. As parents, we need to stay alert for these phases. This is when we need to let our daughters know that we are there for them. It's also when they need our assurances.

Boys are also susceptible to body image distortions, though more often in the direction of added musculature rather than strict weight control. These are the guys who get into serious weight lifting as a means of covering up deeper insecurities. (And this is in no way meant to suggest that all, or even most, weight lifters fit this description.) Unfortunately, this is also the world of steroid use.

All teenagers, boys and girls, need us to broach the topic of body image first, as a way of letting them know that we are aware of some of the temptations they face and that we are there for them. But this alone is not enough and we must do more at least in a couple of areas: media literacy and how we treat one another.

The aspect of media literacy most relevant to this discussion is in helping our teenagers learn to take apart and assess on their own the images, sounds, and attitudes that they are barraged with from the media, whether it is the Internet, television, radio, or print. (By the way, as adults we need to learn and refresh these same skills, too.) This means periodically hitting the mute button on the remote control to talk about what just happened on the television screen, and by no stretch of the imagination do you need to have a graduate degree to come up with the appropriate question or conversation starter. Almost anything will do. *What does this ad appeal to? How do you feel about their thinking that you are actually this naive? Is this effective? What would make it better?* Remember, as sophisticated and as grown up as your teenager can look, inside there is a big part of him that is still a little kid who is very naive about how advertising and the media manipulate his opinions on everything from politics to dress to music. This is where a little information goes a long way. Listen to one high school teacher's experience in her senior psychology class:

As part of the course, I have the students write an end-of-term research paper on a topic of their choosing. Every semester, at least one or two students focus on advertising and the media. By the end of the project, every student who chooses this topic is outraged by how they are being manipulated through the media, from automobile ads to ads for the shampoo they use. Sometimes they even make a video of different television ads to share with their class-mates and show them exactly how the message is crafted over a series of ads for the same products. The best part for me is that from then on I know these students are much more savvy media consumers. They question what they see and hear much more readily. And, most important, they can dissect what they are seeing, in effect dissipating much of the power of the media and advertising.

What's important to note from the above is that once set on the path of media literacy, most teenagers run down it. They don't need much cajoling. The teenager who feels that he is being played for a dupe is a highly motivated teenager. Take advantage of this motivation.

As I was going through the mail one day, I stopped to read one of my daugh-ter's magazines—one of those made for teenage girls—when my daughter walked in. After flipping through it a few more seconds, I paused to look more closely at an ad, at which point I involuntarily uttered under my breath "As if!" This got my daughter's attention.

"What are you looking at, Mom?"

"This ad. It's incredible. This woman looks like a real-life Barbie! It definitely can't be real."

"Earth to Mom. It's a picture of somebody, so of course it's real."

"Do you really believe that?" I asked.

"What do you mean?"

For the better part of the next thirty minutes we took apart that image and a host of others in the magazine. I pointed out to her the signs of air brushing. I talked about the computer enhancement of images. I found examples of one model's legs used with part of another model's torso and a different model's face. My daughter was flabbergasted at first, but she caught on quickly.

According to the Center for Media Literacy, the goal of media literacy is to "analyze and evaluate the powerful images, words and sounds that make up our contemporary mass media culture."[7] You do this by analyzing how mes-sages are constructed; evaluating explicit and implicit messages that go against one's own values; and expressing your own alternative messages through various media tools. The area of media literacy is ripe for connections between you and your teenager. This is when her independence and narcissism work to bring you closer, against the common enemy. Just remember to stay side by side through-out, because if you get ahead of her in this cause, you'll only leave her behind.

Beauty Is More Than Skin Deep

Over the past twenty years, I have had the opportunity to work with many teenage girls not under the spell of eating disorders, and frequently I queried them about how and why they had managed to elude this nemesis. Many gave me odd looks at this request. Rather than search out the pathology of eating disorders, I wanted to know the etiology of a healthy body image.

I was surprised by what these young women told me. Yes, in all these teenagers there were components of media literacy; of enjoying their bodies from the inside out, but more by what they could do with them and less by how they looked; and of identifying with female role models with a wide range of body types. But the one surprising strain that kept coming through had to do with the relationship between their mothers and fathers, specifically the father toward the mother.

> I'm not sure if this is what you're looking for, but I think I got part of my body image from my dad. He just thinks my mom is the most beautiful woman in the world. And he's always telling her. *You look gorgeous today, honey. Doesn't your mom move like a dancer? Your eyes are radiating wonderful energy.* And on and on.
>
>   And I mean, well, I've seen her college yearbook and everything, and she was a babe, but that was twenty-three years ago. But still my dad sees her as beautiful. And I think that's helped me; somehow, he sees the beauty that is in my mom, way beyond the surface. I'm lucky, my dad knows that beauty is more than skin deep, and somehow I think that's helped me to believe and see the same thing. Even to believe that there are other guys out there like my dad who can get past superficial looks.

Believe it or not, I've heard one version or another of the above from many of the adolescent girls who have what I could only describe as a healthy and accurate body image. Besides, there's no downside to playing with this idea for a while. Guaranteed your spouse won't mind. It's win–win, all the way around.

Sex Talks and Gender

Although both parents ideally talk with their kids about sex and sexuality, I recommend that the first big sex talk with your son or daughter happen with the same-sex parent. Because of the shared gender, the conversation comes most naturally from that parent and is more easily received by your teenager.* Yes, even under the best of circumstances, this is an uncomfortable conversation, but still it's also a wonderful time for some close bonding. You are connecting with your teenager on a difficult topic and you are taking the lead. This sends your teenager two essential messages when it comes to her well-being and your connection to each other. First, you recognize that she is becoming an adult and that you have the courage to initiate tough conversations. Second, you show her that the door is always open for these conversations, now or five years from now. Furthermore, make it obvious that you will continue to ask about the subject in the future, just in case your teenager is unable to ask when she has questions.

After those first few talks, it's important to involve the other parent, too, but let the same-gender parent pave the way. The opposite-sex parent helps the teenager realize (both intellectually and experientially) that she can talk about sex not only with other women but with guys, too, something that is vital to her well-being and overall sexuality.

In Chapter 9, I talk about stretching your comfort zone as a way to connect with your teenager. Having the sex talks with your teenager is one of these stretches. It isn't easy and it's worth every ounce of courage it takes to get through the anxiety, both yours and your teenager's. This is true vulnerability in the relationship, which by its very nature implies connection.

There is one essential connection you do need to make for your teenager on the topic of sex: the connection to intimacy. Sex grows out of intimacy, and your teenager needs to understand this in the marrow of his bones. This means that, in a strange way, you're paving the way for the sex talks when he is seven years old and you talk with him about friendship, respect, and trust.

You want him to understand and have experience with the nuances of intimacy before he reaches puberty. Without such an understanding, he is at risk of trying to achieve intimacy through sex, which is always a recipe for disaster. Once someone is familiar with intimacy, he or she would not consider sex without it; or if it did happen without intimacy, it would become a one-time mistake from which the participant would recoil. (Teenagers who do this often reclaim their control and pride over this part of their lives by declaring themselves Born Again Virgins.)

Also, when it comes to these discussions, never underestimate how much your opinion matters. For instance, daughters whose mothers talk with them

---

*Even though I say "teenager" in the text, I realize that these conversations should take place before adolescence. But at the same time, it's only in adolescence that the talks take on a new kind of urgency and level of detailed information. So start the talks as early as possible and prepare yourself for another level entirely when your teenager becomes sexual.

about sex and express disapproval over their teenagers' having sex are much less likely to have sex than their peers who come from families who barely touch on the topic. In essence, during these talks, I like what Jane DiVita Wood, author of *How Can We Talk About That?*[8] has to say: "Help them feel good about waiting."

> We have a nine-year-old girl, Tina, and a thirteen-year-old son, Rick. Rick currently attends middle school, in the seventh grade. About eighteen months ago, I had the "sex" talk with him, the one that I had been putting off for probably the entire year before. My own apprehension and nervousness probably kept me from doing it any earlier. To keep the tension level down, I coaxed him outside to play some catch with the football in the street. As we relaxed while tossing the ball back and forth and slowly making our way around the block, I started relaying information about which I knew he was curious but uneasy—biology of men and women, erections, responsibility, vulnerability, ejaculations, wet dreams, kindness, consideration, procreation, and matters of the heart. After a few minutes, I recognized that he was starting to get uncomfortable and was "locking up," so I pulled back. I began describing the fine points of wide receiver skills by looking the ball into the hands and had him do a few five-yard button hooks and five outs. After a few minutes of football, all the while moving around the block, we again started talking about the different aspects of a maturing body for boys and girls and what that means physically and emotionally. We didn't get too in-depth on any one topic, and as soon as I noticed that he was getting uncomfortable, we returned to football mode by running some timing plays and sideline catches. We probably cycled back and forth from the sex talk to football about four or five times each before we made it around the block and back to our own driveway. It was a difficult talk for him, but I think he heard it and so began our journey toward his understanding of what it means to become a man. Unfortunately, now when I ask Rick to come outside to play some catch, he breaks out in a Pavlovian sweat! I reply by reassuring him that he can relax and that sometimes a request to play catch means nothing more than a wish to play catch with my son.

I love this story because it's the perfect ending to this chapter. This dad had the courage to initiate the big sex talk and the insight into the male gender for how and when to have the talk. He had it on the move, while engaged in an activity, so anxiety was worked through physically. He changed the subject to a familiar one whenever he noticed his son looking overwhelmed. He recognized the talk not as an end but as a beginning to his son's starting to figure out what it means to be a man.

*   *   *

Quite simply, gender matters. At the same time, however, the gender stereotypes tell you nothing about your teenager, which is why the clichés around gender are useful as tools only. They help you to stay curious about your teenager, to ask questions instead of make assumptions. The gender model also assists you in seeing how your teenager is unique and different, which, during adolescence, is perhaps the most important view to have, and certainly the one that affords the best connection between the two of you.

SEVEN

Grandparents: The Secret Weapon

Grandparents have always played a role in the lives of their grandchildren, and, with recent research and observation, it has become increasingly clear that there is an even greater and more vital role for them to play. The old image of grand-parents playing with the kids, catering to their every desire, winding them up, and then dropping them off at their parents' house as they headed home to rest is alive and well. At the same time, many grandparents now have a deeper connection to grandchildren that is worth cultivating. That is, it's well worth acknowledging and working with the more updated image of a grandparenting relationship: they can help to balance the more micro, day-to-day concerns of most parents with the macro hopes and stories around living a meaningful life.

Macro and Micro

Most parents, whether having made the shift from manager to consultant or not, focus mostly on the micro concerns about the daily lives of their teenagers. Did he get to school on time while still eating a decent breakfast? Did she finish her homework and get to sleep at a reasonable time? Any chance he did his fam-ily chores without my having to remind him? Did she remember to speak with her English teacher about writing a college recommendation? All of this is the natural "grist for the mill" when raising a teenager. From our consultant role we want them to begin to exert their independence and autonomy in ways that are in accord with our family values, which means we are paying attention to the details and how they get carried out—or not. It is these small behaviors that give us glimpses into the emergent adults within our teenagers. That is, we observe how they treat their friends in good and tough times. We see how they work through (or not) a tough course at school or a seemingly unfair coach in athletics. We see how they take responsibility when they do not follow through on an agreement. These observations show us the kind of people they are becoming. Having made the shift to consultant does not mean we ignore all the details, just that we don't step in to save as often as we did as manager. (This is also why the exaggerated version of the manager—the agent/lawyer—is so detrimental to our teenager's independence and autonomy.)

Grandparents, while still noticing the micro details, are focused on the macro picture of who your teenager is and who she is becoming. They trust you are tending to the micro, which allows them the expanse to view and influence the emergent adult in your teenager.

I see my grandparents a couple of times a year, for about four days at a time. Sounds weird I'm sure, but I love spending time with them. When I stay at their place they never get on me about cleaning my room, homework, or any of the stuff that my parents nag me about. (And strangely, by the end of that visit I'm doing all those little things on my own!) They are actually interested in me. For example, when I pull out my phone to check Snapchat, Instagram, or whatever I'm into at the time they are curious about how it works. They never judge. Instead, they want me to show them how to make it work, often setting up accounts for them, which we use when we're apart from one another to stay in touch. It's pretty cool.

And:

It's like my grandma never questions me about my grades. All she cares about is that I am working hard. That's all she asks about. Well that, and anything exciting that I'm learning about—whether it is in school or out. I don't know, I just feel so confident about myself when I'm around her. She doesn't artificially prop me up, it's just that somehow she gives me the space to think more about the big questions of living. No lectures either, mostly questions. Damn good questions!

In other words, grandparents, more easily than parents, naturally slip into the anthropologist line of conversation. With their macro perspective grandparents are more easily able to draw out some of the bigger picture thoughts, concerns, and hopes of your teenager. It is actually a tremendous one-two combination that creates both accountability and inspiration in your teen.

My daughter and her wife do an amazing job with their two teenagers. All of their lives are just so much more complicated than when we raised her through the adolescent years. I figure they can use all the help they can get. And because they are doing such a wonderful job of parenting we get to have more of the philosophical and joyful conversations with our grandchildren. They live in such a different world that I'm just fascinated to learn all about. And at the same time, the same values that we brought our daughter up to believe in still apply to this generation of adolescents.

With their ability to focus on the macro it is important that we as parents respect this relationship. Do not undermine it by asking a grandparent to address a microconcern with your teenager. You might like to address poor performance in a class with a questionable teacher by urging the grandparent to give your teenager the classic pep talk: *Yes, I know he is not a good teacher, but you can still learn a great deal from him. In fact, give it your best and you'll probably learn more from this class than any other class you have this year.* Although this all may be true, it is at the microlevel, which overall weakens the grandparent–teenager relationship. Let them stay at the macrolevel even though it may make you cringe: *You know, your dad had a terrible Chemistry teacher, too. No matter what I offered he refused my advice. He is stubborn, just like me, and probably you, too. In the end he failed the course and had to retake it over the summer—just please don't tell him I told you this.* Ironically, this macroview helps your teenager see you as more human, ultimately helping her to feel closer to you.

Family History

We all want our children to have a sense of control of their lives, solid self-esteem, and a belief in their family. When one sifts through the research about what makes some families work while others falter, there are predictable behaviors and attitudes that we know make a difference: family dinners, clear and compassionate limits, regular chores at home, religious/spiritual practices, and family travel. The beauty of research is that it turns up the unexpected at times, and this is especially delightful when what is unearthed is easy to incorporate into our already busy lives. And even better when grandparents can play an ongoing role.

To this end, researchers Marshall Duke and Robyn Fivush[1] from Emory University set out to see if children who knew more about their family were more resilient than those who did not. They created the *Do You Know Scale*, which asked children to answer 20 questions about their family history. The questions asked for information like mother's maiden name, how the parents met, and where they went to school. The results showed that those who knew more of their family's history had the three qualities mentioned above: a greater sense of control of their lives, higher self-esteem, and a deeper belief in their family. Quite amazing for just knowing some family history. See the box below for the scale and the questions.

Do You Know Scale

Please answer the following questions by circling "Y" for "yes" or "N" for "no." Even if you know the information we are asking about, you don't need to write it down. We just wish to know if you know the information.

1. Do you know how your parents met?   Y   N

2. Do you know where your mother grew up?   Y   N

3. Do you know where your father grew up?   Y   N

4. Do you know where some of your grandparents grew up?   Y   N

5. Do you know where some of your grandparents met?   Y   N

6. Do you know where your parents were married?   Y   N

7. Do you know what went on when you were being born?   Y   N

8. Do you know the source of your name?   Y   N

9. Do you know some things about what happened when your brothers or sisters were being born?   Y   N

10. Do you know which person in your family you look most like?   Y   N

11. Do you know which person in the family you act most like?   Y   N

12. Do you know some of the illnesses and injuries that your parents experienced when they were younger?   Y   N

13. Do you know some of the lessons that your parents learned from good or bad experiences?   Y   N

14. Do you know some things that happened to your mom or dad when they were in school?   Y   N

15. Do you know the national background of your family (such as English, German, Russian, etc.)?   Y   N

16. Do you know some of the jobs that your parents had when they were young?   Y   N

17. Do you know some awards that your parents received when they were young?   Y   N

18. Do you know the names of the schools that your mom went to?   Y   N

19. Do you know the names of the schools that your dad went to?   Y   N

20. Do you know about a relative whose face "froze" in a grumpy position because he or she did not smile enough?   Y   N

Score: Total number answered Y.

Now, before getting carried away, it is important to understand that it is not having the literal answers to these questions that made the positive difference in the lives of these children. The qualitative difference lies in the structure in which the information is communicated and the nature of the stories shared. That is, in the process of this research three different types of family narratives were identified:

1. Ascending Family Narrative, which was almost exclusively positive and growth directed. All adversity was faced and overcome, and each generation built boldly on the success of ancestors.
2. Descending Family Narrative, which was almost exclusively negative. The family history is built around being a victim with instances of adversity beating down the family. In essence, "Our family's best days are behind us."
3. Oscillating Family Narrative, which included the good and bad times, but always with the underlying theme of perseverance, resilience, and mutual dependence on family.

As I'm sure you realize, the narrative type that makes a difference in the lives of your children in terms of the qualities we are trying to instill in them is the last one—oscillating narrative. This type of family history gives children the sense of belonging to something bigger than themselves, what Marshall Duke labeled the "intergenerational self." Most importantly, these stories showed how the family had a long history of resilience and success no matter the situation. That is, by trusting one another and working hard they could get through all types of adversity, together.

This intergenerational self was most robust in families where grandparents played a role in the sharing of these stories and in families that had rituals/structures that invited these stories into the lives of their children. That is, family dinners, travel, and time with grandparents.

When I was a kid I loved looking through all my grandmother's photo albums. I would literally sit on the floor next to her in her rocker chair and pepper her with questions about all the different people in the photos. I learned all about distant relatives and how they got to the United States, for better and worse. There were some hard times for sure, but in the end they did just fine.

And:

Every Sunday when I was younger we went to my grandparents—cousins, aunts, and uncles—and they would make a huge paella dinner. The kids played various games and sports, and after the adults had had a glass of wine (or two) we would hang out at the table with them and listen to all the stories of when they were kids and their lives growing up. They were some of my favorite stories growing up.

Knowing this research I think it makes sense for parents to be explicit with their own parents and extended family: Ask them to share their stories of growing up with your children. Not only will it be of benefit to your teenagers but it will also engage the older generation in ways that are meaningful for everyone.

Another way to utilize the findings of this research—especially if your parents are unavailable or deceased—is by using online resources like Ancestry.com. In cases like this, once your teenager is curious—and this won't take long in most cases—you get the extra advantage of working side by side to learn more about your family's history.

One day I just got curious about my family so I went to one of those family tree websites, and before I knew it I was hooked. What I hadn't planned, however, is how it would grab my fifteen-year-old daughter. It was something we could connect on, working together. As it was an otherwise tough time between us I made the most of these late-night research sessions. It was like we had this separate life together away from our daily interactions. We never discussed it either, but I think we both needed time with one another not engaged in the power struggle going on between us at that time.

For Your Parents

Given the importance a grandparent can play in the life of a teenager you may also consider offering your parents a few tips from other grandparents on what makes the teen–grandparent relationship flourish. Here are a few gleaned from conversations with a wide variety of grandparents.

- Trust that your kids are dealing with the details in the home. No matter how tempting it is to cross this line, don't! Stay focused on the big picture.
- When the kids start to melt down (younger children) or tune out (teenagers), leave gracefully. No pointing of fingers, just exit stage left. That is, do your best to allow everyone to save face.
- Spend one-on-one time with each of your grandchildren, even if it is in short bursts. In this regard, don't forget your own children. Give them

time and space, then trust that if they need assistance or advice they'll ask for it.
- Ask big, open-ended questions of your grandchildren. None of those detailed questions about grades and points scored.

Finally, if you find your parents metaphorically stepping on your toes by focusing on the micro aspects of your children's lives, then rather than debating it think about how to use some of the information in this chapter to guide them to new ways of interacting. *The kids really love it when you tell stories about when we were young and about how you and dad met before you immigrated to the United States. Or, I'm the nag around homework, chores, and bedtime so can you be sure to talk about the big picture with the kids? Sometimes I feel like I'm so focused on the little things that I don't get to talk with them enough about what really matters.* And if neither of these works, ask them to sit down and read this chapter.

Deceased or Dysfunctional Grandparents

There are parents whose own parents have all passed, leaving their children with no grandparents. Unfortunately, there are also more than a few parents who are not in healthy relationships with their own parents, which again means that the children do not have access to their grandparents. In both cases, and any others without access to grandparents, there is plenty of room for creative improvisation. In most families there are often a few alternatives to the traditional grandparent—an aunt or uncle, a neighbor, or even the parents of a friend. The key is that this person is from an older generation and therefore has a different perspective on life—a more macroview.

> For our children it was a single woman with a penchant for dogs who lived nearby. Seems like she always had room for another dog and she loved children as well. As both of our parents had died she seemed to seamlessly take over that role of older adult with our kids. From babysitting to unexpected treats she covered the bases. In fact, she took our kids regularly to a little Mexican restaurant down the street where our kids were known as "regulars" even though my husband and I had never been.

Look around and I'm sure you will find one or two people who can play that role in your children's lives. And you'll know you hit the mark when your child asks you if that person can come to his school on "Special Friends and Grandparents Day."

Final Thoughts

At the conclusion of a recent talk, where I talked about the grandparent-teenager connection, a parent approached me with the following story.

I was at my girlfriend's family reunion with her family gathered from all over the Midwest and East Coast. It was a family tradition to have a reunion every five years and it was a full weekend celebration with just over 50 in attendance. As she had never before brought a boyfriend to this event, I was subject to intense and ongoing scrutiny. On top of this, earlier that week we had let our families know that we were moving in together. Her parents did not receive the news well.

On Saturday night at the keynote event her grandmother got up to give a toast, actually several toasts. One of them is permanently etched in my memory: "As I get older some things get cloudier while others become clearer. For instance, in my day they called it trial marriage, but today they call it living together. Whatever. I think what matters is that if two people love each other they should be together, and whatever it takes to better ensure a lifelong, loving and caring partnership I'm for it." At which point, with a twinkle in her eye she looked right at my girlfriend and me—and 31 years later we're still going strong!

EIGHT

Self-Esteem Through Integrity

All parents want their kids to feel good about themselves. High self-esteem in their teenagers, at first blush, appears a worthwhile goal because with it parents believe their kids will do better in everything they attempt and that they will even enjoy life more. It's almost a no-brainer for parents. If teenagers feel good about themselves, they will dare to try new endeavors; they will learn from their missteps and recover quickly from their failures; and they will treat others with more respect, much as they treat themselves.

Although all the foregoing is probably true, kids need to earn their self-esteem; we can't just give it to them because it's good for them. Sure, if we are lousy parents and treat our children poorly, we can increase the likelihood of poor self-esteem. Conversely, if we value them and treat them with respect, we can increase the likelihood of their developing high self-esteem. But, in both scenarios, we can neither parent them directly for high self-esteem nor be certain about how they will behave with high self-esteem. (For example, gang members have some of the highest self-esteem around, and I doubt very much that any parent aspires to gang membership for his or her teenager.)

When parents focus on high self-esteem as a goal, they set themselves and their children up for some disappointing outcomes. Think about it for a second. If you parent for high self-esteem, what kind of behavior does it elicit from you? For most of us, it leads to lots of praise. We praise our kids when they do well. We praise them when they try hard but don't do so well. We praise when they try a little and don't do so well. We praise them when they think about trying but never get out of the starting blocks. We praise them when they don't try at all because we want them to try the next time and not to feel bad about themselves in the moment. And, when it comes to teenagers especially, we praise them when we're not sure what else to say; at least they make momentary eye contact when we sing their praises, even though they dismiss us seconds later as they roll their eyes and turn away from us. In part we understand this dynamic even as we praise them, and we excuse ourselves with the idea that overpraising, although perhaps an exaggeration, isn't harming our children, either. Actually, that's wrong.

Overpraise is the royal road to entitlement, which is one of the last outcomes parents want for their children. When we idly praise our teenagers in the name of self-esteem, we inadvertently give them the expectations that good things and experiences will happen to them because we think they are good people—or simply because they feel good about themselves. In general, this type of entitlement arising from overpraise also leads to more of a focus on outcomes (materialism) than process (engagement with life).

Worse yet, the entitlement resulting from excessive praise leads kids to focus on how to persuade others to get them what they want, especially concerning their materialistic desires.

According to a survey by the Maryland-based Center for a New American Dream, kids between the ages of twelve and seventeen, on average, will ask their parents nine times for something they want, even when their parents give an emphatic no the first eight times. In these instances, instead of their efforts going into the immediate quality of their lives, they are focused on having someone else take care of their desires. Worse, they fully expect that these things they nag their parents into giving them will make them feel better about themselves. This kind of transitory, materialistic self-esteem is the first cousin of entitlement.

Now, don't get me wrong. I've got nothing against well-deserved and genuine praise. Quite the opposite; I believe the praise that is genuine, in the moment, and that hits the mark is of tremendous value. In part because it verifies what the person already knows. Think about a time when someone praised you. If the praise was accurate, you probably quietly nodded your head in agreement and said, "Thanks." You knew that person's assessment was correct, which helps everything go a bit deeper.

On the other hand, think of the last time that someone praised you when you knew the praise was exaggerated. You probably found yourself disputing the praise—"Actually, it was no big deal. If I had been paying more attention . . ."—or changing the subject because something didn't quite feel right, often by returning the praise, even though it wasn't what you were feeling—"Yeah, you did a great job, too." Thus the cycle of pseudomutuality moves forward. That is, false praise is often politely reciprocated with more false praise, all because neither party wants to acknowledge that the proverbial emperor is naked.

A Little Failure Is a Good Sign

Teenagers best come to understand the depths of their resourcefulness and resilience through adverse conditions: failure, disappointment, loneliness, grief, sadness. There is nothing wrong with this, and, fortunately or unfortunately, every teenager has plenty of these experiences. Our job is to let them have these experiences, not try to rescue them from their pain and discomfort in the name of self-esteem.

Or, in the words of newspaper columnist and author Joan Ryan: "Merriam-Webster defines *resilience* as 'an ability to recover from or adjust easily to misfortune or change.' If physical resilience comes from exposure in childhood to germs and bacteria, personal resilience comes from exposure in childhood to failure, embarrassment, disappointment, grief, fear, and doubt."[1]

Yes, it's difficult to watch from the sidelines as your teenager suffers in any way, but it's also the time that your quiet support strengthens the connection between the two of you. That is, your not doing anything except remaining present and optimistic is usually just what your teenager needs during a tough moment. This sends two important messages to your teenager: (1) I will not abandon you, and (2) you can handle this situation. In the end, this respects his independence in a nurturing way; it's the kind of connection that both you and your teenager want with each other.

It really sucked when my girlfriend, Kira, broke up with me. We had been going out for over a year and she was by far the most serious girlfriend I had ever had. I was miserable for weeks, even months. Most of my friends weren't around, in part because I kind of let them slide while I was going out with Kira, so I hung out at home a lot: just sitting in my room listening to music, lying on the sofa channel surfing, or sleeping. But through it all my parents were pretty cool.

Mom made my favorite foods for dinner and got into the habit of bringing me some snack toward the end of the night. She would just knock on my door, bring in some cookies or ice cream, and hang out a bit. She was just waiting to see if I wanted to talk about Kira— sometimes I did, sometimes I didn't.

And my dad made a point of inviting me to all sorts of activities that we hadn't done for years. He even took me to a pro basketball game, and I know for a fact he doesn't even like basketball.

I know they were just trying to cheer me up, even though we all knew that it was going to take time for me to feel better. Still though, I appreciated their efforts and that they gave me the space to do what I needed to do. I also liked that they were around, and even though I didn't talk to them that much about Kira, it was nice that they took the time to hang out in case I felt like talking.

When your teenager goes through a tough event—gets cut from a team, loses an election, does poorly in a class—she needs your quiet support much more than your cheers of self-esteem from the sidelines. Your support allows her to turn inward and address whatever crisis she is facing. Your support tells her that you believe she can handle it. Yes, you encourage her to move on, not as a means of distraction from her pain but as a normal part of healing. This quiet belief in her healing abilities, just when she is doubting herself, is what makes the connection between the two of you stronger.

For teenagers, it's best if parents let them fail while they are still living at home because you will be around to help them through the low spots. It's while they're living under your roof that they garner the experience they need to get through these tough times. Then, when they're older and living on their own, at college or elsewhere, they have experience to fall back on. The last thing a parent wants is a kid to leave home never having experienced suffering or duress in her life because she would lack the requisite experience needed to deal with inevitable down times and failures when they occur.

It's not just about failing; it's more about failing and then picking yourself up and getting back into life again, scarred but better prepared for the world, too. This is the stuff of real, deep-down, authentic self-esteem. It's the kind of self-esteem your teenager makes for himself, and which, if you keep your eyes open, you will witness.

Yet after your teenager experiences a setback, it's difficult to remain on the sidelines quietly and expectantly waiting for him to get back into the swing of things. Yes, he needs your support, but more than ever he needs your honest reassurances. This means you must acknowledge reality as you encourage him to move forward.

In this regard, Milton Erickson, MD, a famous psychiatrist who was a master of hypnotic and trance work with clients and students, was an inspiration. One story of his that sticks in my mind, and that pertains to the kind of support your teenager needs after a setback in acknowledging reality as he moves forward, had to do with what happened when one of Erickson's sons fell and cut himself badly on his upper thigh. At the time, the boy was a small child and when he hurt himself he screamed in pain as only a child can. As I remember the story, the other adults tried to reassure the boy that everything would be fine. Their words had no effect on the boy. As soon as Erickson came up to his son, he paused, looked at the cut, and said something along the lines of "You've fallen and cut yourself badly on your right thigh. It hurts, probably a lot. It stings, too. It hurts a lot, and you are bleeding quite a bit, which is scary." Then he proceeded to touch the blood with his finger, which he held up and carefully examined. "But look closely at your blood. See how deep red it is? That means you have good strong blood, which will speed up the healing. Here, take a close look and see how red and healthy the blood is." To everyone's surprise, except Erickson's, the boy stopped crying and looked closely at the blood on his father's finger, to which he said, "My blood is really red—deep red. That means I'll heal fast, right?" And when they brought the child into the hospital, he was still captivated by the high quality of his own blood and curious about the healing process his body was already engaged in. His father continued to listen and to talk about what kinds of things his son would need to do to heal as quickly as possible.

The principles of this story are wonderful and eminently applicable to your relationship with your teenager. When your child is suffering after a failure of sorts, always start by acknowledging the reality that she is experiencing: *You didn't get the lead in the play, which you worked so hard for. You're disappointed, sad, and angry, which is what you should be feeling. Part of you may even want to quit the cast entirely. Another part of you may be harboring negative thoughts toward the director, even the other kid who got the lead.* All you do initially is comment on reality. Whatever your teenager is experiencing, you put words to it. And don't worry if you're off a bit; she'll correct you before you have time to catch your breath. Let her correct you. Play the student wanting her to clarify a bit more. *What else are you angry about?*

Once reality is acknowledged, you are free to move things forward. *And you'll be down for a while, but you may surprise yourself by what pulls you out of it—a friend, a new activity, maybe even becoming captivated with the part you did get in the play. Anyway, before it's all over, you'll have proved to yourself that you are a hard-working and talented actor.* Then move on.

In the vernacular of hypnosis or sales (two fields too similar for my comfort, especially if you're on the floor of a new car dealership!), this is called developing a "yes set." This just means the person gets used to saying yes. You get his head nodding with questions or comments grounded in the reality of the moment; when his head has gained some momentum, you ask a question or make a comment that might ordinarily meet resistance. As a parent, you want to use the yes set as a means of giving support to your teenager in a way that she will take in and as a way of moving her forward through her healing, all while staying in connection.

You also want to help her learn how to learn from her mistakes as she continues to improve.

As a coach, part of my job, after each game, is to assess how well the team and each individual player performed. I point out both the good and the bad. This clears the air for the next game. The kids gain confidence from knowing their achievements and their mistakes alike. Over the course of the season, I gradually shift from taking the lead on these assessments to sitting down with the team as a whole and then letting each player individually make his own assessments, about the team and about himself. It's gratifying to watch them make this process internal as the season progresses. The only challenge for me is to make sure they aren't too hard on themselves, so often I end up reminding them of some of the positive things they did in the game.

Another successful coach I knew never criticized her players unless she gave them a chance to redeem themselves:

> The last thing I want is players down on themselves at the end of the game, because it'll last through practices the next few days all the way until the next game. So when I take a player out and criticize her, I'm sure to put her back in the game later, so that she can correct her mistake. And I never criticize a player who I don't think has the ability to correct a certain mistake—I accept that as her limit, at least for the time being.

Moments of failure are the hallmark of being human. Your teenager is no different. The key ingredient is not avoiding failure, but what you do with failure, and in that regard parents can be of enormous assistance. The one exception is when a parent embraces the role of agent/lawyer parent. This is when the parent feels their teenager was wronged by the system (poor grade, not enough playing time, etc.) and works to make things right. Whether the parents' assessment is right or wrong, the loser in this dynamic is always the teenager. Let's face it, life is not fair. Resilience needs to be strong no matter the situation. It's almost always best for parents to focus on their teenager and how to help him to move forward and become stronger for facing adversity—whether fair or not.

Self-Esteem and Integrity

With all the attention self-esteem has received in the past couple of decades, the idea of integrity has been pushed into the shadows. (Readers familiar with *Right from Wrong: Instilling a Sense of Integrity in Your Child*, written with Joe Di

Prisco, PhD,[2] will recognize some of the ideas from that book in this chapter, only now in the context of teenagers not children. For more on the general topic of integrity, I direct you to the aforementioned book.) It's time to cast those shadows aside and focus directly on integrity, and by integrity I mean a sense of wholeness, of completeness. Integrity is not some sanitized, politically correct notion. It's something that is internal to each of us and something we struggle with every day. Integrity is messy. In this regard, it's different from a set of morals. Morals are important and help to inform us of a variety of choices in difficult circumstances, but integrity is what we do in those moments, which is not always the same as how we would consider the situation from a distance or in the abstract. And this distinction is one that teenagers are famous for making, much to our shock and disdain. These are the times when they point out our inconsistencies, such as how we preach to them always to tell the truth, yet just the other day they overheard us telling the boss on the phone that we were staying home because we had a touch of the flu, even though we just needed the time to take care of some personal errands. Or when we decline a dinner invitation because we already have plans for that evening, even though the calendar is open. Sure, we can justify fudging the truth, yet at the same time we know that our teenager is correct, that we're not telling the whole truth.

This is the vexing part of integrity—it's also why integrity is such a robust concept—because we learn to value our integrity only by putting ourselves out of integrity. We learn integrity by losing it. Or perhaps even more poignantly, we learn to value integrity only after we give it away. That is, as soon as you violate your sense of integrity, you feel bad: guilt, remorse, anger, confusion, sadness, which are all signs that you're out of integrity. What happens in the next few moments is critical.

You can justify your lost integrity: *He wouldn't have appreciated it anyway. It's really no big deal. I'll do better next time.* But when you do this, you only lose it more and pretty much assure yourself of losing it again in the near future. That is, that first violation of your integrity is when you feel the worst, but each time thereafter, integrity becomes easier and easier to violate. Before long, you don't even recognize that you're out of integrity—it's a chronic state.

On the other hand, if you explore what happened, and wrestle through the concomitant anxiety, you will come to a deeper appreciation and value of your integrity. You ask yourself: What got in the way of doing what I know was the right thing? Was I trying to impress somebody? Was I scared? Of what? How would I have acted if I had been alone? With a different set of people? All these questions lead us into an analysis of what really happened, which allows us to more fully embrace our integrity the next time around.

The psychiatrist and writer Viktor Frankl's inspirational *Man's Search for Meaning* discusses his experiences in the Nazi concentration camps during World War II: "The way in which a man accepts his fate and all the suffering it entails, the way in which he takes up his cross, gives him ample opportunity— even under the most difficult circumstances—to add a deeper meaning to his life."[3] Later on, Frankl goes on to describe how some exceptional prisoners on their march to certain death held their heads high, knowing that despite their imminent deaths, their dignity in themselves was the one thing the Nazi capos could not take from them. By this, I think Frankl meant their integrity. And from his poignant perspective, we need to understand that integrity is the one thing that nobody can take away from us. Yes, we can freely give it away, but nobody can wrest it from us without our permission. And once your teenager understands this, both by your words and his experiences, he is able to make his integrity an organizing crucible in his life.

This brings us right back to the idea of failure. When teenagers let themselves fall short by failing to hold onto their integrity, they simultaneously have a tremendous opportunity to reaffirm themselves and their integrity. That is, without failures, they do not learn how valuable their integrity is to their well-being. And this is the ultimate paradox of successfully raising teenagers: They need to experience a bunch of failures along the way to adulthood. And how we handle their failures and how we teach them to address these missteps is crucial.

Integrity and Intuition

When you speak with teenagers about integrity, they grow fidgety. Whatever you say sounds too much like lecturing to them, and for the most part they are right. Yet, when you talk with them about an idea like intuition, they become engaged and animated; in large part, this is because they see intuition as personal and integrity as something outside of themselves, as some sort of ready-made prescription for behavior, usually foisted on them by well-meaning but clueless adults. Part of every parent's job is to disabuse them of this notion, and once you do so the connection between you and your teenager will grow exponentially stronger.

Teenagers understand and are curious about intuition. They all have experience with knowing certain things without understanding quite how they know them. In fact, most teenagers rely on their intuition to help them forge the identity and independence they are searching for.

> It was weird. I mean, I'm not the kind of person who likes to get up in front of people to speak. And I've never considered myself a leader, either. But when

Self-Esteem Through Integrity

Stephanie suggested that I run for Student Council vice president, I knew it was the right thing to do. It just felt right. And somehow I knew that I would win and do a good job, too. Sometimes you just have to trust yourself.

And,

My mom and dad went away last weekend, and since I'm a senior, they gave me a few options: stay home alone, stay at home and have my aunt spend the weekend, or stay at a friend's house. I was ready to jump at the idea of staying alone, but something didn't feel right about it. I began to imagine my friends and what they would say—actually more what they would want to do. It felt kind of yucky because I knew they could talk me into whatever they wanted. Rationally, I kept trying to convince myself that everything would be fine, but there was this other voice screaming in my head that the weekend would end in disaster. So instead, I opted to have my aunt stay with me. Something about staying alone just didn't feel right.

Every teenager has stories like this; probably not quite so dramatic, but they all have them. Best of all, teenagers are eager to share stories of their intuition at work, in large part because intuition is a first cousin of their narcissism. Therefore, in any conversation you have with your teenager about integrity (and you should have many such discussions), your best bet for success is to start by appealing to his narcissism, which means focusing on his intuition, at least initially.

Intuition is something that most teenagers live by, so why not speak their language? The idea is to meet them at the edge of their narcissism and gently move them into the realm of integrity. Done properly, getting them to focus on their intuition allows them to better understand and value their integrity. That is, when teenagers make integrity important, they also give themselves greater access to their intuition.

The metaphor I use with teenagers is that the connection between integrity and intuition is akin to their stereo system at home. Their integrity is the volume knob on the stereo and their intuition is whatever music they are listening to. Therefore, if they are in integrity and making integrity a priority in their lives, the music is pumping and they can easily hear what their intuition has to say. If, however, they are out of integrity and not making integrity a priority in their lives, the volume is effectively muted and they are unable to hear the wisdom of their intuition. Then, to gain their attention further, I talk with them about what their intuition has to offer them, particularly in two areas.

First, in avoiding danger. Most victims of scams or street robberies report that there was a part of them that was uneasy and suspicious of whatever circumstances they were in, but they just ignored that part of themselves—their intuition. And just to be crystal clear, this in no way means that the victims of wrongdoing are responsible for what happened to them. Sometimes intuition can help us avoid tragedy and sometimes there is nothing we can do. In short, it's never the victim's fault.

Second, in seeing hidden opportunities. Many people, when reflecting upon some success or other, are quick to acknowledge all the hard work that went into their achievements, but a moment later they comment that at some point in the process they made an intuitive leap that didn't make rational sense. Some call this a gut feeling, others an intuitive flash. For teenagers, intuition is what allows a half-back to know when to cut up field, when to employ a stiff arm, and when to wait for blockers. Intuition is what actors depend on to improvise a scene successfully when another actor misses a line. It's also the stuff of relationships: seeing someone for the first time and realizing there is something special about that person. Teenagers quickly understand both aspects of their intuition.

Then, just to seal the deal, I point out the irony contained in this relationship between integrity and intuition—that you need your intuition most when you are out of integrity. Situations that are confusing, quick-paced, highly self-conscious, and socially nuanced are when teenagers most need their intuition. In short, on just about every weekend night. Therefore, it's at these times that they really need to make their integrity a priority. Within a few moments, someone in the audience usually makes the connection to alcohol and drugs during times like these. A few moments later, they make the further connection, to sex. That is, most teenagers are quick to understand that when they drink or use drugs, they cloud access to their intuition; this in turn leads to bad decisions, many of them concerning sex. Research shows that at least 20 percent of teenagers who have been drinking or using drugs have engaged in sexual activities that they regretted the next day.

In general, you want to support your teenagers in struggling to develop an articulate relationship with their intuition. They need to learn how to recognize and trust their intuition; it is what allows them to see and seize opportunity when it presents itself as well as how to recognize trouble and avoid it when it introduces itself. In short, intuition helps to keep your teenager in integrity.

Parents who take this approach to heart often say to their teenagers, on any given Friday or Saturday evening, things such as these: *Okay, get home on time and remember you are a good kid. You know what we think. Pay attention to your intuition, trust yourself, and then do what you think is right. That's all we can ask.*

Bringing It All Together: Discipline

The area in which most parents worry the most about their connection to their teenager is when it comes to discipline. *How hard should you be? What are effective consequences? How do you hold the line and stay connected, too?* These are all great questions, but if you take a minute to consider the role of intuition and integrity in your teenager's life, you will also see a new approach to discipline, one that does not risk the connection between you and your teenager.

But first, you must make one very important assumption. Your teenager—yes, your teenager—knows the right thing to do in almost every situation he will find himself in. From years and years of talking to teenagers across the country, I know this is true. At the same time, I understand that knowing and doing are not the same—not even close. Therefore, your task is to bridge the gap between what they know and what they do, which is not as difficult as it seems.

When it comes to discipline (which at heart means to teach), there are two different, yet complimentary, components: consequences and support. Teenagers need consequences to get them to consider and reflect upon what they have done. In essence, the consequence makes space for the learning. But make no mistake about it, the consequence seldom, if ever, does the teaching. Support is what enables your teenager to realize that she had other options that she could have and should have chosen. But, most important, support helps her to understand why she did what she did, which goes a long way to preventing another lapse in her choices farther down the road.

The research on consequences is loud and clear: You have to have an artist's touch to mete out consequences well. If they are too harsh, your teenager becomes resentful to the point that he misses the opportunity for reflection and growth. If they are too minimal, you never hold your teenager's attention. Always aim for the middle. And when you take aim, make sure you are reasonably calm and not acting in the heat of the moment.

I was furious when my son came home forty minutes after curfew without even bothering to call, especially because we had talked about it just before he left. "We just need to know you're okay. So if you are going to be late, just call so that we can relax. Okay?"

And of course he nodded and mumbled, "Sure." But when I asked him about that earlier conversation, all he was capable of was a shrug of his shoulders as he stared down at the floor.

"I can't believe you didn't call, especially since we talked about it just before you left. This is so rude. You're grounded for the rest of the weekend."

No response, just another shrug of the shoulders.

"I can't believe your attitude! You just don't get it. Well how about we add another week to your grounding, all the way through next weekend?"

Another shrug and some sort of mumbled response.

"Well, if that's going to be your attitude, you're grounded for the next month!"

"Whatever. Can I go to my room now?"

We've all been there and done that. In the moment it's easy to be carried away with consequences out of our own frustration and emotional breakdowns. It's human. At the same time, our teenagers need us to strive to become better human beings, which means if nothing else that we fall into the habits of reflecting on our own interactions with our teenagers and clean up the messes we've created along the way. (More on this in the next section of this chapter.)

Clearly, the parent in the above scenario was falling into the trap of thinking only of consequences. Others might lean toward the support half of discipline, appealing futilely to their teenager's self-esteem: *You're a better kid than this. You don't have to behave this way. You're already wonderful just the way you are. You can't forget this when you're away from us and temptation shows itself.* All nice things to say to your teenager, but not very useful in helping him to learn from his mistakes or in preventing a future incident of the same type.

In connecting with your teenager, both approaches fail. The first is too punitive; the second is demeaning. The best approach to discipline, both in effectiveness and connection, is to focus on consequences and support through the lens of integrity. This will also change your expectations going into and coming out of situations requiring parental discipline. Here are the steps:

1. Catch yourself building to a fury in the moment and buy yourself some time. *I'm too angry to think rationally right now. Go to bed and we'll talk in the morning before either of us leaves for the day.*

2. Sit down with him the next day and review. *You agreed to be home by one. You also agreed to call if you were going to be late. You did neither and came home forty minutes late.*

3. Suggest or solicit a consequence—this depends on your parenting style—and assess his reaction. *Next weekend you're grounded for both nights and you can't use the car until next Monday.* Or, *What kind of consequence do you think we should enforce? And don't worry, if you don't have any ideas, I've got a few of my own.*

4. Move past consequences and into supporting him. Just remind yourself that he knew the right thing to do last night, he just didn't do it. *When you decided to hang out longer at your friend's house and miss your curfew, was there a part of you that was upset—"C'mon, Rikki, you should get home by one*

as you promised." Or when you realized you were going to be late, was there some part of you that said, "Call Mom and Dad"?

5. Wait. When he acknowledges that internal conflict, slight as it was, in some minimal manner—nods his head, mumbles "Yeah"—breathe a deep sigh of relief. *I'm glad to hear that. I'm also confused about why you did not pay more attention to that part of yourself. Actually, this is my overriding concern: You knew the right thing to do, but you didn't listen to yourself. Last night, what got in the way of listening to that part of you that knew and wanted to do the right thing?*

6. Sit back and stay patient. This will take time, perhaps several days. Because now, as he wrestles with these questions, he will eventually figure out how he let himself down—how he gave his integrity away. In addition, as a parent you will eventually learn why your son, as opposed to generic teenagers, broke curfew and did not call home.

In accordance with the thesis of this book, the best aspect of this approach is that you discipline your teenager without severing your connection to her. You avoid, or at least minimize, the proverbial power struggle between teenager and parent. While enforcing consequences, you haven't overplayed your authority card. Instead of her simply having to obey her mom or dad, you turned the tables and put the focus on how she can better listen to herself. You've sidestepped the power issue in favor of staying connected and in keeping her in tune with her integrity.

Or, as one dad confided in me at the end of a talk:

I must have been thirteen or fourteen years old and I was explaining to my dad why I hadn't followed through on one of my responsibilities. In the middle of what I was saying, he leaned in close and gently said: "You can BS your teachers; you can BS your coaches; you can BS your friends; but you can't BS yourself and you can't BS me." Then he looked me right in the eyes and walked away without another word.

I'll never forget that moment as long as I live, because in that brief interchange I learned everything I needed to know about my own integrity and how to keep it important.

Integrity and Guilt

While I was on book tour with coauthor Joe Di Prisco for our book *Right from Wrong: Instilling a Sense of Integrity in Your Child*, one radio interviewer said something along the lines of, "Oh, I get it, the idea is to instill integrity through guilt, right?" Actually, that comment is a little bit right and a lot bit wrong. Here's why.

Before going further, remind yourself of some of the key dynamics at play in your teenager: extreme self-consciousness, idealized independence, and an abundance of ego. Now imagine how guilt plays out in that natural psychosocial triumvirate that your teenager calls self. Guilt is everywhere! No matter that your teenager doesn't give you a glimpse of his guilt, you need to know that it's there, every day. And in huge portions. He just hides it behind the closed bedroom door and the loud music blasting from his stereo.

In brief, guilt is part and parcel of every teenager. If you heap on needless portions, it blows up in your face, which means hasta la vista to the connection between you and your teenager. Focus on his integrity and stop short of playing the parent martyr. *I waited over an hour for you. You should have called, just as we agreed to last night.* And, *We were worried sick when you weren't home on time. We had all sorts of horrible thoughts, from car accidents to robbery.* Although all this is often true, there is no practical use in burdening your teenager with this information. Yes, in the moment, you might feel better—though probably not, as most teenagers will barely acknowledge your guilt; this, in turn, leaves you feeling even more frustrated than before you unburdened yourself. Think about your teenager for a moment. What are the chances that after laying your guilt trip on her she turns to you and says in all sincerity, *I'm real sorry for putting you through all that, Mom and Dad. I had no idea. And I promise not to do it again.* Not going to happen, so stop fantasizing.

Focusing on her integrity—as discussed in the preceding section—uncovers all the guilt the average teenager can handle. Don't push her over the edge. Because once she's overloaded, she will recoil and cast aside all the guilt that you heaped on her and the natural guilt associated with her integrity. In essence, when you add your guilt, all you do is effectively throw out the baby with the bathwater.

Integrity, Identity, and Conflict

At different points in this book, I've talked about various categories of conflict with your teenager: conflict stemming from abstract thinking, from an exaggerated or diminished sense of independence, from unrestrained narcissism, from peers. Within the scope of this chapter, we bump into another order of conflict, one that stems from your teenager's integrity and changing identity.

Sometimes your teenager will have conflict with you because of her high regard for her integrity. That is, sometimes her integrity will cause strife in your relationship with her. At times this stems from a very different take on world events.

It outraged me when Jessica attended the protest last weekend. I fully support what is happening and have little room in my heart for the ingrates who are protesting and objecting to what I feel is the absolute correct action to take. But my own daughter! At first I thought she did it just to shove her opinions in my face.

But afterward I began to have a different take on why she had joined the demonstration. Not only did she believe in what she was doing—equally as strongly as I believe in the opposing view—but not to act on her beliefs would have been to betray herself. Oddly, something I hope she learned from me: If you believe something, then act that way and apologize to nobody for your beliefs. But then it struck me that it was much bigger than our having different viewpoints. In some way she was forcing me to see her as a new person—as a woman capable of her own opinions as well as acting on them. From then on, I saw her differently, and it wouldn't have happened had she not attended the protest.

Sometimes, the only way your teenager can make you see him in the fullness of who he has become is through conflict. In these situations, if you don't see the new person that your teenager has become, the conflict will continue and will escalate. There is no alternative for your teenager. To do otherwise is to ignore his integrity and to forsake the identity he has worked so hard to forge. On the other hand, once you recognize this new aspect to his identity, there is no longer the need for such incendiary conflict. With any luck you may even learn to agree to disagree with one another without attempting to trample over each other's integrity.

It's been a year since Jessica went to that protest and fortunately we were able, for the most part, to discuss our differing viewpoints with a modicum of civility. And down the road, I imagine we'll even smile at that incident. But most important is that we interact differently because of her actions. I see her more for who she is and who she is becoming. It's as if she had outgrown her old skin and shed it right before me. We're both getting used to the new skin.

But sometimes, when and where they choose to create conflict out of their deepening sense of integrity strikes even closer to the heart of your family:

One Sunday morning, my sixteen-year-old suddenly declared that he was no longer going to attend church services with us. "Says who!" my husband and I declared in one voice.

"It's too hypocritical. Everyone acts pious and joyous at church, but once they reach the parking lot, they're back to their angry, cynical selves. It's a waste."

My husband took a few deep breaths and sat down. "What's this all about, Casey? Who appointed you judge and jury of humanity?"

"Dad, it's crazy. I've heard you say how corrupt Mr. Jenkins is, yet he goes to church and acts nice to everyone, even though he's a jerk the rest of the time."

"We all have our crosses to bear, but how is that of any concern to you?"

"It's just so bogus, everyone sort of faking it for each other. I'm going to use the time on my own—maybe I'll go for a walk or a hike, or write in my journal."

How to respond? Depends on you, your family, your faith, and your belief in your teenager. Refuse to hear him out and these astute observations on the everyday integrity of the people around him will pop up elsewhere—perhaps in acting out, but most likely in exaggerated cynicism toward adults, including you. Give him your unmitigated approval and you rob him of the opportunity to dig deeper into himself. Whatever you do, you have to keep several ideas in mind, and probably all at the same time:

1. Slow everything down.
2. Keep your connection with your teenager.
3. Listen to your integrity.
4. Give him the time and direction to pay attention to his own integrity.
5. Meet him halfway.

Another mom I know, after a similar sort of disagreement that also had its basis in her daughter's burgeoning sense of identity, said to her daughter, "I hope you stand up as strong and loud for what you believe in with your friends as you do with me." Then she made eye contact and walked away, leaving her daughter with a perplexed look on her face.

Clean Up Your Messes

When it comes to integrity and raising teenagers it's us, their parents, who are required to gaze into the mirror. After all, our kids, in their saner moments, do have more than a few painfully on-target points about how we can do better ourselves. Raising kids is a messy business. This means we are going to make mistakes: react too strongly to a missed curfew by grounding your daughter for the next six months; continue to yell at your son long after he has understood the point; go through your daughter's belongings with no basis for your worry.

We are not perfect parents any more than our kids are perfect teenagers. But it's what we both do with these imperfections that is crucial. Falling back on your credentials as a mother or father is hardly the responsible modeling that you want your teenager to learn from.

> That is no way to talk to your mother! Besides being rude—kids should never talk to their parents this way—you are also wrong. I never exaggerate and I always seek out as well as hear your side before making any conclusions.

In short, if we want our teenagers to behave responsibly, we also have to behave responsibly. This means cleaning up our messes, which takes far more courage than the more typical wimping out behind the authority of a mother or father. Fortunately, this means that there is plenty of room for our imperfections en route to raising a healthy teenager, but it also means that we must get into the habit of swallowing our pride.

> Sarah, we have to talk about the condition you left the car in after you went out with your friends last night, but before we do I need to apologize for some of the things I said last night. I was angry and tried to get through to you the only way I know how when I'm that mad—I yelled. Yes, I had a right to be upset, but not to yell and carry on. I'm sorry. Now let's talk about you and the car.

This parent stands a much better than average chance of having an effective conversation with his daughter than the parent who simply picks up where she left off the night before—yelling. The dynamic works like this: Your teenager does something wrong, irresponsible, or rude. You get upset, to the point of overreacting. (Remind yourself of the abstract thinking that allows for a strong internal reaction with none of that response reaching the surface for you to see.) Either your teenager engages you at this level and you end up in a shouting match with each other, or she leaves the playing field, goes to her room, and closes the door. You may give chase, but maybe not. You seethe all night. The next morning, you both pick up where you left off the night before. From there, everything escalates and you both say and do things that you know you'll later regret, even as you are saying them.

This all changes when after the first altercation you take a break to look in the mirror and ask yourself how you could have been more effective. Then, the next day, you assume responsibility, in essence conveying *I'm sorry for my part*. This allows your teenager to lean forward, accept your apology, and either implicitly—she is open to what you say next—or explicitly—she, too, apologizes—take responsibility for her overreactions.

This is natural and normal. In any relationship of depth, there are arguments and disagreements, but couples who stay together learn how to work through these stuck places without getting bogged down. And every successful couple has its tricks. In our household, it's my wife who, when we get to that place when everything has been said and we're wondering how to rid of ourselves of this yucky feeling and get back on the same page, turns to me and says, *I'm sorry for my 5 percent of the argument.*

Remember that apologizing means to ask forgiveness for one's faults as well as to make amends. In accordance with the purpose of this book, genuine apology is one of the surefire ways to reconnect with your teenager—and for your teenager to reconnect with her parents, too.

And, yes, kids sometimes apologize because they know that it's what you want to hear and it minimizes the consequences of their wrongdoing. But much more often they apologize because of their integrity. It's the best way for them to get rid of the yucky feelings inside of themselves and to restore their wholeness again. For proof of this, remember when your teenager was five or six years old:

> "Thanks for saying you are sorry."
> "You're welcome, Dad. I promise I won't do it again."
> "Nice to hear, but I'm wondering what it feels like inside to apologize to me."
> "Feels good. Felt yucky before, but feels good now."
> "Good to hear. I feel a lot like that when I apologize, too."
> "Uh, Dad, can we talk about something else?"
> "Sure."

*   *   *

The goal of all reasonable parents for their teenagers is that they learn how to distinguish right from wrong and act on what they know by the time they leave home. For this to happen means that they must make plenty of mistakes along the way. Without these mistakes, they'll never learn to value and trust their integrity. Furthermore, and this is the crux of this book, it's when you have a strong connection with your teenager that you have the most influence over the development of this kind of integrity. Your connection helps your teenager to feel bad when he is out of integrity and forces him to wrestle with the subtle and nuanced issues of integrity.

NINE

Indirect Communication

When poet Noelie Altito uttered the infamous words "The shortest distance between two points is under construction," she must have been referring to parents and their teenagers. Strange, though, because it wasn't this way when your teenagers were children.

I recently attended a workshop given by an infant and toddler specialist who highlighted some of the differences in parental relationships with toddlers as opposed to teenagers. When the presenter was asked how you deal with a toddler who refuses to take a bath, she had a wonderful response—one that is hugely effective with young children:

> I'm a huge fan of food coloring in the bath—it doesn't stain and takes just a few seconds to throw into the water as it's filling the tub. Whenever I start the bathing ritual, I slip right past my son's defenses by asking him if he wants blue water or red water. Nine out of ten times that does the trick. He spends all his efforts on deciding between blue or red, or once in a while he asks for green.

As the speaker relayed this story, I found myself involuntarily nodding in agreement. After all, I've used the same kind of approach with my own young children with generally favorable results. But then I paused and imagined how that same tack might play out with a teenager:

> Mom: "When you take your shower tonight, do you want to try that new soap I picked up at the market?"
> Son: "You think I have BO? Why don't you leave me alone and stop trying to run my life!"

Mom: "I don't think that at all, I just want to know if you want to try this new soap or not."

Son: "Yeah, right. What do you think, I'm stupid? Next thing I know, you'll want me to take ballroom dancing with you and Dad."

The strategic approach that worked so well when your teenager was a child not only falls flat during adolescence but often makes matters worse, whether or not it was an innocent comment or represented some ulterior motive of yours. As the parent of a teenager, it's necessary, at times, to use the direct approach, but it's just as necessary to develop skills in the more indirect methods of communication.

The Direct Approach

Sometimes your teenager needs you to take the direct route, usually in the areas of limits, guidelines, and expectations. Times like this require clear communication and conciseness; they leave no room for doubt or misunderstanding. You also need courage, because during moments like these you are firmly ensconced in the role of parent. These are lonely times.

- "We're going out to dinner after the movie, so we won't be home until after midnight. Remember, no friends over while we're out. No exceptions. Got it?"
- "No, you can't go to a party without adult chaperones present. I don't care if everyone else is. You are not to go to that party tonight, clear?"

Your teenager needs your clarity around these kinds of issues to supplement his courage and assuage his doubt. But as far as these communications leading to an immediate and observable change in behavior, well, they probably won't. (All the changes in your teenager's behavior resulting from your direct interventions happen just outside your view, which is one of the central tenets of an earlier book I wrote with Joe Di Prisco, *Field Guide to the American Teenager*.)

Although the direct approach is important, it's also isolating for you as a parent, and too much of this approach risks a permanent disconnect between you and your teenager. Therefore, for your sanity, the well-being of your teenager, and the connection between you both, you need to supplement the direct approach liberally with lots of indirect communications.

Long Conversations and Short Moments

Given the hyper-self-consciousness and inherent defensiveness of most teenagers, it only makes sense that you will seldom have those long, open, and frank talks you have long dreamed about. That is, if it isn't late at night or you aren't in the car, they will not stay still long enough for you to build up the necessary momentum for long, heart-to-heart talks. This does not mean you give up. Instead, your challenge is to make use of what you know about your teenager developmentally—that deep sharing is not the everyday occurrence between teenagers and parents, at least not on any kind of consistent basis—and plan accordingly. Pragmatically, this means keep the talks short and get comfortable letting the loose ends dangle for a bit.

> I've struggled to persuade my sixteen-year-old son to be more open with me for the past two years, but it's been a total failure. Even when he wants to talk with me, or even if he is in the midst of sharing something with me, it's as if he had given himself a limit of five minutes. It's as if he had set an alarm clock, and after five minutes he stops—sometimes in midsentence. Finally, after two years of this, I've figured out what to do: Just as he is approaching the five-minute mark, I break off the conversation, either by changing the subject, turning my attention elsewhere, or, as rude as it sounds, just not responding. It's strange, I admit, but at the same time it's incredibly liberating, too. It reminds me of the way he talked with me when he was five years old, only now I'm acting the part of the five-year-old. The best part is that, after I have done this a few times, he has taken to pursuing me to finish the conversations—just as I did when he was a child. Talk about a change of dynamics!

You're free to luxuriate in your fantasy about a one-hour conversation with your teenager, but before you actually approach her, do a reality check and shift your expectations from a single, one-hour exchange into eight six- or seven-minute conversations. That is, you bring up the topic while walking to the corner store together. She responds with a few sentences. You ask a question or make a comment that broadens the context. She then turns her attention to the cute boy driving by in a pickup truck. This is your signal that you've reached a resting place, which is different from the end of the conversation. Then the next evening, when you are both bringing your dirty dinner plates to the kitchen sink, you can continue the conversation, picking up almost as if no time has passed between the two talks.

For this indirect, elongated approach to in-depth conversations to work, it's vital that you end each segment having touched upon your teenager's curiosity. *Yeah, these kinds of things always make sense in retrospect, so I wonder what you'll think about this situation a month or so down the road?* You want to end your conversation on a note that starts an internal dialogue with her. Then, later that day or sometime in the next few days, you pick up where you left off because you know that her inner dialogue has carried her farther down the path and that she is now more articulate about the subject as it relates to her than she was the day before.

"Have you figured out which birthday party you're going to on Saturday night—your friend Samantha's or your cousin Elizabeth's?"

"I don't know. I really want to go to both, but they are too far away from each other. And both of them really want me to come to theirs. I don't see Elizabeth that often and I see Samantha every day, but that kind of thinking hasn't helped so far. I just hate to let either one of them down."

"Feel caught in a bind?"

"Yeah. I almost wish I would catch the flu or something."

"I know the feeling."

"You do?"

"Sure. Sometimes I wish there were two of me."

"Well, if you figure out how by Saturday, let me know."

"Absolutely. But which party do you imagine would be the most fun for you?"

"Huh? I haven't really thought about it that way."

"Might be worth the effort. You know, just another variable to consider."

The beauty of this approach is that while you help her process whatever is troubling her, you stop short of taking over her struggles; and this is exactly what all teenagers need from their parents if they are to grow up into responsible young adults. Best of all, once your teenager realizes you are there for her and not trying to micromanage her life, she'll begin to initiate some of these conversations. Here is what happened the next day:

"I decided which party I'm going to."

"Congratulations! How did you decide?"

"I think it will mean more to Elizabeth. Besides, I'm getting a little tired of the same old thing every weekend, so who knows, maybe I'll meet somebody interesting at Elizabeth's."

"Good for you. Have you thought about how you're going to break the news to Samantha?"

"I'm not sure what I'm actually going to say, but I'm going upstairs to wrap her gift now. She can't get too mad if I give her a birthday present when I tell her. Besides, I got her a real nice present. Want to see?"

Take your time. Adolescence lasts for a long time, so there is no rush to get in every point you want to make in every conversation. Think of it this way:

Your teenager is very much like a sponge, and you need to make sure not to soak her with more attention, concern, and suggestions than she can absorb.

Unexpected Moments

When you hone down your expectations to shorter conversations, you set yourself up for pleasant surprises: unexpected moments of sentiment and sharing. (This is especially true if you do this in concert with some of the other ideas in this book.) In *Uncommon Sense for Parents with Teenagers*, I urged parents not to take personally much of their kids' behavior, because most of their moodiness and inconsistency stems from normal development during adolescence, not anything their mom or dad has done.

I still stand by that advice, but at the same time I urge you to take as personally as possible the wonderful moments of sharing and opening up that occur between you and your teenager. They are few and far between, so you need to soak them up to get yourself through the longer dry spells. The key, though, is that once they open up and are vulnerable, you realize that this is the exception to the rule, not the new norm. That is, tomorrow they'll behave as if nothing had happened. Just understand that they are not behaving this way because the shared intimate moment with you was unimportant; quite the contrary, they are defending themselves to protect their growing sense of independence. They got too close and felt as if they might lose themselves. Expect the distance; it's actually a sign of how important and tender the moment was for your teenager.

Notes, E-mail, Texts, Etc. . . .

In even the most harmonious of families there are those inevitable times when the lines of communication break down between you and your teenager. It is part and parcel of raising a teenager. When this happens, more than ever, we need to rise to the task at hand and stay the adult. That is, if we're not careful during these moments, we will behave like our teenager's equal by engaging him in debate and tit-for-tat dialogues:

> "Your room is a disaster! How can you find anything in here?"
> "It's not a problem for me, I know where everything is."
> "Well, I want you to pick up this mess before you go to bed tonight."
> "Why?"
> "Why?!"

"Yeah, why? If it's not a problem for me why should it bother you?"

"Because I'm your mother! And you need to learn to clean up after your-self. That's why."

"I know how to clean up after myself. I just like my room this way. I mean, there's no fungi growing or insects crawling around. Yeah, it's messy, but it's not dirty, so why should it bother you?"

"Young man, this is no way to talk to your mother! . . ."

Catch your breath. I'm not saying that teenagers shouldn't have to keep their rooms neat; well, not entirely. I am saying, however, that engaging them as equals (especially when we are the ones who have regressed back to our adolescent years) is not very effective.

Think back for a moment to when your oldest child was around two years old. This was the first time, during some moment of frustration with your child, that you could hear your parents' words coming out of your mouth. Words and phrases that you swore you would never use with your kids. *Young man, I'm your mother and you need to do what I say without question. Young lady, when I say come down for dinner, I mean right now, not in five minutes.* It's quite a shock the first time that happens, and for some parents it even precipitates an identity crisis that lands them in therapy. For most parents, though, it's simply a wake-up call that demands more monitoring of the feelings and thoughts that course through our brains and the words that come out of our mouths. And for an intrepid few, it's a sign for a long overdue acknowledgment of the job their own parents did with them.

Years later, however, when you have a teenager in your home, you once again experience your parents' words and phrases coming out of your mouth, only this time it's different and your attitude has changed. Instead of feeling horror at this recognition, you find yourself agreeing with what your parents said to you years ago.

Still, though, even the most conscious parents will have many of these cross-generational interchanges with their teenagers. They are part of the land-scape. Fortunately, so is the written word. And notes and short letters from parents to teenagers are the natural redeemers of these train wreck conversations—when we've said something we can't take back and we sort of meant at the time but, with a little perspective, realize that we deeply regret our overreaction. Notes help to reestablish order and tranquility in the parent–teenager relation-ship. More than anything, they invite connection. And all of this is double for handwritten notes—a lost art for many of us:

Dear Ray,
These last few weeks have been rough between us. I've said some things I regret, and I hope you feel similarly about some of what you've said. I feel bad

about this, but I'm not sure what else to do. I'm human and sometimes I just react instead of thinking things through more thoroughly. It's a difficult time, one that I hope in a couple of months we can look back on in astonishment. But for now, this is what we have to deal with.

But the reason I'm writing you this note is not to state the obvious; quite the opposite, to state what isn't so obvious. Despite what you might think and despite how you might interpret our recent interactions, I want to be crystal clear about one point: I love you. I never want you to lose sight of that fact. Sure, you're stubborn and self-righteous these days (a lot like me), but no matter what, I love you and am proud of the young man you are becoming. And I don't want you ever to doubt that one important point. It's just that right now, and I'm being frank, I'm having trouble liking you, but that has nothing to do with how much I love you and always will. I have no doubt that we'll get through this, but just don't forget how much I love you.

Love,
Dad

The father who relayed this story to me also mentioned how terrific he felt after writing the note late one evening and slipping it under his son's door early the next morning. He felt that he had communicated something important to his son. He felt that he was a good dad. He was sure it would have the intended impact on Ray, so he was caught off guard by his son's response later that morning at the breakfast table: Nothing. Ray didn't mention the note. Instead, he just slurped his cereal, grunted a "good morning," and read the newspaper. And he didn't mention the note later that day, either—on the car ride home from play practice, at dinner, or before going to bed.

For the next week, Ray said nothing, and his father didn't know how to bring it up. Then one morning, out of the blue, Ray's father heard the whoosh of a postcard sliding under his door. The handwriting was Ray's, but the postcard had only two words written on it: *Me, too.*

Needless to say, breakfast that morning was like breakfast every other morning: Ray just slurped his cereal, grunted a "good morning," and read the newspaper. Neither of them spoke of the first note or the subsequent postcard, but the father did say there was more patience between the two of them and a whole lot more felt optimism about the future.

Not all notes need be this poignant, nor should they be. More often they are about some mundane observation that for one reason or another you were unable to voice when you noticed it. The note is something little that tells them you are paying attention, believe in them, and are there for them should the need ever arise.

Hey, Sam,

Walking by your room last night I heard you laughing on the phone with some friend or another. I just love the sound of your laugh.

Hope you slept well. Have a good day at school and see you at dinner tonight.

Love,
Mom

And:

Susie,

While I was drinking my coffee this afternoon, I was watching you and Oscar [twelve-year-old Labrador retriever] play together in the backyard. It brought back memories of when we first brought him home, when you were just three. You were so responsible for him back then, and you still are. It was just great watching you two play together—brought back great memories. Thanks.

Thinking of you.

Love,
Dad

The advantages of writing notes to your teenagers are twofold. One, writing notes involves you more in your teenager's life. You are actively making observations and taking time to communicate them in a way that your teenager can take in. You are doing something concrete to strengthen your connection with your teenager. Two, you are respecting your teenager's world. You know he is self-conscious and defensive, so you write a note because it slips by the self-consciousness and the defensiveness. You also give him the best opportunity to take in fully what you have written—he reads it in privacy somewhere, in his room or car. And best of all, it's something that he can keep and refer to in the future, perhaps even when he is down on himself or his relationship with you.

To a lesser extent, the same is true for texts. Often the quick text with a playful emoji from work while your daughter is at school or sitting down to do her homework serves the same purpose. At a time in her life when she is overly defended and often inaccessible, you are exercising your creativity to reach around her defenses and let her know that you both see her in her best light and still believe in her. This is the kind of understanding support teenagers need from their parents. Notes, texts, and e-mails are not intrusive and don't even require responses. From your teenager's perspective, can you imagine a more wonderful way to stay connected?

Notes and Teddy Bears

Remember the teddy bears, dolls, and blankets that were so special to your kids when they were toddlers? Many a family trip was delayed if your daughter couldn't find her favorite doll or your son couldn't find his special blanket. Then, when they reached school age, many of you made sure that this distinguished object of affection accompanied your child to her first day(s) of kindergarten. The teachers at the school understood and expected this onslaught of cuddly animals and blankets, and silently nodded in affirmation as you began to explain why Todd was clutching his ratty old blanket. No words were necessary.

Psychologists have named these wonderful exhibitions of love and trust transition objects—a terrible name if ever there was one. These manifestations of security were essential to your child's well-being way back then, and at certain times will resurface as important once again. When going into a new situation with relative strangers, your fifteen-year-old will regress and take comfort in her proven transition objects. That is, as she embarks on an overnight at a friend's house or a week at camp, she might grab that old teddy bear and toss him in with her other luggage.

> My thirteen-year-old was preparing to go to her first boy–girl party at her best friend's house, where she and a couple of the other girls were going to sleep over after the party. On the way out, we had an argument about how she was dressed—in my opinion her shirt was too short and her spaghetti straps too thin. She disagreed, strongly. After lots of give and take, we finally compromised on a different top, not my first choice by a long shot, but not hers, either. When her ride arrived, she was quick to run out the back door, shouting "Bye" over her shoulder. My husband and I just looked at each other. Our little daughter was growing up. We sat together quietly. As he was about to say something, our daughter sprinted back through the door, up the stairs, and into her room. A moment later, she emerged with her favorite childhood stuffed animal, Sally. As she flew past us for the second time, she said, "Can't forget old Sally. See you in the morning. Good night." My husband and I looked at each other in disbelief at the incongruity of my thirty-minute argument with her over her provocative clothes and her teddy bear. Then we shook our heads as it dawned on us that for her, there was no incongruity.

All parents will hold in their mind's eye snapshots of their teenagers simultaneously reaching forward into adulthood and backward into childhood. Practically speaking, your teenager's need for these childhood objects of security pops up at the most unexpected times. But for the most part, teenagers are upgrading their transition objects. And believe it or not, some of these updated transition objects are your notes.

> I still remember packing for the beginning of my freshman year at college. I had everything and was doing a quick run-through, just to be safe, when I saw the manila envelope filled with the notes that my mom and dad had written me through high school. We had never talked about them, but I had saved every one of them—I had even reread most of them a bunch of times. Anyway, for some reason I just popped the envelope into one of my bags.
>
> Later on, after I got to college and settled into my dorm room, I stayed up late rereading all the notes they had written. They just made me feel good about myself, and they helped me to remember who I was. I'm naturally shy, so meeting new people at college was pretty scary for me and I was worried about losing myself as I got to know these strangers. But the notes from my mom and dad helped. For those first few weeks of college, I must have reread those notes four or five times. Each time they seemed to go into my soul a little more deeply . . . I'm a junior now and I haven't looked at them since my freshman year, but I'm never going to throw them out.

We all need our little transition objects when we enter a new environment: family photographs, mementos from the past, favorite art pieces. Your teenager is no different. If you want to include yourself in your teenager's box of transition objects, then writing notes is one of the most direct routes.

In this same vein, when your teenager graduates high school (it will happen sooner than you think) and moves away to his first apartment or off to college, you need to exercise your creativity in forging this distant connection. One of the best suggestions I ever heard (and this is applicable to summer camp as well as all other extended stays away from home) is to ask them to take photos of their surroundings and who they are spending time with and text them home or post them on social media where you can see them. It's a great help for you to have some visual references to your teenager's new surroundings.

Transitions

In general, during any transition, we all step back a bit from our normal patterns of behavior, a change that opens the door for a variety of experiences: from reflection to frustration; from anger to vulnerability; from increased flexibility to increased rigidity; from diminished consciousness to increased consciousness. But no matter how you experience a transition, all transitions are opportunities for connection between you and your teenager. Some of the transitions your teenagers face include the obvious ones such as the shift from school to summer schedule in the spring; and back from summer to school schedule in the fall; and graduation from high school, beginning with all the changes that occur during the second semester of senior year. With a second glance, all sorts of other adolescent transitions are discernable in a variety of normal developmental areas: friendship, romance, employment, extracurricular involvement. There are other transitions that stem from the family: an older sibling moving away, the birth of a younger sibling, an illness, a divorce (often creating weekly, even daily, transitions if there is joint custody), income loss through unemployment, and relocation to a different community and school district.

According to author William Bridges, there are three stages in every transition: ending, middle, beginning.[1] At first this seems obvious, but with a little examination many of us often realize that we act as if there were only two steps to transitions—endings and beginnings—which leaves us rushing from one activity to the next. Behaving this way leaves little room for genuine reflection, which is the precursor to change. That is, when you don't embrace the middle step, you miss some pivotal opportunities for improvement.

A powerful example is what happened on September 11, 2001. Our old way of living came to a sudden halt, and for a long time many of us were in the middle stage, unsure of how to move forward. During this time, we instinctively reached out to one another and reconnected with what was truly important in our lives. Many people changed their lives for the better in the ensuing months. Some reconfigured employment to make family a greater priority. Others sought out spiritual roots. But just about everybody engaged in serious reflection, essentially asking themselves what was important in their lives. Although the tragedy that initiated this reflection was egregious in its horror and beyond words in the pain and suffering it caused, some were able to use this event as a catalyst for change and reconnection to the priorities that are so easily pushed aside in the chaos of everyday living. It was the middle stage of this transition that forced people to reconceptualize their lives and who they had become, most often for the better.

In every transition, your teenager has ample opportunities to reaffirm, reconnect, and redefine, just as long as she acknowledges this in-between state, a state that is neither ending nor beginning. This is where you come in. Your job is to get her to pause long enough to catch her breath and to recognize the upside of not rushing into a new beginning. The key to success here is a combination of knowing your teenager, observing the details of her life (or at least the ones that she lets you glimpse now and again), and your intention.

When basketball season ends and your son has afternoons free, you adjust your schedule during those first few days and invite him to do something special with you. Maybe you take him to see the local professional team play or you go out to dinner at a nice restaurant or you take him shopping or you excuse him from school for the day and drag him to the golf course with you. What you do depends on how well you know your teenager, and this helps you come up with ideas about what he would like to do, even with you.

Then, whatever you end up doing, you casually talk about your son's basketball season. You relive the highlights, shake your head at the bad breaks, laugh at the lucky ones, and generally listen to each other's stories. When this goes well, there are moments of silence—maybe during dinner, maybe during the ride home—when you both naturally reflect. This is also when you gently ask questions that encourage your son to recognize the opportunities of the middle stage that he is in. These questions come from your own experience with reflection as well as your observations about your son's life, in particular the just completed basketball season. *Where did you surprise yourself this season? When did you let yourself down? If you could go back and change anything about this season, what would it be?* As in other areas, don't expect ready-at-hand responses.

The next time you spend time with your son, or perhaps even during the first time, depending on how things go, you ask some of the same types of questions about the new beginning at hand. *How do you want to use the time that has been freed up since basketball ended? Any ideas you're wrestling with?* Then wait. Listen to what he says and then fish for more. *Anything else?* And feel free to throw out suggestions. *Do something new at school, maybe go out for the play? Get a part-time job to save for car insurance? Volunteer at the camp you worked at last summer?* Put the ideas out there, but don't get too attached because most likely whatever he decides won't come from your list, which is the whole point. Your intention of encouraging him to think about the new beginning in front of him paves the way for him to create and choose from his own list.

Predictable and recurring transitions (such as the end of a season or a school year) are often ritualized into some annual event for the family. This is when you celebrate an ending and when the reflection begins. In this regard, there is no greater transition for a high school student than graduation, and for all intents and purposes it begins at the onset of second semester senior year.

Quite simply, your teenager is vulnerable for the entire second semester of senior year. This is the beginning of the end of his high school career, and every senior knows this and outwardly celebrates the ending while inwardly suffering from a range of self-doubts. For most seniors, their final semester of high school is all about friends: solidifying old friendships, meeting new friends, and taking flyers with new acquaintances. It's also a time to test their wings, to try new activities and behaviors: from taking an independent study in poetry to playing intramural softball; from teaching a Sunday school class to racing their parents' cars on a Saturday night; from deepening a commitment to community service to experimenting with drugs, sex, and rock and roll. For better and worse, they try all sorts of new things.

In the midst of this second semester, parents are hard pressed for time with their seniors, so the idea of deepening your connection to your teenager during this time seems, at first glance, far-fetched. Take a second look. Sure your teenager's focus is outside the family, but the extent to which she extends herself in a healthy way during this time is to a large degree dependent on how secure she feels at home. The more connected she feels to you, the more able she is to explore the world about her.

> The last few months of school were a little strange. There was so much I wanted to do, and then there were my parents looking so sad and forlorn because I wasn't spending any time with them. They just couldn't understand that you only graduate high school once in your life, but your family is always there. I know it sounds like a cliché, but it's true. They kept inviting me to do all sorts of things—go out for dinner, camping, movies—but I said no practically every time. But what's really weird is that their constant invites helped me to get more outside of myself during this time. It was as if I knew that they loved me and wanted to spend time with me, which set me free to go and explore things I would have otherwise been too tentative to try.

I have heard the above account one way or another too many times to count. They need you to reach out to them to feel connected, which in turn allows them to say no so that they can explore the world around them. It reminds me of the consummate salesperson: *In my business, the percentage of sales to calls is steadfast at 10 percent. The way I figure it is that sales people who are better than I am haven't been able to make that percentage budge, so my best bet is to work on the other side of the equation by making as many calls as possible. That's the secret of my success: I make three times as many calls as my colleagues, which is why my sales are roughly three times theirs.*

Parents need to take this pragmatic advice to heart. Your teenager will say yes to your invites at the going rate (whatever that is in your family), so your best bet is to invite him more often and not take a no personally. Therein lies the danger to your connection to your teenager. If you take a no personally, then you'll feel hurt and as a result stop tendering invitations, just when your teenager needs you to reach out. The reaching out is what deepens the connection, especially during the huge transitions such as senior year.

Changing Bodies, Changing Connections

When your teenager was an infant and a toddler, you carefully monitored his physical growth. At each appointment with the pediatrician, she probably updated you on where his weight and height were in relation to the norm for that age. You also became a great observer of your child and how these growth spurts affected his behavior. Most parents intuitively recognize the signs of a growth spurt in their child: irritability, clumsiness, increased appetite, sleeplessness, and often tears. Just before the big growth spurt, which can measure as much as one centimeter, or three-eighths of an inch, in one twenty-four-hour period, the body seems to implode on itself. After the spurt, your child probably returned to his more normal behavior and perhaps slept a bit more than usual.

Well, guess what? Your teenager is still going through these same spurts, but you're just not tuned into them the way you used to be. When you spotted the growth spurt in your infant, you allowed for the irritability and all the rest. In fact, you probably put your arm around your spouse and together said something along the lines of "Ah, a growth spurt. Isn't it remarkable?"

Fast-forward thirteen years.

You've just had a barbed interchange with your teenage daughter as you cleared the plates from dinner. You each got in a couple of good shots before she stormed out of the kitchen and up to her room. In the meantime, after your deep breathing exercises have failed, you've taken the dishes out of the dishwasher to wash by hand—a strategy you learned in a recent stress management class. Now imagine, really imagine, how you would feel and respond if minutes later your daughter came back down to the kitchen, stood next to you with her arm around you, and said, "I'm sorry for what I said, Mom. It's just that I'm in the midst of a growth spurt and it's making me crazy!" In all likelihood, you would sympathize with her; indeed, you would offer to get her some ice and aspirin to help with the inevitable joint and bone pain associated with growth spurts.

Sometimes his moodiness is as simple as a growth spurt, and you can use this information to further your connection with him. Take a moment to consider how a growth spurt affects your teenager's basic sense of coordination. During a spurt, or just thereafter, he needs to readjust to this new body of his. Nothing is quite as it was before, most noticeably his hands and his feet, the parts of his body most out of his awareness. For proof of this, take a second look at your teenager the next time he spills his glass at the dinner table—you probably won't have to wait too long. Rather than immediately picking up the glass and cleaning up after himself (as you would do and as you wish he would do), he'll stare off into space for a while. Actually, it's a specific type of staring. First at the spilled glass, then at his hand, and then up and away, off into the distance. It's as if he were corroborating for himself that it was his hand that knocked over the glass; but he is also going further than that, because in the last look—up and away—he is actually updating the mental image he carries of his body.

If your eyes are open, this is magic in action. Growing one centimeter over the course of a single day makes anyone clumsy; for most of us, that lack of coordination plays out mainly in our hands and our feet, where a miscalculated centimeter is the difference between bumping into the coffee table or not; between tripping on the step or not; and yes, between spilling the glass or not. In short, intermittent bouts of clumsiness and uncoordinated movement are normal for teenagers.

I'm not saying that this explains every instance of knocked-over milk in your teenager's life, far from it. Sometimes their miscalculations are caused by inattentiveness, sometimes by fatigue, sometimes by boredom. But more than a fair share of their awkward crashes with the dining room chairs are a result of their changing bodies, which gives you a golden opportunity to connect.

Pause for a moment to imagine how these inevitable periods of clumsiness interact with the typical teenager's heightened sense of self-consciousness. It's quite the one–two combination. It's especially lethal in the train of thoughts and conclusions it can lead your teenager to make: that she's a spaz, that he's uncoordinated, and much worse, as I'm sure you can imagine. Your job is to save him from himself by severing these conclusions. You do this by accepting these moments as normal and, when he lets you, even explaining them to your teenager.

I was attending a middle school dance with a friend of mine who was the vice principal of that school. Toward the end of the evening, the DJ had all the kids up and dancing, and they all had huge grins plastered on their faces. My friend was subtlety pointing out various kids to me. One in particular stood out: *He's the social climber. Doesn't have a group that he hangs with and is desperately trying to crack into the echelon of the "cool" kids.* At this point, he was trying to impress the cool kids with his wild dancing, and I could tell that there was a disconnect between his mind and his body, which meant he was on the verge of going out of control. Seconds later, he jumped into the air and landed on the back of his left heel, catching the cuff of his pants underneath, at which point he lost all traction and slammed to the floor on his rear end. The music continued to blast, but all the dancing had stopped and you could have heard a pin hit the gym floor. My friend didn't miss a beat. She handed me her glass of punch and raced over to the boy on the floor. About twenty feet from the student she did a slide on her knees, ending up three feet from the boy on the floor as she made like a baseball umpire yelling *Safe!* at the top of her lungs as her arms made the safe signal. Within seconds everyone was laughing and the boy was up on his feet dancing once again.

"Wow, that was quick thinking. You know you just saved that guy from some heavy humiliation—probably years of therapy, too."

She smiled at this. "You're probably right. Think I should send the parents a bill?"

The more you can normalize or minimize the bumps and bruises that come from their growth spurts and other physical changes, the stronger the connection. Remind yourself of when they were in kindergarten and you used to explain away the bumps, bruises, and scrapes that covered their knees and legs: *It's all a part of being a kid. You wouldn't be a normal kid if you didn't get banged up some. And from the looks of those knees, I would say you're doing better than average as a kid.* Now imagine how you can translate this same sentiment to that same child now that he's fifteen instead of five.

Show Up

As is discussed in Chapter 13, "Know Your Village," your teenager is two people in one: a regressed child who lives at home and an emergent adult who shows herself outside of the home. (Remember the image of the thirteen-year-old girl headed to her first girl–boy party with her teddy bear.) Therefore, one of your primary tasks is to catch glimpses of this emergent adult whenever possible so that you have a connection with both aspects of your teenager—her regressed part and her emergent adult part. This habit helps you to have confidence in your teenager and keeps the connection between you and her strong, vibrant, and robust. The difficult part is in learning to read between the lines as to when you are invited to show up on your own, or at least with minimal initiative on your teenager's part, and when you need to stay away.

In this regard, it's vital for you to understand that although most adolescents tend toward overstatement and exaggeration as a matter of course—*It was totally awesome! It was, like, the most amazing time I've ever had!*—there is one notable exception: expressing their vulnerability with you. In particular, leaving themselves open to your rejection, and, believe it or not, they feel vulnerable with you more often than you might realize.

Imagine it's a weekday evening and you've just learned that your sixteen-year-old daughter has a home soccer game the next day. Here are five scenarios and the translations for what your teenager is really thinking, but can't say for fear of appearing too vulnerable.

- First scenario:

  "Want me to come to the game tomorrow?"

  "Guess so. If you want."

  Translation: She really wants you to come to the game.

- Second scenario:

  "Want me to come to the game tomorrow?"

  "It's up to you. Probably won't be much of a game—they're not very good—so I may not even play in the second half."

  Translation: She really wants you to come to the game.

- Third scenario:

  "Want me to come to the game tomorrow?"

  "I don't care. You've been to the last couple, so no real need to come, unless you've got nothing better to do."

  Translation: She really wants you to come to the game.

- Fourth scenario:

  "Want me to come to the game tomorrow?"

  "You want me to decide whether you come to my game or not but you won't let me decide on my own whether I can go to the party on Saturday night?"

  Translation: She really wants you to come to the game.

- Fifth scenario:

  "Want me to come to the game tomorrow?"

  "Absolutely not! I don't even want you within a block of the field. Understand?"

  Translation: She does not want you to come to the game—really!

Most of the time, the best your teenager can do is to leave you an opening in which to invite yourself. Any more than that is felt as too vulnerable, like going out too far on the limb and risking unnecessary exposure and liability. Sure, your teenager will risk this from time to time, but it is much easier if you become conversant in their world and recognize the invitation for what it is without making them speak so explicitly. That is, the more you learn to read between the lines during the little interchanges, the stronger your connection, which in turn lays the groundwork for your teenager to express more vulnerability in the bigger conversations.

The Information Drop

Every parent has some book or article that contains information that you would love your teenager to sit down and read. Usually it has something to do with hormones, puberty, and sexual behavior. The big question is how to share these resources with your teenager in a way that captures his curiosity, or that at least doesn't nauseate him. In general, what worked so well when he was younger usually falls short during adolescence. That is, years ago, if you said something was important he accepted your evaluation and treated it as important, too. Now it's the opposite. If you want him to evaluate something as important, you need to undervalue it.

> After raising four teenagers, I've come to realize that there are only two ways to get them to read something that I think is important. The second best option is to leave the newspaper or magazine open to the article and leave it lying around on the coffee table or in the dining room. But far and away the best option is to leave it in the bathroom. That's a surefire read—just be judicious and save it for the really important stuff.

If ever there was sage advice from the front lines, that is it. At the same time, there are other ways, too. Besides leaving reading material in the bathroom (which I agree is the best), it's also effective to leave it lying around in her room, preferably on her bed or desk. And after you leave said book, do whatever it takes to not ask her if she saw it. Just trust that she found the book and will use it in a way that makes sense for her, which you probably won't find out about for at least a few months.

> I was at the bookstore and found this great book on all the changes teenagers' bodies go through during and after puberty. I bought it and tossed it on my son's bed, but he never acknowledged seeing it. Given the state of his room, I couldn't even be sure that he had found it. Then one day out of the blue, he says, "That book you left in my room talked a bunch about how the hormone changes affect my skin, so I'm not too freaked out by this acne, since pretty much everyone gets it." I was shocked. Then he just went on to talk about the movie he was going to that evening, as if I had known all along that he had found the book and read it. Of course, when I stopped to consider that if he had read the parts about acne he had surely read the parts about sex and sex-uality, I gave a huge sigh of relief.

The reality of these books is that they become references for your kids, something they turn to as various issues arise in their lives. Here's how one high school teenager described how she read and used an earlier book that I wrote for kids, *Surviving High School.*[2]

My mom bought it for me, or at least I think she did because I just found it lying on my bed one day after school. At first I just tossed it aside, figuring that if my mom bought it for me it was just some adult lecture dressed up to look cool. But a couple days later, I spent a couple of hours thumbing through it and reading around. Nothing major. But the strange thing is that I sought it out at different times during high school, when I came face-to-face with some of the things you talked about: stress, girlfriends, alcohol, cars. It was kind of cool that way, and don't take any offense, but I liked what the kids had to say way more than what you said in the commentary.

For me, this was the best review I could ever hope for from a teenager. She had glanced at the book and kept it around, which means a general thumbs up. Then she used the book as a reference when various issues came up in her life. And, most important, she told me what she liked and disliked, which is something all parents need to prepare themselves for when providing any kind of reading or listening materials for their teenagers. The nature of adolescence is never to accept in entirety anything an adult has to offer in this realm. The only way teenagers can take in this kind of information is to wrestle with it, which means deciding what is useful, what is relevant, what isn't worth their time, and what is irrelevant. Listen when they talk to you this way, because, much as in Chapter 4, "The Car," they are catching you up on what they know and what they don't know on whatever topic they are discussing. It's a great time to play a student and ask them to explain further, which, once they shift into the teacher's role, they are more than happy to do.

Be Careful What You Wish For, or, Wish Carefully

Robert K. Merton is credited with first describing the concept of a self-fulfilling prophecy in 1948 and how it works. There are three steps:

1. We have expectations of people that we communicate to them in a variety of ways, both verbally and nonverbally.
2. These people in turn respond to these cues and adjust their behavior accordingly to match our expectations.
3. With their adjustment of behavior, they now match our original expectations, hence the term *self-fulfilling prophecy.*

In short, what you expect is what you get. Research—from rats running mazes to children learning in the classroom—supports the idea of the self-fulfilling prophecy. When research assistants and teachers believe (of course, erroneously in research experiments, because there is indeed no difference between the rats or children in the control and experimental groups) that the rats or children they are working with are inherently more intelligent and capable than the norm, these subjects do indeed perform better. When researchers think they have smart rats, these rats learn more quickly how to navigate mazes than their counterparts. When teachers think their students are more intelligent than other students, these students perform better in their classrooms.

There are New Age philosophies predicated on the idea of a self-fulfilling prophecy, and the problem with this way of thinking is that it easily leads to denial. *Repeat endless mantras, hold only positive thoughts and expectations, and your life will be bliss.* But then again, if you're the parent of a teenager, you already know that this type of New Age philosophy is doomed when it comes to your adolescent. There are, however, a few points that wise parents can take from this concept to improve their connections with their teenagers.

First, while you read the daily newspaper, listen to the radio, or watch the latest shocking news stories about teenagers, stay skeptical about the stereotypes. Challenge your thinking. Questioning the prevailing view pushes the stereotypes to the side and reduces your chances of expecting the worst from your teenager.

> Both of my parents were wild teenagers, and I can tell they expect me to be the same. Thing is, I don't feel like being wild or anything. Sure, I've tried alcohol, but it's just not my thing. I'm kind of quiet and nerdy. I like to read, watch movies with my friends, and just be a kid. But the bizarre part is that I find myself thinking about getting drunk and passing out on the sofa so that my parents catch me. Kind of so they think I'm a chip off the old block. Weird, huh?

Second, when in doubt, expect the best. When you are perplexed about your teenager and not sure whether to feel excited or scared, choose the middle ground. Simply remain optimistic. Often your perplexed feelings are a result of his ambiguity, so your quiet optimism can help him choose the more responsible alternative as a means of resolving his confusion. Even if you are not there, your resilient optimism goes with him and will often carry the day—or night, as more frequently happens.

Third, face reality. When bad things happen (and they will), expect your teenager to make a full and responsible recovery—that she will learn from her mistakes. Perhaps not right away, but eventually. Part of the difficulty of staying connected to teenagers is the tendency for parents to anticipate the worst: to take one mistake, say a poor grade in tenth-grade English, and extrapolate it into an inevitable downward spiral—imagine that she'll flunk out of high school and work minimum wage jobs for her entire adult life. This kind of thinking is of no use to your teenager and quickly takes its toll on your connection with each other.

For proof that a few mistakes (even some big ones) don't ruin the rest of your life, take a few moments to reflect on your own adolescence—as well as the adolescences of some of your friends. From your parents' perspective, were you the perfect teenager? What were your shortcomings in their eyes? Most of us, at some time or another, walked the edge just to see what it was like: cars, alcohol, sex, bad grades, negative attitude. Nothing major, but we did test the limits. Your teenager will need to do the same. Stay concerned, but don't take it personally. It means that your teenager will experiment. If you're lucky, it'll happen just out of your view and you won't hear about it until she is in her second or third year of college. And yes, this is the time you have to play the parent role, and while doing this you can still expect the best. For me, the right mixture of vigilance, towing the line, and perspective comes from a story I read in *Sports Illustrated* in the 1960s.

To paraphrase, the story was about a man driving along the streets of a New England city just after a snowstorm. As he was driving along and minding his own business, he was pummeled with snowballs from behind some parked cars. The driver narrowly avoided an accident, pulled his car over, and shook from head to toe with anger. His blood pressure was through the roof. Then an image popped into his head: He remembered how, when he was an eleven-year-old boy living in New York City, on a similar kind of day he and his two best friends had plastered another unsuspecting automobile with snowballs. He also remembered how that driver had pulled over and given chase to the three friends, who as soon as they realized what was happening divided and ran for cover. He remembered running for many city blocks and scaling a few alley walls in his efforts to escape. Hours later, when he felt the coast was clear, he made his way home and found his two friends. They rehashed the story for hours—the fear, the excitement, the surprise, the solidarity. And with each retelling, the story became a bit more embellished than the previous one. It was a big moment in his life. And, in retrospect, the author realized that from that moment on, he and his friends never again threw snowballs at moving vehicles. It was never a stated decision, but one that all the boys implicitly understood. Suddenly, years later, while still sitting in his car, his blood pressure elevated, he realized what he had to do. He got out of the car, put on his best angry look, and gave chase to the boys. Fifty yards later, he stopped to catch his breath. He had done his job—the kids had scattered to the wind. And as he walked back to his car, he realized that twenty years ago that guy had probably chased him and his buddies for a short distance only, but that the effects had been long lasting.

Expect Normal

In our country, there's an alarming trend for parents to expect their children to display above-average talents across the board. Average is no longer acceptable, which is more than just a little bit unfortunate for teenagers.

It takes only a cursory glance at the research on human development to realize that development is not a linear process across the board. Rather, because it is more steplike, it shows sudden spurts of growth alongside slow and steady progress. If we think of this as normal, we are afforded a healthier and more realistic perspective of our teenagers' worlds. That is, if your son loves history and thrives in all his history classes, you are proud, but don't be too alarmed if he does not feel the same way about math and does not do nearly as well in his math classes. Similarly, if your daughter is a great athlete but not very artistic, respect where she is naturally gifted and where she requires more work. In other words, have a different set of expectations for where she has a developmental advantage and where she has a developmental disadvantage.

Again, your history as an adolescent is helpful. Think of your personal strengths and weaknesses when you were in high school. How have they changed in the intervening years? (Probably not that much.) More important, when it comes to career and family, how did you manage to capitalize on your strengths and push your weaknesses to the side?

In many ways, schools are designed for certain types of kids to shine and others to fade into the background. Fortunately, this is not true for the rest of life. Kids who are good at analytical thinking do well in school. Kids who are extroverted and social are rewarded at school. Kids who are athletic are valued at school. Kids who have an extraordinary talent shine at school. The rest of us more or less make up the background. But as adults there are careers, families, and opportunities for success for every type of person, not just the analytical, extroverted, athletic, and gifted. Never forget this when thinking about your own teenager.

Because I have a degree in psychology, it is normal for me to observe the behavior of those around me in psychological terms. In this regard, I'll never forget one of my first meetings with a group of television producers. All in all, there were about six or seven of us in the room. We were trying to come up with an angle for a new project when I was struck with the behavior of those around me; it was as if I were at a meeting of people diagnosed with Attention Deficit Disorder—most suffering from hyperactivity, too. Only a couple of people seemed to pay much attention to what was happening; the rest were off consulting their iPads/tablets and speaking into their cell phones. But after a few minutes of this, to my amazement, it became clear to me that I was the stranger in their world. They were listening to everything and were moving ahead quickly to imagine how to turn the ideas into something worthwhile. They only looked as if they weren't paying attention. These producers had found a world where their natural way of thinking—divergent, fast, creative, three steps at a time—was valued, not disdained. Later on, when I pressed some of these same people about their experiences in school, it came as no surprise that most considered themselves rather unsuccessful in that regard. School was tough on their way of thinking.

Being well-rounded is a great goal—for adults. Teenagers are always better off following their passions. Engaging in what they love helps them to escape their excessive self-consciousness, gives them confidence, reduces their stress, and buoys them with optimism. Once they get through adolescence by riding their passions as far as possible, they can focus more of their attention on becoming well-rounded. But it's an unfair expectation to have of your teenager during her adolescence, unless, of course, that is her natural predilection.

*   *   *

Expect the best, don't get bowled over by the bad, and expect a full recovery. Most of all, make this an attitude you convey rather than a lecture you deliver. This belief in your teenager throughout adolescence sets the stage for some spectacular leaps of growth. Yes, there will always be plenty of two-steps-forward, one-step-backward learning in any adolescent's life, but when your teenager sees belief in him spread across your face and show in your demeanor, then there are times when the one step forward becomes a giant leap forward, much to the delight of you both. And, most important, this indirect communication further strengthens the connection between you and your teenager.

TEN

Technology: Social Media and Gaming

I still remember the first time I viewed the 2011 viral video of a one-year-old girl alternately playing with an iPad and a magazine. Understanding how to navigate the iPad, including expanding photos by using the touch screen with her fingers and pushing them apart, she was at a loss as to why that same technique did not work with the magazine. As she went back and forth between iPad and magazine with her attempts to expand the photos in the magazine repeatedly failing, she looked at her fingers as if somehow they are what was broken.

Our kids are growing up surrounded by computers, mobile devices, tablets, and more, and it is apparent that there is no turning back on the role of technology in our children's and teenagers' lives. That has both its benefits and costs, and much of the talk on teenagers and tech use focuses on potential negative effects. However, if you have an understanding of adolescent development, social media and gaming can actually be useful tools to make and deepen the connections with our teens.

Social Media

At a minimum, social media keeps your teenager connected to friends, especially during daily transitions, like coming home after school.

> When my daughter gets home from school I know she's not fully home until she has had something to eat, spent some time alone, and checked all of her various social media accounts. It frustrated me for the longest time until my

mom reminded me of what I was like at that same age. Like my daughter, I needed both food and time alone, but since there was no Internet it was the phone with the long extension cord that I dragged into my room so I could call my friends. Even though there was nothing to talk about I just needed to connect. So now I get it. Still frustrated, but much more understanding of her relentless need to stay plugged in.

It is important to remember that the developmental norms and needs of teenagers have not changed that much since you were a teen. However, the way these needs are met has shifted, especially when it comes to social and friendship development. And technology, especially through social media, has made this process both more expeditious and more treacherous.

One of the prime benefits to adolescents of the phone or texting is that they literally are not in visual contact with the other person. Therefore, there is no physical self-consciousness, which unto itself is a huge relief for the typical teenager. Think about how much time the average teen spends staring into the mirror. Or, as one mom told me, "It takes my daughter twenty minutes to get her T-shirt untucked in just the right way!"

Because of the increased relaxation associated with the phone, it might seem perplexing that along with social media there seems to be an increased use in FaceTime and Skype by teenagers. Both these video calling services literally bring physical self-consciousness back into play. But within the context of social media, there are two different occasions when visual connection is preferred. The first is when they're goofing around with buddies. Teenagers expect a great deal of the communication in their conversations—read, adolescent humor—to be nonverbal, especially with boys. That is, these communications frequently include a variety of sound effects and the facial expressions that go with them, both natural and unnatural. The second exception is when teens are communicating with a romantic interest. Then they can both stage their background to highlight their best parts, and, more importantly, fully take in one another's presence.

Your Education in Social Media

At the Brentwood School, I teach a course on Influence and Persuasion to juniors and seniors. As a way of introducing the subject matter, I ask them a straightforward question: If you want someone to do a small favor for you, what is the single most important word to use in your request? Typically the first word mentioned is *please*. Although that is a good guess, as well as a sign of good manners, in this case it is not the most powerful word. From there, the list of guesses balloons: *demand, beg, need, require, save, why*. To date, none of my students has guessed the correct word. As a parent, it is important to know this word and how to use it, because it will help you positively influence your teenager around the use of social media.

Social scientists have shown that when a stranger makes a simple request to cut in line to make a copy, 60 percent of people grant that request. When the stranger includes the word *because* along with a reason—*because I'm in a rush*—the compliance rate jumps to 94 percent. Interestingly, in requests that don't require significant inconvenience simply using *because* with a meaningless rational—*because I have to make copies*—the compliance rate still jumps, this time to 93 percent. When, however, requests require more sacrifice, the use of *because* diminishes somewhat depending on the strength of the rationale.[1]

All of this is to say your teenagers need to hear your perspectives on their technology use. Please understand, this does not mean a lecture, but rather a quick, to-the-point *because*. *Another 15 minutes because you need to get to sleep at a reasonable time. Please turn off your phone because we want to have a conversation at the dinner table. Time to turn off the game because you need to get outside for awhile.*

When it comes to social media, and because it moves so quickly and with potentially hurtful consequences, your teenagers need education from a variety of places, especially you. Fortunately, this does not require you to become a social media guru. It does, however, mean that you must be ongoing in your education about social media in several different aspects.

To this end, it often surprises me how many parents lean on their teenagers for guidelines as to how to use social media. This is akin to letting them set the timeline for when they are ready to drive, which none of us would ever do. The good news is that there are many great organizations out there ready to provide you with the needed information. In my mind, Common Sense Media is a good starting point for this type of information, though, as always, you have to balance your beliefs and practices with their suggestions.

> When it comes to social media I always consult a few of the expert websites for some background information and suggestions. Then I always compare their thoughts with my intimate knowledge of our family and my son, as well as our family values, and from there I get pretty clear on whatever I'm researching. Whether it is video games, movies, or social media platforms, I end up feeling like I've got clarity before sitting down to hear what my son has to say. And I usually let him start these conversations.

As you gain greater knowledge around social media you need to stay balanced between potential pitfalls and gains. Keeping your perspective balanced while engaged with your teenager will keep the connection fruitful. As you listen to what he has to say you can point out your concerns and see how he responds. And make sure you let his responses influence you, especially in terms of your willingness to share some of the nervousness/risk and what you need behaviorally from him in order to take the risk. (See Chapter 3 for more on giving back the problem to your teenager.) If your teenager perceives you as beyond any influence around any topic, especially social media—your mind is made up and that is the final word—then your influence will drop precipitously. Therefore, it is important to educate yourself on some of the basics around technology. Here are four key areas to keep in mind.

1. **Privacy and Safety:** It is important for all of us to understand that, pragmatically, we should not expect privacy on the Internet, whether it is the sites we visit; the messages, images, and videos we post; or personal information we share. In this regard, teenagers are incredibly naïve. They think they are beyond hacking of any sort, or of people researching them by viewing their various social media. In this area, they do need the proverbial splash of cold water across the face. One educator I know of regularly tells the students at her high school something along the lines of:

   > I'm not here today to lecture on the evils of social media. I do, however, want to educate you on two aspects of social media that could cause you harm down the road without your ever knowing about it: college admissions and employment. More and more colleges and businesses regularly check on applicants' social media outlets. They do not probe deeply, but if they discover disturbing information on a cursory viewing then that is often enough for them to pass on you for the college acceptance or the job. And they will never share that information with you, so you will never know why you did not get accepted into that college or for that job.

2. **Relationship Building:** Through social media, relationships both broaden and deepen. Sometimes this is where similar interests are discovered, or where creativity is expressed in unexpected ways, or even unabashed kindness. There are even times when teenagers have exclusively online relationships with one another based on a shared Internet game or media platform. And these connections can be robust and healthy.

   > My son has a couple of kids he plays *Minecraft* with that he met at camp a couple of years ago. They don't even go to the same camp

anymore but they play online together a couple of times every week. Their friendships are no longer bound by geography, a concept I'm having a difficult time getting my arms around.

3. **Relationship Damaging:** Unfortunately, this is the area we most often see in the headlines and hear about in the carpool—cyberbullying, exclusion, and generally disparaging posts. Sadly, it is all true. This is where the independence and immediacy of social media cause real damage. Sometimes this hurt is intentional, when kids are out to sabotage one another, and other times it is a spontaneous reaction to something that has happened or something someone else has posted.

   When I walked into class I was part of the group (four other eighth-grade girls) but when I walked out 50 minutes later everything had changed. Not sure why, but one of them posted a terrible comment about me and the others responded in kind, even with a few bad photos of me. Suddenly I was all alone, and everybody knew it. That was the worst part, everybody knowing.

4. **Self-Directed Learning:** The resources available via the Internet are truly extraordinary. Teenagers can learn to code, write poetry, draw, or make a robot. Practically the only limit to what they can learn online is their imaginations.

   My ninth-grade son really wanted a mask of his own making for Halloween. So once he designed it he went online and learned how to make a mask that molded to his face. It was a complicated and drawn out process, but he stuck with it all the way. And it was a pretty cool mask, too.

The Internet itself is neutral, and we need to keep this in mind as we observe and engage with our teenagers over their various uses of it. This means they will make mistakes along the way. It also means they will have some wonderful interpersonal and intrapersonal moments. Our job, like in every other area, is to encourage the positive, discourage the negative, and be there after they make mistakes to both hold them responsible and love them.

Negotiate Guidelines Through Listening and Modeling

Given how quickly technology changes and grows, along with how well versed our children are in all aspects of their increasing social media options, it only makes sense to start the conversations with them about guidelines after you have done some of your own research, as outlined above. One interesting place to begin is with what teenagers are thinking about our technology use and misuse. Researchers at the University of Washington conducted a survey along these lines—"What Tech Usage Rules Would Kids Make for Their Parents?"[2] The rules that teenagers proposed for their parents fell into roughly seven categories, with the major insight that teens really do take their behavioral cues regarding technology from how parents handle it in their own lives. Their bottom line, like ours, is that they want their parents present, and not involved at all in technology, when they are trying to talk to us.

> When my dad gets a text in the middle of a conversation, he is famous for holding up one finger, saying "Just one minute," taking at least five minutes to text back, and then expecting me to wait patiently for him to get back to me and our conversation. Worst part, he gets mad when I walk away/roll my eyes/ exhale loudly.

They also want us to learn to balance our use of technology with other activities that do not involve it. Sound familiar? This is the exact same thing we are aiming for with them—balance and moderation. Quite explicitly, they do not want us texting while driving or sitting at a traffic light. They notice every exception to the rule that we make for ourselves, and each instance like this undermines our influence with them as well as our connection to them. When they see us breaking our own rules, they feel unencumbered to do the same. In short, they want us to practice what we preach 24/7. As teenagers, more than just about any other developmental age, they have a nose for sniffing out hypocrisy of any kind, especially when it comes to their parents. This doesn't mean we have to be perfect, but it does mean we need to own up to our shortcomings and not just passively accept them.

Finally, the top guideline that was suggested for parents by their children was not to overshare about them (teens) online. That is, do not put up photos or stories about your teenagers without first getting their okay. This was mentioned twice as often as any other suggestion. If you think about it in the context of adolescent development, this makes perfect sense. As they become more and more self-aware they also tend to try and overcontrol what is "out there" about them for fear it will embarrass or humiliate them down the road. And nothing can be more embarrassing to a teen than a well-intentioned parent.

> I can't stand it when my mom posts photos of me as a little kid. Sure, they're cute and all, but she just doesn't get how public they are. I mean the last thing I need is someone from school reposting them with an entirely different tag line. I've seen this happen to other kids and it's just too painful to watch. But

my mom just doesn't get it and keeps telling me not to be so sensitive . . . I just wish she would be a bit more sensitive around me!

In conversations with teenagers about social media, ask them questions about how they use it and what it does for them. Be patient, as these exchanges tend to come out in bits and bursts. For instance, you may ask about how they use something like Snapchat and get a terse response: *Because I like it!* And later that day or the next, while on a walk or in the car, you might ask again and get a much more elaborate response. With teenagers, sometimes you have to prime the pump a few times before you get what you are looking for. Just don't take personally their lack of response to the first few prompts.

As technology is such a part of all of our lives it is essential that it become the topic of an ongoing dialogue with your teenager. Add it to the ongoing conversations about alcohol, drugs, sex, and driving. According to recent research by the Pew Foundation,[3] more and more parents are having conversations with their teenagers about online behavior and content, though the regularity of these exchanges is questionable. That is, although 92–95 percent of parents report having had these discussions, only 36–40 percent report doing so frequently. And remember, from your teenager's perspective: *Out of sight, out of mind.* That is, unless they are regularly hearing from you, it is as if you have never spoken with them.

Nobody ever said it was easy to raise a teenager. But, at the same time, the more often you talk to your son or daughter about these topics, the less anxiety you'll have about them—and you'll have increased attention for listening.

My teenage boys know that I will give them the benefit of the doubt just about every time if they will take the time to teach me how to use some of the different apps and sites they love. We literally sit side by side as they walk me through all the steps. For me, there are three huge benefits to this. First, practically, I learn about a new site or app, which I frequently enjoy for a long time afterward. Second, I get to see a more patient, adultlike part of my boys— they explain well and both use humor to enhance my learning. And finally, and the best by far, we end up talking about much more than what I'm learning about—from how his friends behave online, to bad parental behavior by some of his friends' parents, and many other subjects that would otherwise be off limits.

In this same vein, other parents have shared that after having their teen teach them about a site or an app, they "friend"/follow each other on this new piece of social media. Now granted, this is probably an account/username that your child set up just to share with you and a few other family members, which is fine because you probably do not want all the details of what their friends and teenagers in general are sharing. But this does establish another connection between you and your teenager—whether it is texting one another encouraging comments, funny photos/selfies, or simple updates; this is another vehicle for ongoing communication and connection that is respectful of privacy and context.

Side by Side

Connection is almost always best fostered when side by side with our teenager. Whether it is in a car, on a walk, or in a theater, side by side is always best.

> For us it's the family hike. Every month or two we just insist that, as a family, we go for a nearby hike. It's usually only 3–5 miles. There's plenty of grumbling and excuse making before we start, and truthfully for the first couple of miles as well. But after that second mile we hit our flow state as a family and all sorts of wonderful exchanges happen. We laugh. We talk about hopes and desires. It's like our teenagers grant us access to them as long as we keep moving. It's beautiful. And we've now done it enough that my husband and I take it on faith that if we can get everyone on the trail then we'll hit that flow state. Works for us.

Technology is no exception. The screen of just about all technology is also perfect for naturally putting us in this position as our focus remains on the screen, assisting to circumvent the self-consciousness inherent in adolescence. Without sneaking up on your teenager, learn how to approach and ask the obvious, "What are you up to?" Then, exercise patience and simply wait and read the signs. The nature of the immersion of technology is that the response will be delayed (unless there is something on the screen that will cause embarrassment) so expect the hesitated response, which may feel like rudeness but is not. Take a look at the screen, read your teenager's body language, and ask a straightforward question, often pointing at something on the screen. Then play it by ear. If you are lucky she will begin to explain something to you, even unconsciously making room for you to sit nearby. Stay interested. In fact, learn to be interested in this technological world of your teenager if for no other reason than to create another common reference point. That is, it is irrelevant whether or not you are really interested in what's happening on the screen.

> My daughter just loves Snapchat, the app that lets you make and share stories, and since she's taken the time to explain it all to me she also shares with me

some of her favorites as well as the latest ones she has done. Now I'm not naive. I know she has a couple of accounts and that this is the PG one that she shares with me, but still, it's a fabulous point of contact. I even made my own video story the other day and shared it with her. She was impressed, but then couldn't stop herself from pointing out all the ways I could have improved the story. Come to think of it, it was kind of like how I read and comment on her papers.

As a side note, you will notice that when discussing or disagreeing with something on the screen both of you are not nearly as defensive as you might otherwise be. This is natural. In fact, successful companies like Pixar use this to maximize feedback. Typically, when working on a movie, the team gathers in the morning to look at the previous day's work up on the screen. From this vantage point whoever is presenting the work is not the focus, what is on the screen is the focus. And when the person responsible is not the visual focus defensiveness tends to diminish. While looking at the screen together, the same is true for you and your teenager. That makes it an ideal place from which to discuss political debates as well as to edit papers.

Engaging your curiosity in how teenagers use and enjoy technology is beautiful in that it allows you to enter important aspects of their world, and most teenagers are more than willing to share their expertise in whatever is in technological vogue. They do this for a couple of reasons. For one, they are proud to share with you important parts of their lives, just as long as they are in charge of the limits. For another, they enjoy being in the role of expert while mom or dad is the student. This is a role reversal that just about every teenager enjoys. Parents do, too, as they get to see a different side of their teenager in these reversed roles. Deeply empathetic parents also experience daily life with their teenager from the other side.

My son explains things well, but he tends to go too fast. So when I ask him to repeat himself I can tell that it is trying his patience. I try to take it all in during the first explanation but somehow he thinks I can take more in than I'm capable of in one sitting. Honestly, sometimes after he teaches me something I go back on my own to try and clear up what I've missed just so I don't trouble him . . . And this has helped me to realize how I have a similar dynamic with him when I'm the expert. The most recent example was in teaching him how to drive. It's so simple to me that I would get impatient when he did not understand something the first or second time through. I've also come to appreciate why the DMV picked 50 hours of driving before they can take the driving portion of the driver's license exam, which means I need to lower my expectations, especially at the onset.

Video and Online Gaming

Online gaming is the norm for today's teenagers. Research in 2015 from the Pew Foundation reported that of teenagers between the ages of 13 and 17, 72 percent of them play video games. Of these teens, 84 percent are boys and 59 percent are girls.[4] For the majority of teenagers there is a vital social component that comes with game playing. Sometimes this social connection comes about simply by playing games in real time with others. At other times it's talking with friends about games in common and the newest trends. And often, while at a friend's home, it's taking turns playing and having conversation about a wide range of subjects while watching others play the game.

> I've got a few controllers and a bunch of games, so my friends like playing at my house. It's really a blast, playing the games and even more, just hanging out and goofing around with one another. And my parents are pretty cool about giving us our space when my friends come over.

With the advances of high-speed Internet, teens can also converse with one another while gaming together, from the privacy of their own homes. In fact, 59 percent of online players use a voice connection with other players.[5] Still others take it a step further by Skyping or FaceTiming together while they play the game. In short, our teenagers' friendships are no longer bound by geography. Indeed, more than half of teen gamers report having made at least one new friend online.[6]

> It's actually pretty cool that I can lie in my bed while playing online and talk with my friends. We help each other out in the game plus talk about lots of other stuff, too. And my parents are fine with it as long as all my homework is done and lights out by the agreed upon time. Heck, even once in awhile we do homework together!

Many parents have wondered how much is too much when it comes to gaming. The standard response, and it's a good one, is that it is fine as long as it does not interfere with the rest of their lives and their normal development. That is, they are working hard in school and getting their homework completed. They are participating in extracurricular activities of some sort: athletics, arts, a part-time job, or involvement with the church or community. They are getting exercise and a reasonable amount of sleep. All of this is straightforward. From a strict time perspective, and as a general rule of thumb, however, I agree with what Andrew Przybylski, an experimental psychologist from the University of Oxford, said in an NPR interview: "If there was a magic dose, it would be less than one hour (per day), and if there was a dangerous dose, it would be more than three hours (per day)."[7] Less than an hour is hardly a cause for concern and your teen is probably just using it as a transition or a break in his day.

> After my son gets home from sports practice he likes to play a video game until dinner. It's sort of a break from school and helps him shift back to the family, and then homework later in the night. He shares his room with his two younger brothers so I also think it's a way for him to get some personal space.

As easy as it is to appreciate these connections and friendships, the first-person violence contained in many of these games is still troubling to many. Again, it's a matter of how much, how often, and most important, what is the impact on your teenager. In general, research has shown that for a short while after playing the game teenagers are more aggressive. (Of course, the same can be said of parents after watching the home football team lose a particularly close game.) In general, this postgame aggression is short lived, and always worth pointing out to your teenager so he becomes aware of this pattern.

A lost opportunity for many parents is when your teenager first requests a new game as to whether or not *the game* makes you uncomfortable. That is, every request is an opportunity to assess. And almost always *the ask* comes in a natural setting for them to talk—in the car, late at night, eating a meal together, during a commercial break while watching a show together: *Okay, you know the drill. Let's talk about how you think you're doing in the whole game-playing arena. First, walk me through the Big Four: schoolwork, sleep, exercise, and friends. Second, tell me about the game. And third, send me two links about the game—one positive and one negative.*

It is easy to see how this approach, or some variation thereof, actually empowers your teenager. She can figure out for herself the responsibility you need to see to go along with a purchase of the new game. That is, after a few times of this there should be few, if any surprises, and you will get a good glimpse of the emergent adult in your teen. Also, because the expectations are clear and consistent, it will also deepen the connection between the two of you.

Along these lines, *the ask* is also a good time to remind them of the kind of online behavior you expect of them. This is important to do and easy to forget once you have had the conversation once or twice. In fact, a great idea is to ask them for examples of responsible behaviors online. In this respect, the research is quite encouraging. That is, online gaming is a place where teenagers are learning how to respond to and stand up to inappropriate behavior. Researchers at Cornell University found that 63 percent of game players saw or heard other gamers acting too aggressive whereas another 49 percent saw or heard others being racist or sexist. That's the bad news in terms of parents concerned about the behavior their teens are exposed to online. The good news, however, makes up for much of this concern. That is, 75 percent of gamers reported that at least some of the time they responded directly to the aggressors, asking them to stop. And beyond this, 85 percent of those who reported witnessing these inappropriate behaviors saw other players being exceptionally kind and helpful.[8]

This research indicates that not only is it nice, but it is vitally important to ask your teens about the negative behaviors they see online as well as how they and others respond. That is, you want to reinforce high expectations and actual positive behavior. In many ways it is safer to confront others online than in person, so getting this experience online is hopefully a precursor to doing more of this in face-to-face relationships, which is something you can and should support.

> "I'm really proud of you for calling out that other player on all the racist comments. Just wondering, do kids talk that way at school, too?"
>
> "Yeah, sometimes."
>
> "What do people do?"
>
> "Depends. At first we usually ignore it and hope it stops, but if not we generally just try and change the subject."
>
> "Anyone ever directly say to stop?"
>
> "Hardly."
>
> "So, easier to stand up to this kind of thing online than in person?"
>
> "Pretty much."
>
> "I get it. It's still a struggle for me, too. But truth be told, I think you're ahead of me when I was your age. And I hope you can do a better job at standing up to these kinds of comments than I did at your age . . . I expect you will."

Video games and online gaming have positive and negative aspects, so a large piece of your job is to do what you can to maximize the positive and minimize the negative. You do this through ongoing conversations, clear guidelines, and paying attention. This gaming world is also a rich opportunity to deepen the connection between you and your teenager through your interest and curiosity. That is, beyond your parental role learn to take an anthropological perspective. Be creative in this approach, and learn to question rather than judge.

> I was surprised to note that when starting or ending any of his online gaming sessions he never said "hello" or "good-bye" to whomever he was playing with. They just stopped. At first I thought it was an opportunity to teach some basic manners, but I caught myself and instead just asked about it. He did not have

any explanation other than that's just the way you do it online. I was fascinated, because in daily life he always greets friends. I think it's just something about jumping into the middle in the online world. As opposed to beginnings, middles, and ends, the Internet is one, giant middle.

Not Your *Playboy/Playgirl* Magazine

This is a difficult topic to write about but as the parents of teens it is important not to bury our heads in the sand. And compared to when we were teenagers, pornography is a much more powerful influence. For instance, according to research, most teenagers in the late 1980s and early 1990s "had looked at or read *Playboy* or *Playgirl*."[9] So clearly, teenagers have always used pornography as one avenue of exploration when curious about sex and sexuality. But it was an entirely different game back then. That is, pornography today is more readily available, more explicit, and more diverse.

Or as Philip Zimbardo, *Man Interrupted*, sums up: "All of the most popular porn sites offer free content and also offer more exclusive features . . . You can find pretty much anything you want free of charge, and you can access these videos nearly any time, anywhere in the world that Internet exists."[10] Zimbardo further speculates about the potential for what he has labeled an "arousal addiction" in teenagers with too much exposure to Internet porn (and online gaming). Due to the availability, variety, and explicitness of porn through the high-speed Internet this type of disorder leads individuals to "seek out novelty in order to achieve or maintain a high level of arousal."[11] That is, with more porn consumption comes both less satisfaction and more negative consequences, and the subjective need for more porn.

For instance, as teens watch more porn they come to see sex as more of a physical or recreational act, rather than one of intimacy. This is especially so if they believe the porn they are watching is realistic. Repeated viewing can also leave them feeling intimidated and inadequate, as male porn actors are all unusually endowed and female porn actors practically all have had implants. Alexandra Y sums this up in an article she wrote for *Psychology Today*:

> Pornography shows us a world where relationships mean nothing and immediate sexual gratification means everything. Therefore, the adolescent viewer's brain is being wired to expect that sex and relationships are separate from one another, and that men's and women's bodies should be sexually exaggerated as they are in porn—which can lead to shame about one's own body as well as failure to be aroused by the bodies of others.[12]

These are scary statistics and theories, especially for the parents of boys as teenage guys watch porn more than girls, though girls are catching up in their watching of Internet porn. What's a parent to do? Let's begin by taking a deep breath, and then let's get a little perspective.

Developmentally it makes perfect sense that teenagers are curious about sex and sexuality. After all, the beginning of adolescence is marked by the onset of puberty, which most of us have worked hard to forget. Here are a few reminders of what puberty is like:

- Wide mood swings due to the rapid and abrupt release of hormones
- Growth spurts leading to wide swings of energy from boundless to lethargic
- Body parts changing beyond your control
- Periods of seemingly nonstop feeding
- Acne and clumsy growth spurts just as you are experiencing full-blown self-consciousness for the first time
- And finally, unexpected and unpredictable urges around sex, with certain body parts seemingly having a mind of their own.

Therefore, and this is essential to remember, if you discover your teenage daughter or son viewing pornography online it is not the end of the world. They do not necessarily have a porn addiction, nor is it necessarily deviant behavior. At the very least it is a call for some conversation, but not panic. That is, if you overreact by focusing on discipline, and miss the curiosity that is driving the behavior, you in essence are punishing your teen for his or her trajectory of normal, adolescent development, which undermines your connection to one another. Better to take to heart the advice of George Vaillant, *Triumphs of Experience: The Men of the Harvard Grant Study*, when he wrote, "When you're just getting the hang of grief, rage, and joy, it makes all the difference in the world to have parents who can tolerate and 'hold' your feelings rather than treating them as misbehavior."[13]

With any luck, your teenager's middle school and/or high school has a decent Human Development course where this was covered. But even with this education, parents still have their own responsibility to educate. For example, when your teenager took the course, it may or may not have coincided with her going through puberty. If she had yet to enter puberty then she probably missed much, if not most, of what was being taught.

I hated learning about sex in Human Development! I wasn't even close to hitting puberty—had not even gotten my period—so it felt like science fiction.

Of course I knew better, I mean I watch TV and have seen R rated movies, but none of it connected. I just felt embarrassed the entire time and hoped nobody would notice.

Furthermore, your teenager needs to hear at least some of what is taught in Human Development from you and it needs to be ensconced in your family values. Yes, it is an awkward conversation, and still one that needs to occur.

I knew I had to have the conversation one day when I forgot to knock on my son's door . . . Anyway, I recovered. Ended up purchasing a couple of copies of *It's Perfectly Normal: Changing Bodies, Growing Up, Sex, and Sexual Health.*[14] One for him and one for me. I simply put his copy in his room, on his desk. Then periodically I would ask him about it—nothing pushy, just curious. He hated it, and one day I finally came clean: "Hey, I'm not comfortable with this topic either, but it is too important to not talk about. Just bear with me a bit, okay?" It did get less awkward after that, but never comfortable.

The good news here is that when parents weigh in on Internet content it makes a positive difference in the attitudes and behaviors of teenagers. That is, research looked at parenting styles and found that the teenagers of those parents who were authoritarian or authoritative—having rules and expectations around Internet viewing—in turn internalized their parents' messages and cut back on or eliminated inappropriate viewing.[15] Finally, if you hang in there with these conversations there is a decent chance that, when your teens are in their twenties, these will be the stories of good-natured and humorous bonding.

Not All Online Time Is Equal

One of the basic tenets of improvisational theater is the idea of *Yes, and . . .* This means that when one actor picks up after another the best recipe for success is to simply accept what has been said and add onto it or change directions. This is opposed to the all too common *No, but . . .* When it comes to the connection with our teenagers this is one of the golden rules. Listen to yourself. Learn to catch the *No, but* before voicing it and replace it with at least some form of *Yes, and.*

This one idea has made a huge difference in my relationship with my sophomore son. He asks me something, say about purchasing a new video game. "That might be possible, and let's think about what that will take." It was really difficult at first but the more I practiced the more I realized that frequently my "No, but's" just blocked our connection and his creativity.

One of the concerns of technology is how much time is spent sitting indoors in front of a screen. Yes, and just as the second edition of this book was nearing completion Nintendo released *Pokémon Go*, which quickly became a phenomenon across the United States and beyond. As opposed to the original *Pokémon* cards, first released in 1996 and quickly expanding to the handheld Game Boy device, this groundbreaking version requires the use of mobile devices while moving through the world looking for *Pokémon* that are linked to actual geographic places. Thus, small groups of teenagers are seen walking through neighborhoods, downtowns, and all around trying to capture various *Pokémon* and increasing their levels of expertise. That is, the game had the amazing effect of pulling players out of the confines of their own rooms and homes and into the real world—walking, biking, and driving slowly to find and capture *Pokémon*.

> I've never seen anything like it. Suddenly my fifteen-year-old son was fixing up his bicycle to join some of his friends as they rode around town in search of *Pokémon*. And over the course of one weekend I went from worrying about him getting out of the apartment enough to worrying about him riding his bike around town too much! Ironically, in both cases it was behind a screen—his computer at home and his phone on the bike. And it was the bike and screen combination that had me concerned, especially after I read about two kids walking off the edge of the road because they were so focused on their screens.

The point is that *Pokémon Go* motivated teenagers to explore the outdoors with their friends, and for insightful adults, their parents, too. For instance, teenagers were now eager for family walks as long as they could plan the route. And as the walks unfolded so did conversation—about *Pokémon Go* and much more. My hunch is that by the time you read this *Pokémon Go* will have passed or be one of many games taking advantage of increased mobility. From Snapchat to Instagram the social networking/gaming world will continue to evolve. The point is that with every evolution you'll want to keep your eyes open for the new opportunities to connect. They are there, just as long as you are watchful.

*   *   *

There is no doubt that technology will continue to evolve and, in this regard, that teenagers will always be one or two steps ahead of their parents. As best you can, keep your eyes open and stay current with trends. At the same time, trust your relationship with your teenager and trust your intuition. In the long run, your relationship and your informed intuition are the two best tools you have in influencing how your teenager makes use of the myriad of social media and gaming options.

ELEVEN

Extend the Comfort Zone

We all have a comfort zone. You feel calm, relaxed, and confident whenever you are engaged with an activity or behavior inside your comfort zone. Throughout your youth and during school your comfort zones were systematically stretched and extended. This is the nature of education. It's also the nature of parenting, especially when it comes to teenagers.

The Swiss psychologist Jean Piaget articulated and labeled this process of acquiring new skills and new information that requires you to toggle back and forth between comfort and discomfort as equilibrium and disequilibrium. Take learning a new card game as an example. When you come to the table you are in equilibrium—you're looking forward to learning and playing a new game. Then, as you learn the basics and some of the nuances of the game, you begin to experience a state of disequilibrium. This is when doubt and confusion creep in. How you deal with this state dictates whether or not you'll extend your comfort zone to include this new card game. That is, if you become overwhelmed by your confusion, you give rise to all sorts of defenses and rationalizations for not learning the game.

This is a silly game and it's not worth the time and effort to learn. People who play this game are lame. Besides, I've got better things to do with my time. If, however, you do manage to get through your confusion, you are on the path to learning the basics of this new card game. In Piaget's terms, you've reached a new and higher state of equilibrium for having endured your earlier state of disequilibrium. In terms of the comfort zone, you have successfully expanded your comfort zone to include a new activity.

When engaged in learning of any kind—whether it is a new skill or the continued development of an old skill—we experience the learning process as roughly one step backward, two steps forward. Visually, moving left to right, it looks something like this:

Equilibrium ----------------- **Disequilibrium** ------------------ **Equilibrium**

(Looking forward to learning the new card game.)

(Confusion and doubt.)

(New skills and knowledge; understand the basics of the new card game.)

Those who understand and appreciate this necessary progression to learning—from calm to confusion to clarity—and who are motivated to learn through genuine curiosity—develop ever-expanding comfort zones. They have a thirst for new knowledge and proficiencies grounded in the present. If your parents or friends of theirs possess this quality, they are on the path to wisdom.

Think of it this way: Adults well into the second half of their lives who take pleasure from expanding their comfort zones are a delight to spend time with. We look forward to visiting these people. For one thing, we know we'll never experience boredom around them. For another, we feel that somehow they'll give us a boost of energy, a sense of rejuvenation, perhaps even inspiration. This feeling is a result of how such people live and approach life more than anything they say to us or compliments they bestow upon us.

On the other hand, folks of this generation who have made a habit of staying well within their comfort zones and who are fearful of extending their comfort zones are tough to hang around for very long. Thirty minutes with them feels like several hours. And instead of feeling rejuvenated afterward, we are exhausted. They tell the same stories over and over again. They ask the same questions and respond in the same way almost no matter how you respond. They are predictable, and they suck the life right out of you.

Your teenager understands, at a gut level, the difference between expanding and constricting comfort zones. My favorite example of this, one that hits the mark with most teenagers, has to do with learning to drive. Teenagers are motivated to earn their drivers' licenses, and doing so requires them to expand their comfort zones and experience Piaget's ideas of equilibrium and disequilibrium. To reinforce this idea with their parents, I ask the parents in my seminars to remember or imagine their first time in a car with their teenager behind the wheel, learning to drive. You will recognize the process, which goes something like this.

Your daughter gets into the car on the driver's side, with you sitting next to her in the passenger's seat. She adjusts the seat so that her feet are comfortably touching the brake and gas pedals. (Note: If there is a third pedal, the clutch, she shouldn't take her first drive in this car!) Then she adjusts the rearview mirror, then the side mirrors. Then, maybe, the rearview mirror, one more time. She remembers to buckle her seat belt—every adult she knows has already warned her that failing to buckle up means an automatic failure on the driving part of the exam. But the seat belt throws off the seat adjustment. So she read-justs the seat, and now the mirrors again, just to be safe.

Then she puts her foot on the brake pedal and pushes—probably with more force than necessary, but again, better to be safe than sorry. Next, she shifts the car out of Park and into Drive. Finally, with equal parts anticipation and trepidation, she slowly lifts her right foot off the brake pedal. Nothing. Then she feels the blood rush to the surface of her skin as she puts the car back into Park and remembers to start the engine. You do your best to hide your smile.

Now, with the car started and the engine idling, she puts the car into gear and begins to lift her foot off the brake pedal. Then, as soon as the car begins to move, her right foot involuntarily slams down on the brake pedal—at which point you lurch forward toward the dashboard. At this point, you are neither a confident nor a happy passenger.

Over the next minute or so, through a series of lurches, sudden stops, and a few more lurches, she gets the car out of the driveway and onto the open road. Within minutes, she is aware of the cars following her closely, trying to get her to speed up. She glances down at the speedometer and it reads twenty-three miles per hour. She is shocked. Even though the posted speed limit is thirty-five miles per hour, she can't ever imagine anyone traveling that fast down this street and feeling safe. She refuses to be intimidated and sticks to her speed, which makes you both proud and self-conscious. (At this point, I ask the parents in the seminar to fast-forward to a time when their teenager has had her license for a few months.)

She is now a model of efficiency: She enters the car, starts the engine, makes minor adjustments to the mirrors and seat as she backs down the driveway, tunes the radio to her favorite station, continues an in-depth conversation with her friend in the passenger seat, and checks her hair in the rearview mirror. Seconds later, she is barreling down that same thirty-five-mile-per-hour street at forty-five miles per hour and tailgating the slowpoke who is just ahead of her. Under her breath she is muttering, "Are you going to drive that car or take it for a walk?"

By the end of a story like this, parents have a much better sense of what a comfort zone is and how and why their teenagers would choose to expand it.

It's important that, as a parent, you are successful in supporting your teenager in expanding her comfort zone, because whenever you do so you deepen the connection you already have with her. If, however, you push too hard or are too cautious, you miss golden opportunities. Striking the right balance in this arena is an art form, and it is due in large part to two interrelated factors.

First, we all have areas of our lives in which we are confident and motivated to expand our comfort zones regularly. We also have other areas in which we resist any kind of expansion.

> When it comes to physical activities, I'm game for just about anything: bungee jumping, in-line skating, parachuting, dancing. You name it and I'm there. I've always been confident in my physical self and enjoy pushing the limits. But when it comes to learning new things, unrelated to my physicality, well, that's a different story. For example, take social media. I hate it, but also understand that most of my resistance is grounded in anxiety, not in any sort of philosophical stance.
>
> I swear, I'm like a whiny little seven-year-old making crazy excuses to keep away from the world of social media.

Helping your teenager reach an expanded comfort zone requires that you know your own areas of comfort and discomfort as well as those of your teenager. This is never easy because we tend to project the discomforts and comforts we have onto our children. This is when perceptive parents realize exactly how their teenagers are like them and unlike them. This is crucial to understand if you want a solid connection with your teenager—some of the things you take for granted (and are well within your comfort zone) are huge leaps for your teenager (and are way out of his comfort zone). This does not mean that we shouldn't push our kids when they hit the edges of their comfort zones, but it does mean we should push differently. For example, sometimes we have to help them through their laziness, something every parent is familiar with and capable of addressing. The approach here is direct—*Turn off the television and put your dishes in the sink or we're not going shopping*—and usually effective.

There are, however, other times when we realize it's not laziness holding them back; it's something else, often that they are out of their comfort zones. This has an entirely different feel to it. Yes, we still have to push them but we must do so with more patience, more understanding, and more compassion. Sometimes we help them unpack their emotional resistances: *You seem nervous about this; are you afraid of something? What's the worst that could happen?* Sometimes, we support them by helping them build momentum: *Imagine how good you will feel about yourself after you do this. Once you do this, all that other stuff that seems so difficult now will be a snap to get through.*

Sometimes we listen to their anxieties and remind them of their past successes under similar emotional circumstances: *I understand that you're not sure what you'll say to Talia about all this, but I do know you'll get through it successfully. Remember last year when you had that blowup with Jeff? You didn't know what to do then, either, but you figured it out somehow and got through it. You're still good friends today, perhaps better than before the argument. You'll get through this, too, just as you did back then.*

Important to understanding what your teenager's resistance is all about is knowing what he looks and sounds like when he is at the edges of his comfort zone. For some, it's psychosomatic: stomach aches, headaches, muscle soreness, dry throat, diarrhea, light headedness. For others, it's self-critical thinking: *No way I can do this. I'll mess up and everyone will laugh at me. I'm such a jerk for wasting everyone's time like this when I know I'm just going to fall flat on my face and embarrass myself.* For yet others, it's exaggerated behavior: they become very quiet or very extroverted, throw temper tantrums, get the giggles. The point is that your teenager won't tell you when he is out of his comfort zone, because, bearing in mind the foregoing array of uncomfortable states he is experiencing, he is unlikely to be able to explain it to you. Instead, through your observations of him, you must familiarize yourself with what he looks and sounds like when he's on the edges of his comfort zone. He has to trust that you'll do your homework so that you'll understand without his having to tell you.

The first time I heard about the idea of comfort zones, it set me to thinking about the kinds of things that are out of my comfort zone and how I behave when I'm on the edge of my zone. I was sitting at the kitchen table thinking about all this when my seventeen-year-old daughter walked in, looked at me, and said, "You okay, Dad? You've got a strange look on your face." So I told her what I was thinking about, and it really got her attention. Next thing I knew, she was sitting next to me, hanging onto my every word, and before long telling me what it's like for her to go out of her comfort zone. I learned a great deal about my daughter in that one conversation. But most of all, I was shocked by how self-aware she was and how different she was from me in how she responded to being pushed out of her comfort zone. Whereas I become quiet and internal, she's the opposite—she gets irritable and nitpicks at everything and everybody around her. Had I known all this a few years earlier, we could have avoided some of our worst arguments.

The second consideration in knowing how to be artful in pushing your teenager to extend his comfort zone is to realize that whenever he pushes his limits, your comfort zone is pushed, too. Think about driving and dating as examples. When your teenager first learns to drive and begins to date (often uncomfortably close in proximity to one another), it forces you to see him in a more mature, adultlike image—your comfort zone is pushed and extended or he would never drive or date. Therefore, you need to pay close attention to what is happening with you as well as your teenager when these kinds of changes are occurring: *Are you just uncomfortable from seeing him grow up or is there legitimacy to your discomfort that means you need to get him to slow down?* This is a huge question, because, without a doubt, once a teenager successfully pushes his comfort zone, the next step is to push it even further to discover the absolute limit. In other words, for his own safety and well-being, he needs limits; this is, like it or not, where you come in. And nothing feels more like being a wet blanket than trying to constrain your teenager's excitement at pushing his limits—especially after you've encouraged him to extend those limits in the first place. But conversely, abdicating this responsibility is terrifying for you and unsafe for your teenager.

These two points taken together—different comfort zones for you and your teenager and your shifting role as limit-setter and advocate—illustrate the fragile balance you are attempting to strike. But learning when and how to distinguish when you need to encourage him to push the limits and when you need to insist that he pull back forces you always to expand your comfort zone with your teenager, and this knowledge is something that no teenager fails to notice and appreciate. That is, when your teenager sees you stretching for him, it instantly deepens the connection between the two of you, even when you eventually have to change stances and set some limits. This is when he grouses in the moment, but later on, in the car or before bed, he'll want to reflect with you about how cool his new accomplishment was.

> I still remember when my dad taught me to drive. At first, he had to encourage me, which was cool. But now that I've been driving for a while, it's the opposite: He's always telling me to slow down, stop at the yellow lights, and drive more carefully. I don't like it when he says these things, but I know he doesn't like it, either. He just wants me to be safe. Truth is, I could be a safer driver.

Moments of Connection

When your teenager is stretching her comfort zone, the critical time is during the unsettling middle phase of disequilibrium. When she is uncomfortable, confused, and filled with doubt, she instinctively reaches out to you. If you are there, waiting for her with positive expectancy, you will share a moment of connection. She experiences you as "there for me." On the flip side, if you are not there or are not aware of what she needs from you—which, of course, she cannot tell you—then she'll feel abandoned during a moment of vulnerable need, something no parent or child wants. Therefore, knowing how to respond during these moments of disequilibrium requires that parents learn to read between the lines, something that is much easier once you understand just what your teenager needs from you during these exposed moments.

In Chapter 9, "Indirect Communication," we discussed how teenagers periodically invite you into their lives, albeit indirectly. What we need to remember about the comfort zone is that whenever teenagers are attempting something new or taking a big step in skill levels, they could benefit from our support. When they hit those moments of disequilibrium they need our reassurances, even if they are nonverbal or limited to just a few words. *You can do it. Go ahead. It'll be okay.* It will help if you remind yourself of what it was like years ago, when you taught your teenager, then a child, to ride a two-wheel bike.

Stan was five years old when he insisted on learning to ride a two-wheeler. We walked out to the driveway together and ceremoniously removed the training wheels. (At that point, I double-checked the chinstrap on his helmet.) Then he got on the bike and I gently pushed him around the driveway as I held onto the seat.

"Okay, Stan. I'm going to let go now. Ready?"

He whipped his head back toward me in panic and said, "No! I'll fall down. Don't let go, Daddy."

I kept my grip on the seat and pushed him around for a few minutes before trying again. "You're doing great, Stan. How about I let go now? Ready?"

"No, Dad! Not yet, please."

It was at about this time that I had to stop pushing. I had underestimated how long it would take Stan to take off on his own and hadn't even considered what the effort would do to my lower back. We rested together for a few minutes, Stan screwing up his courage and me massaging my back muscles. "In a bit I'll push you some more and this time I'll let you go on your own once we get going. Okay?"

"But I'm scared, Dad."

"I know you are—that's normal. But I also know that you're ready to ride all on your own."

"Are you sure?"

"Absolutely."

"But what if I fall?"

"Then I'll help you up and we'll try again. I fell a few times when I was learning, it's no big deal. And you're way better than I was when I started riding."

"Really?"

"Really. Now let's get back on the bike."

He started to get ready to protest, but then our eyes met and locked. I could almost feel him tuning into the confidence I had in his ability to ride the bike by himself. It was as if he were borrowing my confidence. It was a powerful moment for me, very emotional, too. I broke eye contact. Then Stan said, "Let's go, Dad. Give me a push."

A few minutes later he was gliding across the driveway all on his own, a huge smile plastered across his face. He had fallen a couple of times, but the scrapes and bruises were long forgotten in lieu of the excitement he felt over learning to ride a two-wheeler.

I hung out with him and watched him ride the bike for a while longer, only now the tables had shifted—instead of looking to me for support, he was showing off for my benefit. He was back in charge. And believe me, I was an appreciative audience.

This same process is as true for your teenager now as it was for her when she was a child; it's just a little trickier to spot. Take a big high school project such as a term paper as an example. Almost all term papers stretch your teenager's comfort zone—that's what they are designed to do. As a result, this is when you have to combine your unique knowledge and insight into your teenager with the inevitable episodes of disequilibrium she will experience with just about any long-term classroom project. Believe it or not, some teenagers actually appreciate their parents' direct help in projects of this magnitude.

I like it when my mom sits down with me and helps to break up my big assignments into smaller chunks. I even write down all the steps: Read the two books, make an outline, write a draft, get feedback, write a second draft, edit, write final paper. When we're done, I feel more relaxed and in control.

Most teenagers, however, are not that open to such direct input from their parents, which is why this is one of those times when you have to exercise your creativity. At the heart of success in this area is recognizing when and how your teenager needs your assistance. (Again, knowing what she looks and sounds like when she is out of her comfort zone is the key.) That is, when she's up against a deadline of less than twelve hours, she won't appreciate a talk about organization and pacing. She may, however, appreciate your feedback on her first draft at 11:00 p.m.; editing assistance at 5:00 a.m.; and a ride to school at 7:55 a.m. Take your cues from her.

Believe me, I know what some of you are thinking right now, and I've heard it many, many times before. *But doesn't this just teach her to procrastinate? What about consequences for her irresponsibility? Isn't this just codependent behavior?* To all these questions I say maybe. It all depends on the context and the state of your relationship with each other. If you are writing the paper for her, that is no good for either of you, and it definitely gets in the way of her receiving feedback on her work. If, however, you are assisting her to focus on the work, and not on all the logistical details of putting it together, then this is supportive.

If it is the same pattern for every paper, then yes, to some extent you are acting as a codependent and perpetuating her disorganization. If, however, you recognize yourself in her behavior, you may instead regard this as teaching her successful, though less than graceful, coping mechanisms to deal with an "inherited" trait.

Sheri dropped the bombshell right before she left for school: Although she had done all the research for her end-of-term history paper, due the next day, she had not yet written an outline or first draft. Her lower lip trembled as she told us, and her eyes and tone of voice cried for our help. Her dad and I are both suckers for this kind of presentation—we assured her that we would help out that evening.

But minutes later, after Sheri had left for school, Kurt and I locked eyes and explained to each other how we urgently needed to attend to our own work, and therefore the other parent would have to help Sheri through the crisis of her research paper later that night. We were both sincere and even convincing in our arguments, but still, neither of us budged.

Having reached a stalemate, we took a break and turned our attention to the common enemy: Sheri. *Why does she sabotage herself this way? What will happen when she goes to college and we're not around to bail her out? Is this the time for the hard truth of natural consequences? But what are the natural consequences? Is the angst she's going through now consequence enough? Is a poor grade what she needs to make her change this behavior? The realization that your parents abandon you when you need them most?* Clearly, these consequences are not all equal, nor are they desirable, especially that last one. Then we had a flash of insight: Sheri is us! The reason Kurt and I were fighting over who would help Sheri was because both of us had put ourselves in the same situation, only at work instead of at school. And, just like Sheri, we both do this regularly.

Of course, this revelation did not help us to decide who was going to help her that night, but it did rid us of the frustration and impotence we felt about how ineffective we were in persuading Sheri to change this pattern. Now, instead of anger, we felt a great deal of compassion, and we lowered our sights from a complete change in behavior to helping her learn how to work with this pattern—which both of us have in our lives.

In the end, both Kurt and I brought our work home and we pulled our first-ever family all-nighter. In a strange way, it was bonding, though I hope I never have to do it again.

Sometimes, a cigar is just a cigar, and other times it's much more than a cigar. With your teenager and your family, you are the judge. The point is that during these moments of need and disequilibrium, as you watch your teenager regress before your very eyes, know that she needs to feel connected to you. But what she needs from you is not predictable—firm insistence, gentle support, quiet presence, clear directions—it all depends on the context. During these moments, what is most important is patience, creativity, and perseverance. If you can maintain these qualities during her moments of disequilibrium, a warm connection will follow during the ensuing equilibrium that's just around the corner.

Shared Risk

A variation of staying available to your teenager during moments of his disequilibrium is to intentionally do something together that stretches both your comfort zones. A great way to do this is to learn some new skill together, perhaps even something that your teenager chooses and that is a bigger leap for you than for him. This way, you become equal partners on a level playing field. Learning together to in-line skate, play a musical instrument, ski, garden, or ride a horse can deepen your connection in some profound ways. Not only do you risk disequilibrium with one another, but you also support, compete with, and encourage each other. On top of that, you also have a shared experience, which during the adolescent years is a monumental achievement.

We've all heard the cliché about the greater the risk, the greater the reward, but one dad I knew took it to the limit, and it eased the complications of a long-ago divorce and a recent remarriage. More important, the project of their shared risk formed the basis of his relationship with his daughter throughout her adolescence.

When Carrie was fourteen, we were driving home together. As we came to a stop at a traffic signal, a 1966 Mustang convertible in mint condition pulled up alongside us. I heard Carrie gasp. Then she said, "Cool car! I would love a car like that."

The sarcastic voice inside my head was saying, "Yeah, right. You and millions of other teenagers." But something entirely different came out of my mouth. "Really? How badly do you want a car like that?"

"Are you kidding? I'll pay you back every cent if you loan me the money. Honest. Even if it takes until I'm, like, thirty."

"Whoa. Who said anything about a car loan? I just want to know how much you want an old Mustang."

"I'll do anything. Really. I'll even babysit my pain-in-the-butt stepsister all summer if you want."

This was actually tempting, but I passed on the offer and said, "No, nothing like that. Here's the deal." And I was more shocked than Carrie by what came out of my mouth next. "If you find an old fixer-upper Mustang, I'll buy it outright for you. No loans. Then we'll put the car in my garage and together we'll completely restore it to mint condition, maybe even better."

"That's crazy, Dad. I'll be lucky if it's ready when I get my license."

"True, but then again you won't need it until then, either. Tell you what, you've got until we get to your mother's house to decide. After you get out of the car, the deal's off."

I glanced over at her in the passenger seat. She couldn't tell if I was serious or not. Then she said, "But Dad, you don't know anything about cars, let alone fixing them. You can't even change the oil—even you say so."

"Well, neither do you. Besides, that's the whole point, we'll learn together. Oh yeah, that's the only catch to this deal—we have to do everything together on the car. What do you say?"

"When it's done, it's totally my car, right? No strings attached?"

"No strings. It'll be your car free and clear, I'll even buy you six months' worth of insurance once it's done."

"Cool. You've got a deal. When can we start looking?"

I pulled over to a convenience store. "How about right now? Let's run in and get a copy of the Auto Classifieds."

As we walked into the store, I felt great about myself as a father, my daughter as a young woman, and, most of all, about our relationship as father and daughter. Then I felt a twitch in my solar plexus—Carrie was absolutely right. I knew nothing about cars. This was going to stretch both of us. I just hoped I could hold up my end of the bargain.

Whenever you can find an activity that represents a shared risk for you and your teenager, jump at the opportunity. In fact, make yourself active and use your creativity to come up with a range of such activities. Connections built on this kind of foundation easily withstand the normal ups and downs of adolescent behavior. This kind of connection also makes relationships durable and resilient.

Negotiating

In many ways your relationship with your teenager is one big shared comfort zone between the two of you. If your relationship is expansive, you both feel safe to address difficult topics with one another. You trust each other and do not breech that trust once it is given. And that trust is built on your ability to negotiate with one another. But the difficulty with staying open to negotiating as a part of your parenting style is that it causes more anxiety all around than any of the other typical parenting approaches. In the overcontrolling style (*My way or the highway!*), parents experience little anxiety because if their teenagers don't follow their rules, the problem is with the teenager. In the undercontrolling style (*You decide. Besides, you never listen to me anyway, so do whatever you want . . .*), there is a minimum of anxiety because the kids are making the decisions and the parents are claiming no responsibility and ignoring all the bombs bursting around them. But in the consultant model (with the notable exceptions of health and safety issues), there is plenty of anxiety to go around because both parties are taking responsibility and constantly negotiating the terms of the relationship. It's plain, old-fashioned hard work.

When you are open to negotiating the nonhealth and nonsafety issues with teenagers—curfew, dress, car privileges, friends—you are sending a few important messages. First, you are open to their input if they can make a strong and reasonable case for themselves. This means that they can stretch your comfort zone when it comes to them; this, in turn, means there is room in the parent-teenager relationship for them to develop a stable identity by exercising their independence. Second, you expect them to understand, acknowledge, and consider in all their requests your perspective on what they are asking. That is, they have to put themselves in your shoes before trying to negotiate, which helps them to internalize your views and values to succeed in their negotiations. (This is exponentially more effective than lecturing your teenagers about what you believe they should do.) Third, their past behavior matters; they know this, and it increases the likelihood that they will behave responsibly in whatever they are negotiating for. That is, they know that if they screw up, it will come back to haunt them the next time around—something no parents I've ever met fail to point out to their teenagers when making concessions during a negotiation.

But negotiating with your teenager is never painless. Afterward, you are the one left holding the ball of anxiety as you wonder aloud whether you made the right decision.

Kim seemed too happy when I let her stay out with the car an hour past her normal curfew. Had I given in too quickly? But she made a strong case: She made points about safety, reminded me of how much I like and respect the kids she was going out with that night, talked about the last time I had granted her a special request and she had done so well, and she even swore that there would be no alcohol before I could ask. As if to hammer that last point home, she said that she would wake me when she got home "just so you can get a good whiff of my alcohol-free breath." Her case was almost too good, which made me nervous. But then again this is the kind of behavior and negotiating I am after, right? Regardless, I knew there was no need for her to wake me when she got home because I doubted very much that I would fall asleep until she was home safely.

There are a couple of salient points to take from the above reflection. First, it's never a bad idea to slow down the pace of the negotiations. Even when your teenager makes a compelling and comprehensive case (as in the previous story), it's wise to put the negotiation on hold, even if just for a short while. This is the equivalent of sleeping on it.

> "You've really thought this one through."
> "Thanks. So can I stay out an extra hour with the car?"
> "I'm not sure yet, give me an hour to think about it. I want to see if any more questions come up before I decide."
> "But I need to know now."
> "If you make me decide now the answer is no, but if you can wait an hour or so there is a good chance I'll say yes. You decide."

At the end of the above dialogue, it's your teenager who gets to hold the anxiety for a while, at least long enough for you to try on her request for size. (This is not too dissimilar from what we discussed in Chapter 3, "Give Up on Lectures and Advice," about giving the problem back to your teenager.) If your teenager is negotiating in earnest, she'll hesitantly, but willingly hold on to the anxiety until you make a final decision or come back with one or two more questions. (This does not, however, mean that she won't hover about your elbow until you finally decide.) If, on the other hand, she presses for an answer right then and there—I need to call Jessica now because her parents need to know what she's doing tonight before they go out to dinner in ten minutes—she is no longer negotiating; she is using a sales technique, bullying, or conning you, a variation of *My manager will only let me offer you this price on that car for another hour.*

If she pushes for an immediate response, which earns her an emphatic no, let your initial disappointment fade. She may have actually needed and secretly wanted you to deny her request so that she could save face with friends. "Yeah,

I asked my mom, but no way. She was like a total bitch." (This is a variation of the code words we talked about in Chapter 6.)

The second point to keep in mind about negotiating is that it always leaves you anxious and unable to sleep. There is no way around this.

When my kids were infants, like most parents of newborns I was chronically sleep-deprived because of their immediate needs—nursing, diapers, cuddling—and now, as the parent of two teenagers, I'm nearly as sleep-deprived. The only difference is that now they have different needs. And these needs keep them away from home at night and leave me pacing the floors and halls while I worry about their safety.

Family Travel

In her book *See Jane Win*, Sylvia Rimm[1] asked women who considered themselves both happy and successful to look back on and describe their childhoods. In this manner, she hoped to identify common behaviors and attitudes that made a critical difference to these women's eventual success and happiness.

The second most frequently cited experience by Rimm's respondents, across all developmental levels and careers, was family travel. Participants said that family travel was a time of adventure and bonding. These findings fit in with our discussion of stretching your comfort zones together. Travel, by its nature, is an intentional stretching of the comfort zone, so it only makes sense that travel to new places as a family strengthens your connection to your teenager. Kids who feel alienated from their families often discover aspects of deep kinship during a family trip, levels of connection that had previously gone undetected. This is especially so when the travel takes the family to a foreign culture. There are several reasons for this.

First, everyone in the family is more or less equal in their ability to learn and adapt to the ways, subtle and not so subtle, of this new culture. Sure, the parents are still the parents, but that doesn't mean they will be the ones to figure out the local train schedule, greeting customs, or how to order lunch. Furthermore, families are united together as they work to figure out and explore this new environment. This is when many of the at-home differences between parents and teenagers simply slip away.

Second, many people travel to learn about different approaches to life and to discover or reconnect with aspects of themselves. Some love the feel of their curiosity as it is stimulated by a new culture. Others rediscover a resourcefulness they had forgotten about. Some experience travel as a respite from long-held assumptions and as an opportunity for reflection. All these lay the groundwork for new and deeper connections among family members, especially between parents and teenagers. Not only that, but it is during this family travel that you will see, often for the first time, some wonderful and unexpected qualities in your teenager, qualities that you were blinded to by the normal routine of home.

It's so bizarre, but when we went abroad with Jason, all his eating habits changed. At home he adheres to the typical male adolescent diet of burgers, pizza, soda, and the like. But when we were away, he insisted on eating all the local dishes and vehemently eschewed his normal diet. But the real crazy part is that as soon as we got back home to the States, it was right back to burgers, pizza, and soda.

And:

At home Sarah lives on the phone and the Internet, usually at the same time, and is totally dependent on us or friends for transportation. She would never think of using the local bus lines. But recently, when we visited New York City as a family, this all changed. Suddenly, she was an explorer. She got a map of the subway system and led us all around the city—Sarah and her map. Now we were dependent on her! This was a side to her that was brand new to all of us, but knowing it's there is a great relief, especially when we think about her going off to college next year.

Third, when you plan your travel to another country, consider making use of your teenager's expertise over your own. That is, if she has been learning a foreign language, visit a country where that language is spoken. It's great for her to have the experience of you turning to her for help on how to say whatever it is you want to communicate. You will both end up listening to one another in different and better ways. Or, better yet, build a trip around one of her interests and let her pull you along in her enthusiasm.

A couple of years ago, Barry got into learning everything he could about bull-fighting. I think it was something he picked up from one of his history teachers. Anyway, at his bequest, we planned a summer vacation to Spain, all built around the traditional running of the bulls at the fiesta of San Fermin in July. (Don't worry, before we even purchased the tickets, we made him promise not even to ask us if he could participate in the run!) The whole trip was built around the themes of matadors and bulls, from a visit to the Bullfighting Museum in Bilbao to attending a bullfight at the bullring in Seville.

The trip was a huge success for all of us. Even before we left, we saw a different side to Barry because he did all the research and most of the planning of the trip. That was our agreement from the beginning. He was incredible. Hard to believe it was the same kid who has waited until the last second on every long-term project he has ever had. He printed out historical information on some of the events that we were attending so that we could appreciate them more. He even cranked up his efforts in Spanish to get ready for the trip—going from a steadfast B-minus student to an A student in one quarter. It was so relaxing, like having your own in-house tour guide.

We came back from that trip a much closer family, and that sense of intimacy has only faded a tiny bit in the six months since.

Of course, travel with teenagers is seldom all peaches and cream. There is the initial resistance to leaving their friends, to leaving behind their familiar daily routines, and frequently—though you don't want to hear this—the dread of spending unending days in the exclusive company of their family, especially their parents. Don't take their resistance personally or too literally. Instead, stay steadfast in your intention to have a pleasant family vacation and deal with each bit of resistance separately, as it comes up. If you keep in mind throughout the planning and the travel that your teenager's resistance has more to do with the discomfort that accompanies stretching his comfort zone, it will buoy you with confidence and vision to keep moving forward, even while you're doubting yourself. Finally, the reason travel is effective is because it stretches everyone's comfort zones, which means you don't necessarily have to go to exotic regions all over the world to have this experience. Sometimes it's a weekend in the big city near where you live, or a weekend away from the city and in the country. In other words, it's closer than you think.

Friends and Travel

Psychiatrist Harry Stack Sullivan postulated in his developmental theory that once a person reaches puberty, the strongest organizer of life is the avoidance of loneliness. Simply put, your teenager's friends are more important to her than she can say. Therefore, rather than trying to knock that wall down—*Don't worry, Samantha will still be your friend when we get back. Besides, we're pretty good company ourselves*—go around it. Whenever feasible, let your teenager invite a friend along for the trip if that's the difference between whether he goes on the trip or not. Or even better, invite the friend for a portion of the vacation. This strategy makes for a winning situation for you, your teenager, and your family.

Since the first year we got married, we have rented a cottage at a lake a few hundred miles away—just us at first, then after the kids were born, just us and the kids. We haven't missed a summer in twenty years. It's our escape and our time for reconnecting to each other and what is important in our lives, individually and as a family.

But last year was a disaster. Billie, our oldest at fifteen, behaved like the quintessential teenager: moody, bored, angry, and for all intents and purposes attached to both the phone and his laptop. All he did was communicate with his friends back home. Finally, we took the phone and laptop away. Then the moodiness and anger escalated to new heights and he was like a time bomb. We all avoided him and counted the days until we went home. It wasn't a very rejuvenating vacation. More like something out of the *National Lampoon* vacation movies with Chevy Chase.

This year we still rented the place at the lake, but we made one huge exception to our only family rule: We let Billie bring a friend for half the vacation. In fact, we insisted upon it. What a wonderful addition his friend Will made to our vacation! Sure, he and Billie were often off doing their own thing—sailing, miniature golf, meeting girls—but when they were around the family, Billie was a joy. (Well, maybe not a joy, but nowhere near the pain in the neck he had been the previous year.) We chose quality over quantity time on this vacation and we'll do the same thing again next year. Already, Billie's younger sister, Sasha, is asking when she can bring a friend, too. I guess we've begun a new family tradition, at least until they're both out of adolescence.

This is not to say that you should include your teenager's friends on every trip you take as a family because there are definitely times when it's appropriate to be together just as a family. Still, though, bringing along the friend every now and again greases the wheels for more success during your family's getaways.

Alcohol, Drugs, and Comfort Zones

We all know that there is no surefire means of guaranteeing that your teenager never gets into life-changing trouble through alcohol and drug use. Sure, you can abstain in the hope that your model will guide them through the slippery choices around drug and alcohol use. And, of course, you can supply them with the latest research that points out how negative an influence these substances have on brain development. You can even talk about friends of yours who used drugs and alcohol to cope with their problems and the world around them, the same friends who now attend daily AA meetings and are trying to develop the coping and problem-solving skills they missed out on during adolescence. You can even arm them with the knowledge that substance abuse runs in your family and therefore they have a much higher risk of developing a problem than most of their peers. And still there is no guarantee that they will listen to your warnings. This does not, however, stop us from doing most of the above as well as anything else we think might stack the odds in their favor. Well, you can add one more idea to your list.

We know there is no one reason why teenagers use drugs and alcohol, which is why there is no one means of stopping them from using it and getting into trouble in the first place. Although I have no empirical proof of what I'm about to say, I believe that one aspect of why teenagers turn to drugs and alcohol is connected to their relationship to their comfort zones. Some teenagers, in fact many teenagers, use drugs and alcohol simply because they are bored. These substances spice up their lives. Therein lies an opportunity: For those who use out of boredom, a regular stretching of their comfort zones offers a wonderful alternative. So use that to your advantage in working to counteract the attraction of normal adolescents to drug and alcohol experimentation.

> I flat out told my son that part of why I tried alcohol in high school was because I was bored. He was surprised by my honesty, but shook his head as if he understood. Then I told him that's why I like him to try new things, to test himself, to take some risks. Because if he is doing that kind of thing regularly, at least he'll feel less drawn to alcohol out of boredom. Sure, there's still peer pressure and the appeal of the unknown, but I'll just take them one at a time. My goal is to reduce the odds, that's all. At bottom, I'm a realistic mom.

For your teenager, regularly stretching her comfort zone won't necessarily turn her into a teetotaler, but it will reduce the draw these substances have on her and diminish the chances that she'll get into trouble with alcohol or drugs during her adolescence.

> Seems like more than half our grade does the same thing, weekend after weekend. They find a place to have a party—someone's house, a park, an empty field—and they meet there and drink. Then people do crazy things and behave in all sorts of strange ways—stuff they would never do if they were sober. I tried it a couple of times, but truth is it's so predictable that it's kind of boring. I still go to those parties once in a while, but the truth is I prefer to go to the indoor climbing wall on weekends. There are a bunch of excellent climbers there most weekend nights and we really push each other to do some crazy things. It's way more fun than the parties, at least for me.

If you support your teenager in stretching her comfort zone and allow her to extend your comfort zone (through negotiating and taking risks together), your connection to each other will deepen. And when all is said and done, your connection is as strong a deterrent to drug and alcohol use as there is.

Confusion Is Good

Throughout this chapter, and much of the book for that matter, I have made an implicit assumption; namely, that for the most part, confusion is good. In this regard, your teenager's relationship to confusion (as well as your own) is essential to articulate and understand. Or, as one successful teacher regularly told her students:

> I teach psychology to high school juniors and seniors, and in the first class of each new year, I always start out the same. I talk about confusion. Most kids, especially motivated, grade-oriented students, are afraid of confusion. They see it as the hallmark of an unintelligent mind and the unsuccessful person, and my job is to convince them, through their own experiences, of the opposite. This is what I tell them:
>
> *One thing we have to get straight at the outset: In this room, in this course, despite what you think you have learned elsewhere, confusion is good. That is, in terms you can understand, the more confused you are throughout this course, the better grade you will get.* At this point, there is always some wise guy who raises his hand and says, *I'm confused.* And I always respond, *Good. Then you are on your way to learning a lot and getting a good grade, too.*

It takes time and experience for teenagers to understand that the relationship between success and confusion is the opposite of what they first think. Successful people are the ones who can tolerate large amounts of confusion without being overwhelmed and without becoming indecisive. Clarity, commitment, and passion usually grow out of confusion. Quite simply, if something comes too easily, there is a tendency to undervalue its worth and never develop a deep commitment.

There is a famous poster of Albert Einstein that hangs in many adolescents' rooms. It's a photo of him thinking hard, along with a quote attributed to him: *Genius is 1 percent inspiration and 99 percent perspiration.* When it comes to teenagers, I think we should add to the end of the quote, at least in parentheses, *usually experienced as confusion.* In the vernacular of what we've discussed in this chapter, confusion is a sign of disequilibrium and of extending one's comfort zone, which we've seen are positive developments.

In academics, a reliable predictor of how well a student will do is seen in her relationship to confusion. Most students who do poorly in school (and this is not just limited to the classroom because the relationship to confusion is a reliable predictor of success in all sorts of other activities—from clubs to sports to community service to leadership) respond to confusion with the fight-or-flight instinct. Some attack by pointing out the real-life uselessness of what they learn in the classroom. *I'm never going to use this complicated math in my life so why do I have to learn it now? Besides, if I do need it, I can get it done hundreds of times faster on my computer.* Others attack through distraction. That is, they act out and create chaos in the classroom so that nobody has the opportunity to address the material that is causing their confusion. This is when kids talk to other students incessantly, come to class late (or not at all), or mouth off to the teacher. Other students embrace the flight instinct by refusing to engage with material that is potentially confusing. These kids sit in class but don't do the work, seldom hand in homework, and are generally passive in their education.

The worst part is that both sets of kids—fight or flight—do so out of fear of confusion. They take the experience of confusion as indicative of their incompetence and lack of intelligence. That is, they think that smart and successful people never experience confusion— thus the approach of the psychology teacher mentioned earlier.

When your teenager encounters confusion, you want her to take a deep breath, roll up her shirtsleeves, and say to herself, *Okay, now it's getting interesting. I'm confused, which means I'm on the verge of learning something, so I just need to take my time and relax. It'll all come clear with just a little bit of patience and persistence.* Your job as parents in all this is to make sure that your teenager gets plenty of direct and indirect messages from you telling her not to fear confusion.

This means that you are explicit with them as they do the work and when you ask them about their work afterward—much like the idea of thinking like an anthropologist, only with a narrow focus.

How do you handle confusion? Do you get anxious? What kinds of things do you say to yourself? Some people get down on themselves when they are confused, calling themselves stupid and things like that. Others get excited with the expectation that they're on the verge of learning something new.

What about you? And: *Anything confusing in your homework today?*

Any place you got stuck but worked your way through? How did you do it? See, that's what I mean about confusion—if you can handle it there's always a light at the end of the tunnel.

This also means that you simultaneously embrace the indirect approach, too. You can do this through observations: *When the other team changed defensive strategies late in the game, I saw that it confused you. Then a few minutes later I could see that you had figured out a way around it. Good job.* You can do this through reporting back what others have told you: *Your drama teacher says that you're terrific at handling last-minute changes. She says you get this confused look on your face, take a few deep breaths, and then make the change better than she had even imagined you would.*

You communicate the most about confusion, however, by the way you relate to confusion in your own life. Teenagers need parents who are transparent in their relationship to confusion, not parents who never experience it or never show their own confusion and doubts. Of course, you never want to overwhelm your teenager, but you don't want to overprotect him to the point of misleading him into seeing confusion as a sign of weakness, either. This means that when you're wrestling with a new recipe, a problem at work, a backed-up drain, you voice aloud your confusions. *I'm not sure what to do next, but I do know I'm starting to get too stressed out by it all. I need a break to let my confusion sort itself out. And: I sure messed up that recipe. And I'm not even sure what I did wrong—think I'll go through it again and see if I can figure out what happened.*

One former student of mine told me the transformative experience in his high school life around understanding the role of confusion occurred in his eleventh-grade math class:

Mr. J. was far and away the best math teacher in the school—he used to be a big-shot engineer but walked away from the corporate life after his last kid went to college. Said he had always wanted to teach but couldn't afford it until his kids had finished their education. Everyone loved him, in part because he loved math so much and in part because it really mattered to him that his students understood math.

One day, he was doing a homework problem on the board that nobody in the class could figure out. He was writing on the board while he was telling us what he was thinking and how he was approaching the problem, just as he usually did. Then, at the end, he circled the answer and said, "There! Did it."

"Uh, Mr. J.?" It was Tammy, the best student in the class. "The book says you should get a different answer."

"Really? What do they say?"

She told him, and he put it on the board next to the answer as he had worked it out. I remember being embarrassed for Mr. J. I mean, he was the teacher and he's supposed to know this stuff. But then I noticed that instead of looking embarrassed, he seemed to be having fun. He was smiling and his eyes were scrunched as if he was really interested in what had gone wrong.

"What did you do wrong, Mr. J.?"

"I don't know." And he just kept staring at the board.

A few of us made suggestions, and he tried each one, but after each one, he shook his head and said, "No, that's not it."

Then he just stared at the problem for a few minutes. "This is like being an engineer again. We would get problems that just drove us nuts for hours, sometimes days. The only thing to do was to take a break and come back with fresh eyes. So how about we take ten minutes and talk about good movies anyone's seen lately?"

Fifteen minutes later, Mr. J. said, "That should have been long enough, so let's take another look at that problem now."

After a minute of us all staring at the board, one of the other students, Aaron, said, "I'm not sure what it is, but there's something off in step three."

Thirty seconds later, Mr. J. shouted, "Brilliant, Aaron! That's exactly where I went wrong." Then he explained and showed us exactly where his mistake was.

Minutes later, the bell rang and Mr. J. said, "Great class today—best yet, in fact. Remember it well because it's what it's all about. This is where the real joy comes from, hanging in there when you're stuck and then bursting through the other side. Wonderful!"

I think about that class all the time. I had never seen another adult enjoy getting confused, and suddenly I understood that that was my problem—I was scared of confusion. But it all changed for me that day in Mr. J.'s class.

There are more Mr. J.'s teaching than most adults realize. When you talk about confusion with your teenager, remember to catch the names of the teachers who teach the kids to embrace confusion, then let those teachers know that you appreciate what they do.

A Final Exam

By now you might be remembering your own experiences with extending your comfort zones, coming up with ideas about how to facilitate the same in your teenager, and, most important, how to make comfort zones a part of your connection with your teenager. Not so fast.

It's time for a final exam of sorts. Stretching your comfort zone with your teenager on something that you believe in but that runs contrary to how most other parents think gives you a glimpse into the peer pressure your kids face from friends and acquaintances. But if you believe in whatever you are doing, it's probably worth moving forward. How you stand up for what you believe in with other parents is huge for your teenager—through your actions she vicariously learns how to stick up for what she believes in, how to stay in relationships with friends, and how to hold on to the confusion of standing alone while friends and peers point out the downsides of what she is doing.

So the question is this: How far are you willing to stretch your comfort zone to do something that you believe in when everyone around you has a different opinion? Here are a couple of examples:

A famous Bay Area radio talk show host, Ronn Owens, encountered this firsthand one day on the air. Before the show, he discussed with his colleagues at the radio station the HBO hit *The Sopranos*—Ronn was a huge fan, and *The Sopranos* was his favorite show on television. During that conversation, he mentioned something that most of his colleagues disagreed with, so during his show, he asked his listeners what they had to say.

The issue at hand was that he had let his younger daughter, when she was eleven, watch *The Sopranos* with him. Two years later, his older daughter and his wife joined them on the sofa each time a new *Sopranos* episode aired.

Ronn defended his choice to let his younger daughter watch the show by stating that she heard the kind of language used in *The Sopranos* on the playgrounds anyway and, besides, watching it together gave him the chance to explain the context, discuss the issues, and generally bond with his daughter. His listeners asked poignant and tough questions—about language, violence, sex, racism, ethics—but Ronn was undeterred and responded calmly with well-thought-out replies. Several times, he had to agree to disagree. The point is that he had thought it through, was comfortable with his decision, and didn't need to bring anyone around to his point of view. His daughters should have been proud.

Now, I'm not necessarily saying that you should watch similar shows with your kids, but I am saying that once you have thought through the issues, you need to stick to what you believe, especially when those around you don't agree. Yes, you can always change your mind, and not because the peer pressure makes you uncomfortable but because your viewpoint actually shifts. To do otherwise is to cave in to peer pressure on center stage in front of your teenager; you then have a huge disconnect rather than the opportunity to deepen the connection.

A few years ago, when my son was in eighth grade, he wanted to go to the carnival in town and then to a friend's to sleep over. This was a big deal in our family, not only because of the sleepover after the carnival but also because this family was going to let him and their son stay out much later than we normally allow our son to stay out. While we were talking about it, I could tell that he expected me to interrupt him with something along the lines of *Are you nuts? You can't sleep over and you can't stay out past curfew. Get real!* But actually I was ready to be talked into the idea—he has been a responsible kid and I felt it was a good test for him before high school.

But once I realized how pessimistic he was about what I would say, I decided to take advantage of the situation. I wanted to take the opportunity to let him see me in a different light, perhaps even become closer as a result.

"Well, that's a big request. How about you give me a couple hours to think it over?"

"Sure."

Then I went into stealth mode. I picked up the phone and pretended to call several different friends, explaining to each of them the situation—making sure my son could overhear each phone call—and seeking their input. Then I carried on my end of the conversation as if they disagreed strongly with me. I pretended to listen, but still held my ground. After a few of these calls, I stopped, and I could tell my son thought his chances of going to the carnival and sleepover were slim to none.

"Steve, I've thought it over. I'm uncomfortable about letting you stay out so late, but I also think you're ready for it. So if you can help me resolve some of my worries, you can spend the night at your friend's house."

He looked stunned. And I had to hold back a huge smile. Then we talked about my discomfort and what he could do for me.

The carnival and sleepover went off without a hitch, but best of all, Steve and I bonded that night in a way that has carried over into our daily relationship, which makes the risk worth it.

If you're up for it, here's a final exam question that is sure to test your conviction in extending your comfort zone. There is no right answer, it just depends on the ground you cover and how you cover it. Here you go: Your fifteen-year-old daughter comes to you and asks to host a coed sleepover. What do you say? Remember, laughing in her face and shouting *Absolutely not!* is not an option, at least if you want to deepen your connection—and, for that matter, neither is *Sure! Sounds great!* because that won't deepen the connection, either. Instead:

1. Catch your breath. If you've instinctively said *no*, step back and reconsider.
2. Make a list of your concerns: sex, alcohol, sex, drugs, sex, no sleep, sex.
3. Now share them with your daughter.
4. Listen to what she has to say. Listen some more. Is she sincere? Do her suggestions help?
5. Ask some more questions.

6. Point out the stakes—a mess-up here would cost her for a long, long time.

7. Take some time alone. Slow everything down. Ask yourself the following important questions:

   • Is the concept of a coed sleepover something you can legitimately consider? If not, 'fess up. Don't pretend it's your teenager's fault. If it's too much for you, it's too much for you. *Sorry, honey, but I just can't do this. The risk is too high; wish I could be more flexible, but I can't on this one.*

   • If there is a coed sleepover structure you can live with, what is it?

   • If you and your daughter agree to a structure, will you hold up your end? That is, if even one agreement is breached, will you act? If not, you need to say *no*.

The whole point is that when your teenager asks you something that at first glance seems crazy, don't dismiss the idea too quickly. The more time you take and the more sincere you are the more you strengthen the connection; that is, the more you let her push and extend your comfort zone—which does not mean that you necessarily go along with her request. When you negotiate in good faith, allowing the other person to extend your comfort zone, the relationship grows stronger. Who knows, you may even end up surprising yourself by what you finally decide.

*   *   *

The nature of adolescence is that it's a time of many firsts, and more happens then than at any other time of our lives. We remember most of the pivotal life experiences that happened during adolescence, probably more than during any other four- or six-year period in our lives. From driving to romance to risk to identity to independence, the adolescent years have every other developmental period beaten hands down.

I was talking to a colleague I was chaperoning a high school dance with about all the firsts that happen during adolescence, and we were both commenting on how the firsts become fewer and fewer as we grow older. (Or at least as we get older.) Then we paused our conversation and turned our attention to the dance. As with most high school dances, mostly freshmen and sophomores were there—the upper classmen feel that the dance is beneath them or they show up at the tail end, often after having done some partying themselves, which is another category of problems. Anyway, about halfway through the evening, not too many kids were dancing and the boys and girls had pretty much staked out their own separate groupings, the occasional coed group here and there. Then I noticed what could only be a ninth-grade boy begin to walk from his group of friends across the floor to a group of girls. In particular, he had his eye on one girl, who noticed him walking and gave a shy smile before she looked away. The smile added a bounce to his step. As he got closer, she opened her stance toward him and looked up with the smile still on her face. You could see him fill with confidence. Then, just a few steps away from the girl and her friends, she abruptly turned her back to him and leaned in to her friends. He froze. A moment later, I could see his mouth move, then watched the girl's smile freeze and her girlfriends giggle. Seconds later, he was coming back across the gym floor—alone.

At this point, my colleague turned to me and said, "Never mind. Some of those firsts aren't worth remembering, repeating, or living through again. I'll take midlife any day."

An engaging conversation with a teenager—usually not your own—precipitates the beginnings of a midlife crisis in many adults. Mainly this has to do with feeling the teenager's excitement at facing all the firsts just ahead of him. But it also has to do with all the dreams that have faded from our lives since our own adolescence. This is why the idea of stretching your comfort zone is as applicable now as it was twenty years ago.

TWELVE

Applying to and Selecting a College

The process of applying to college is fraught with built-in obstacles pushing against the parent–teenager connection. That is, it is incredibly vulnerable for both sides of the relationship. First, from a teenager applying to college:

> Most of the kids at my school go to college so it's a pretty normal expectation. And while I'm really looking forward to college the whole application process has me freaked out. I just don't want to disappoint anybody, especially my parents, if I don't get into a decent college. I've got good grades but I have no idea what to write for my essay—I just feel so normal and so boring. I've already had the same nightmare more than a few times: Just seeing pages and pages of rejection letters coming at me and no way to escape.

Second, from the parent of a high school senior beginning the application process:

> I think I'm more nervous about this than my son. Sure, I want him to go to college and have a great experience, but I can't imagine not having him around every day. And I want him to stretch in the schools he applies to, but I don't want him to have to face the pain of rejection. I want to tell him what to write for his essays but I want him to do this and own it all himself . . . I'm really stuck and I'm sure of no help to my son.

Your job as a parent is to be a supportive resource for your teenager. It is not your application to college. Nor does where she applies and/or gets accepted affect your self-esteem. This is about your teenager taking the next step their life and applying to and attending college. And although some of you—and many of your teenagers, like the one above—have doubts about getting into any college, please hold the thoughts of what Charles Shields pointed out in *The College Guide for Parents*: that 9 out of 10 students that apply to two or more schools get into at least one school.[1] Your teenager will get admitted to college, just as long as she gets those applications in on time and fully completed, which is where you are the supportive resource.

By the way, the placement of this chapter near the end of the book is quite intentional. For you to successfully deepen the connection with your teenager through the college process you are going to need all the attitudes and skills discussed thus far. From late-night conversations to anthropologist-like questions to car rides to supportive texts, you'll use it all through this process. And it's worth all the effort, as you will watch your teenager grow up right in front of your eyes as you lay the groundwork for the next phase of your lives together.

Your Research: Timeline, Vocabulary, and Application

Before getting into any of the details of connecting with your teenager through this process you need to get a clearer view of what is required for a complete and successful application to college. Do your homework prior to engaging your teenager. This is a very different approach than say with technology. In those instances your role as student and their role as teacher works exceptionally well. They know the area well, are relaxed in using it, and delighted to share their knowledge with you in ways that make them the expert. It is a role reversal that is win–win. With college, however, it is the wrong approach. In this instance your teenager is not an expert nor is he relaxed about the process. He is anxious. Think for a moment how you respond when you are anxious about something that you do not know well and someone asks you to explain it to them. The vast majority of us are not very patient or understanding in these situations. Therefore, when it comes to applying to and selecting a college it is best for you to make yourself a knowledgeable consultant. And please note the difference between knowledgeable and know-it-all, as the latter is a complete relationship breaker for your teenager.

I suggest you start your work by getting an arching overview, and one of the best resources for this overall timeline—ninth grade through college acceptance—is the National Association for College Admission Counseling's website. It's a fabulous snapshot that includes course selection, standardized tests, financial aid, and extracurricular activities.[2]

Their pdf—Countdown to College—is an incredible overview of everything you need to know as a parent. It helped me understand course planning at his high school as well as gave me lots to do in terms of supporting him by registering him for his standardized tests and a host of other logistical requirements that I was happy to take off of his plate—as was he!

After you have this overview you need to familiarize yourself with the vocabulary of college admissions. You want a basic understanding of these terms when you meet with the school's College Counselor or Guidance Counselor as misunderstanding these terms can have some very real, negative consequences. Below are some of the basics, just to get you familiar.

- Early Decision: This is for students who by the start of their senior year have a clear top choice college. Early decision applications get turned in sometime in October or November—all colleges are different so if your child is applying for early decision, make sure you have the deadline for that college. If accepted—schools let applicants know in mid-December—this is a binding decision (legally and financially), which means no backing out.
- Early Action: This process has a similar timeline to Early Decision, with the major difference that if accepted it is not a binding agreement. That is, like the regular decision process, your teenager will not have to let the college know until May 1.
- Regular Admissions: Applications are usually due in early or mid-January with decisions coming back to applicants in late March or early April. If accepted, students have until May 1 to let the college know of their decision.
- Waiting List: This is the purgatory of the college admissions process. In essence, this means the student is qualified should a space open up, which could happen as early as a couple of weeks into May or as late as the day before classes start.

As you review these terms you start to glimpse some of the chess game of getting into college.

My daughter was torn between two schools, with a big drop in excitement for the third school on her list. She wanted to try for Early Decision, but wasn't sure for which school. She spoke with the College Counselor at her school who said all being equal between school X and Y, she should apply to X school. The reason was that the counselor knew of four other students applying to Y school—two of whom were legacies and a third was a recruited athlete—and of only one other student applying to X school. So it came down to a strategic choice for my daughter.

Finally, there is the application itself, which fortunately has been significantly consolidated since most of us applied. Now there is the Common Application, which just under 700 colleges accept. As a parent, you should explore the Common App website[3] as it offers a host of resources, including the most recent prompts for the essay portion of the application. This is something to do either on your own or, if your teenager is willing, together. If you do it together, however, do not expect a long attention span from your teen, as the site may elicit too much anxiety for him to spend any real time exploring. But trust that your teen will explore the site on his own at a later time.

> I know it sounds a bit crazy, but after we visited colleges in the summer of my daughter's junior year, she got so excited that she actually completed the common app just to familiarize herself with it and as a kind of rough draft. I never would have done anything like that but it helped her enormously.

Given that your teenager will speak with you in fits and spurts about college it is essential that you do your homework such that when she opens up to you, you have the background to understand what she is saying and what she is not saying. This way you can both support her and gently guide her through her blind spots, even if you have to use *My friend Sally* . . . stories.

> My friend Sally just told me a sad story. Seems her son planned on applying early to college a couple of years ago, but the school he wanted to apply to had a different deadline than the schools his other friends were applying to. So, long story short, he missed the deadline. Such a shame.

Chief Organizer

This is one of the areas where you can be of tremendous assistance to your teenager, and most will appreciate it from the beginning. It's not that you complete the application, select the colleges, or write the essays. Rather, you guide the organization of the various components. This is why it is important to familiarize yourself with the Common App ahead of time—it asks for a lot of information and the website is an incredible resource for advice and expertise.

The nuance here is that you can only do whatever your teenager is comfortable with, and this will vary from teenager to teenager—even siblings! Start early with them, asking how you can assist. Get in the habit of asking questions rather than making statements. After all, *Let me proofread your essay* is very different from *Want me to proofread your essay?* Some teenagers will welcome your assistance with open arms while others prefer to do it on their own. Just a word of warning if your teenager is part of the latter group: do not be surprised if further along in the process they panic, revealing they are woefully behind and hugely disorganized and suddenly, desperately, want your help. Like everything else with your teen, it's an ongoing negotiation.

> He first showed me his essay two days before the deadline. I'm proud of myself because I held it together. The essay was terrible—poorly written and no depth. "You have some decent ideas here. Want some feedback?" And then we took it slowly. I pushed for more depth but stopped short of prescribing. I held higher expectations than he had for himself without demeaning him. And I made the coffee as we were both up all night! The next morning was the only time all through high school that I let him sleep in.

Areas that are ripe for your organizational prowess include timeline for application completion, financial aid forms, booking tours for college visits, keeping track of the college list, and registering for standardized tests—SAT or ACT. One other assignment to keep track of is what college counselors call a *brag sheet,* and it's one of the most difficult tasks for many students. And yes, it's exactly what it sounds like, a list of all their accomplishments and roles. It's incredibly narcissistic. Ironically, it is also something that we have preached against much of their lives. That is, not to be a braggart but to let our accomplishments and attitudes speak for themselves. In the application, however, it is important for them to have these examples at their fingertips. Also, from this sheet many students discover a topic for their application essay.

Finally, here is one piece of pragmatic advice from a colleague of mine at the Brentwood School. Dr. Jawaan Wallace, the Director of College Counseling, suggests that families applying to college pick one time each week to discuss the process. Maybe it's Sunday afternoon from 4 to 5, dinner on Wednesday evening, or Friday after school. Just pick a time and hold all your questions and thoughts for that time. Without this structure, families run the risk of allowing the college conversation to loom over every family interchange, which will send your teen running for cover faster than you could have ever imagined.

The College List

Contrary to what many people believe at the start of this process, the college list often goes through many changes from start to finish. In general, as you help organize your teenager you want to create a list based on three different categories of probable admittance: safety (very high likelihood of admittance), probable (good chance, but no guarantee of admittance), and reach (a long shot). Throughout the entire application process your teenager needs to view and review every school on the list to make sure she would feel good about attending any of them.

The big question many students and parents have is *How many schools should I apply to?* The Common App tops out at 20 applications per student, though some get around this by registering two different accounts—a bad idea. Although the Common App makes it easier to apply to more schools, other factors to consider are the cost—you have to pay for each, individual application—quality of research into the schools on your list, and, finally, that your teen is quite sure she would be happy with any of the schools on the list (more on that later in this chapter). In general, college counselors recommend applying to anywhere from 6 to 12 schools, with as even a spread as possible across categories.

In terms of putting this list together your teenager will gather information from peers, teachers, counselors, friends of the family, and published materials on the different colleges. Additionally, if your child's school subscribes to Naviance,[4] it is one of the best resources possible for putting the list together. Naviance has succinct and thorough descriptions of just about all the colleges and shows the test scores and GPA generally required for admittance and how students from your school have fared in terms of admissions. (For schools that subscribe, it also serves as a repository for all the application materials.) Unfortunately, there are no individual subscriptions so your teen should check with her school.

> Putting that list together was tough for my son. He really had to come to grips with reality in terms of schools he could get into. He's a decent student but not a top scholar. He had to face that. In the end, he had 8 schools on his list and got into 5—all of his safety, all but one of the probable, and neither of the reach schools. But by the end, I know he would have been fine, even happy, attending any of the schools on his list.

If your family is counting on financial aid then it is imperative that you have this conversation with your teenager at the outset. In the end, your teen may get into one of his reach schools but attend one of the safety schools due to significant differences in the aid packages offered. Unfortunately, the amount of aid offered is not all that predictable from college to college.

> My daughter got into her dream school, which was wonderful. Unfortunately, the financial aid package was minimal, especially compared to a few of the

other schools. It was hard on her. She was both proud and devastated. It took a while for her to recover, but one night in late July she just turned to me and said: "Well, I really wanted to go to Y but it sure feels like X wants me because of all the financial aid they offered. I like that they want me that much, and I think it'll be a great four years."

Visiting Colleges

If the high school your teenager attends has any sort of college trip, then urge, bordering on insisting, your teen to participate. Typically these trips include visits to a dozen or so colleges of all types and sizes—state universities, small liberal arts schools, all black schools, and young women's colleges. It's the best way for teens to see a range of what is really out there, and hopefully to narrow down the type of school that is their best fit. Best of all they end up debriefing each college with their friends as they ride the bus from school to school and stay up late hanging out and naturally reflecting on each school. The only downside to these visits—and you'll see this when you visit schools with your teens—is that a great deal of the assessment of that school depends on the student tour guide. That, and the weather.

I thought I would really like X School, but after visiting I'm not even sure I am going to apply. The tour guide was a real jock so I didn't connect with his perspective at all. Plus there was this dad that I thought was going to adopt the guide by the end of the tour—I felt bad for his daughter who was with him. And, of course, it was raining the entire time.

It is also great if you can visit some schools with your teenager. This way you both have common ground for future reference and from which to evaluate different schools. Also, driving away from a campus together and, frequently, stopping for lunch on the road, leads to a natural debriefing while also keeping the door open for bigger conversations. That is, after the school is discussed it may lead to conversation about areas of study, or friends from school your teen will miss, or what it will be like to live away from home for the first time. It can get existential pretty quick.

While on these visits, take the tour the college is offering and don't be afraid to wander on your own as well. The two best wandering spots are the library and the food centers. Watch how students interact with one another and don't be afraid to ask a few about their experience at the school. When students open up to you like this, they provide the most honest assessments you'll get.

In the name of efficiency, if you have younger children at home bring them on the tours whenever possible. It keeps the family together and gives them a glimpse into what lies ahead.

We were visiting schools with our daughter and brought along my son who at the time was in sixth grade. He was neutral on the whole experience other than liking all the food options at each campus. But along the way he tuned into the differences between the schools. "That was a lousy presentation. The Admissions Associate didn't answer any of the questions. She just said what she wanted to say. Besides, this school is too small. I already know I want a big school."

And it allows for some common reference points, some quite humorous.

When we visited this one school—I won't give you the name—we were on the tour and it was fairly neutral. There was, however, this one girl who kept interrupting and spouting off facts and highlights about the school. She must have thought the tour guide made the admit decisions. Anyway, when we got to the library this girl came up to our tour guide and proceeded to climb on his back. He kept talking as if nothing out of the ordinary was happening. Everyone just looked at each other in disbelief—it was so strange. And she stayed on his back for a full five minutes as he walked us through the library! Whenever this comes up in our family we all get a huge laugh. It was the most bizarre tour experience I had. And no, I did not go to that school!

In arranging these visits you also have some latitude in the schools you visit. That is, you definitely need to take tours at the schools on your teen's list, and, with a bit of luck, you can add a couple of schools you think might surprise your teen. And yes, this can include your alma mater, just as long as you don't get attached.

Truthfully I didn't think my son would click with my alma mater, but still, I thought there was an outside chance. It was worth a try. Fortunately I knew the president of the college as he and I went to school together. As a result we got the VIP tour complete with a thirty-minute coffee in the president's office. I was impressed. At dinner that night, my son was gentle with me. "Dad, I can see why you loved it here. It's totally you. But I don't think it's for me." I was quiet, and fought as hard as I could not to look disappointed, nor to interrogate him with questions. "Yeah, I can see that. Thanks for taking an open look."

Outside Assistance

If you are fortunate enough to have the resources, a question that may arise is whether to use a private college counselor or not. There are a few issues to consider in making this decision. First, if there is too much tension between you and your teen you may need someone more neutral. (A good litmus test for this is how you did together teaching him how to drive.) This is especially true around the essay. In fact, I usually recommend that most students have an English teacher read their essay at different points along the way. Or this might be the time to hire outside assistance, just for writing the essay. Just be careful, whether you use an outside person or not, that the essay is your teenager's. I once attended a panel discussion of College Admissions directors from some of the top schools in the country, and one of them commented to the audience of largely parents: "I've literally read thousands and thousands of essays over my twenty plus years in college admissions, and let me tell you, it doesn't take more than a paragraph or two to discern whether the writing is that of an eighteen-year-old senior or a forty-five-year-old parent. And in the latter case, I pretty much stop reading."

Second, if you are too anxious about the horizon of your teenager going off to college such that your anxiety is contagious and undermining your teen, then consider an outside counselor. Just understand that in this case the counselor is more for you than your teenager.

Third, if your school does not have a college counseling professional you may want to seek outside input along the way. Though, again, the Common App website is a huge resource, including a range of videos on just about every topic related to college admissions.

Finally, if your teen's school does have a College Counselor and you do decide to get some outside assistance, make sure to let the College Counselor at school know. Ideally, you should share the name and contact information of the outside person with the professional at school. At the very least they have two areas of expertise that need to synch together. The outside person will have the details of your teenager's application. The school person will have knowledge of the school's relationship with the various colleges (as well as the status of peer students applying to the same colleges).

Making the Decision and Healing Wounds

Once your teen has received her decisions she has a choice to make. For some this is easy, especially if they have gotten into one of their favorites. For many others, however, the choice is not so easy. In these cases, if at all possible, return for another campus visit. It's an entirely different experience when the shoe is on the proverbial other foot. The school will not work to sell itself—your teen will make the case for herself. And this is definitely when to get away from the prepared tour and talk to some of the students hanging around campus.

> It came down to two schools for me, which fortunately were both within driving distance. I visited both with my mom. I was pretty skeptical going in so it was a surprise when after just a few minutes on one of the campuses it was clear that this was the school for me. I can't explain it, I just knew. Then that night my mom took me out for a celebration dinner and we just had the best time. We were both in the best of moods and stayed up late into the night just talking.

Thus far, most of this chapter has had to do with the logistical information about your teen applying to and getting accepted to college. Now, we return to the need for your teen to feel good about all the schools on his list: safety, probable, and reach. For this to happen, there is one idea you need to embrace, never let go of, and remind your teenager of frequently. The reality is that every teenager applying to college is being judged by some invisible third entity—and will receive a final judgment from every school in the form of an e-mail. This goes against the grain of all adolescents who are doing their best to not judge and to not be so impacted by others' judgments of them. This leads to the most important role you play throughout this process. You are your teen's taproot of confidence and faith. And here is how you ensure a healthy, strong, and vibrant taproot.

You need to remind her of all that she has accomplished and the person who she has been in her first eighteen years on this planet. (This is where the brag sheet comes in handy.) From her successes and efforts as a student, athlete, artist, leader, community activist, and friend. Along the way, periodically unpack these areas with her. Let these memories remind her of who she is and what she has done. The goal is that in the end she realizes she is ready to go to college, she will do well in this next phase of her life, and that whatever college she attends will be better for having her as a student.

> I was really hurt when I did not get into any of my top choice schools. It felt wildly personal. But all along the way my dad, in some subtle and not-so-subtle ways, reminded me that I was more than could be captured in a college application—how hard I work, my sense of humor and empathy, my

deep commitment to social justice. And it all helped to cushion my fall from not getting into any of those top choices. It took a few weeks, but honestly I'm excited about next year at college. I actually feel much better than I ever imagined feeling, even if I had gotten into one of those other schools.

Believe me, when teenagers hear this message from a parent, or even a teacher or administrator, it makes a world of difference. This is also why, from the start, your goal has to be to assist your teen in finding the college that is the best fit for her, which might not be the aspirational one you had in mind.

My parents are trying to be good about college, but they clearly believe I should go to X school, which is only one of the toughest schools to get into in the country. Talk about pressure! If I don't get in I know I'll feel like a failure. Sure, they'll never say anything about it, but I know they'll be seeing me that way. Hell, my mom doesn't think I know, but she has already bought the school's bumper sticker!

It's also essential to remember that getting into an Ivy League (or Ivy Like) school is no guarantee for success or a meaningful life. In fact, the vast majority of students end up quite happy and satisfied about the college they attended.

*   *   *

In ending this chapter, I want to leave you the letter from a mother and father to their son prior to his first college response. (It is from a 2015 article by Frank Bruni in the *New York Times*: "How to Survive the College Admissions Madness.") My hope is that if you follow the tenets in this book you can and will write a similar note for your teenage son or daughter. Trust me, it will mean the world to your child.

Dear Matt,

On the night before you receive your first college response, we wanted to let you know that we could not be any prouder of you than we are today. Whether or not you get accepted does not determine how proud we are of everything you have accomplished and the wonderful person you have become. That will not change based on what admissions officers decide about your future. We will celebrate with joy wherever you get accepted—and the happier you are with those responses, the happier we will be. But your worth as a person, a student and our son is not diminished or influenced in the least by what these colleges have decided.

If it does not go your way, you'll take a different route to get where you want. There is not a single college in this country that would not be lucky to have you, and you are capable of succeeding at any of them.

We love you as deep as the ocean, as high as the sky, all the way around the world and back again—and to wherever you are headed.

Mom and Dad[5]

THIRTEEN

Know Your Village

Many parents can't help observing and commenting on how politely, respectfully, and responsibly most of their teenagers' friends behave toward them, which is diametrically opposed to how their own teenagers treat them in private. Furthermore, it's tempting when you find yourself in this situation to suggest to your teenager that she pick up on some of the behaviors and attitudes of her friends. *Jessica seems very responsible for her age—her parents must be proud. Stephen is so polite, it's a pleasure when he's around.* This never fails to make her roll her eyes, let out a deep sigh, and walk away, mumbling something to herself that you can't quite make out and probably wouldn't want to hear anyway.

The irony here is that when in the presence of his friend's parents, it is your teenager who is receiving their accolades, much to the disdain of that same teenager whose company you enjoyed in your kitchen. Teenagers often present the best parts of themselves to the adults who are not their parents. This is because, although they have fired you as the manager of their lives, they still have a need for adult input, just not yours. They seek out nonparental adult input because they experience it as less intrusive and therefore less threatening to their burgeoning independence. They look for this input from teachers, coaches, friends' parents, clergy, employers, relatives, neighbors, older siblings. Although it is tempting to take their search for adult input other than yours personally, don't. The reality is that their need and desire for increased adult input away from home is a sign of their healthy development.

How and Why Your Teenager Makes Use of Other Adults

In Chapter 3, "Give Up on Lectures and Advice," we looked at the role of and desire for increased independence on the part of teenagers. Bearing this in mind, you realize that they need and want a diversity of adult opinions, ideas, and choices about how to assert this independence. They are closely watching all the adults around them and making mental notes about different approaches to life. What's more, because these other adults are not your teenager's parents, they have less of an agenda and less of an emotional and psychological bias about your teenager, which frees them to reveal more of themselves when they are around your son or daughter.

> Sometimes I think I'm more self-conscious than my sixteen-year-old son, at least when I'm around him, that is. I seem to be hyper aware that he is watching everything I do, looking for inconsistencies and information he can use against me later on: how much I drink, the size of the tip I leave waitstaff, how fast I drive, if I come to a complete stop at every stop sign, how I treat strangers—the list is endless. As a result, I often feel I'm not myself with him, that I'm trying to be the mom I think he needs.

Unfortunately, this is exactly the kind of spontaneity your teenager is searching for and is so difficult for you to provide—because no parents can separate what is happening in the moment to their teenager from how it will affect the long term. This is huge. Take a moment to let it soak in.

Imagine, for instance, that your teenager skips his homework one night. The nonparental adult might say, *It was your choice not to do the homework, so stop whining and deal with the consequences.* Then the nonparent would move on with whatever he or she was doing. But, for a parent, it's an entirely different matter. Now you hear yourself saying, *Why didn't you do the homework? This is going to lower your grade in that class and maybe even for the semester. How can you expect to get into a good college when you keep doing this kind of stuff to yourself? Can you go talk to your teacher and see whether you can make it up by doing the assignment and a few extra-credit questions?* Then, of course, this deteriorates into an argument that ends with your teenager walking away from you just when you're getting warmed up.

Other adults, by virtue of not being your teenager's parent, are free to comment on what happened, no more or no less, and move on. Parents, on the other hand, comment on what's happened and extend their concern into the future in an ever-downward spiral, along the way relating the behavior to how it connects to their teenager when he was in fifth grade and extrapolating to what it'll mean for him when he's in his twenties.

I've been teaching high school Spanish for seventeen years now and am generally known for my ability to connect with kids—I was even the Junior Dean for six years. I still get e-mails every week from former students who stay in touch and are continuously grateful for our relationship during high school. But when it comes to my own teenager, I'm as bad as, if not worse than, most of the parents of the students I've helped so much during these past seventeen years. I can't help myself. Even though I know when what I'm saying or lecturing my son about is only making things worse, I just can't stop myself. Sometimes, I even imagine what I would say to another kid, but those are never the words that come out of my mouth. Instead, I sound like every other parent. Somehow I'm starting to think we're hardwired this way when it comes to our own teenagers.

Other adults—say, the English teacher at school—have no shared history with your son that gets in the way of their seeing him with clear eyes. And this is when magic can happen. Because a teacher is seeing him through fresh eyes, your teenager loses the need to defend himself, his history, and his choices and leaves himself more open to the ideas, opinions, and suggestions that come his way from the teacher. What's even more shocking is that your teenager is open with this other adult to some of the very ideas and suggestions that he has steadfastly rejected from you at home.

Making Use of the Important Adults in Your Teenager's Life

Though it seems to be an admission of defeat or too daunting a request to make of someone outside your family, you need to learn to risk your vulnerability and enlist the assistance of the adults closest to your teenager. If you behave as if everything is wonderful all the time in your family and with your teenager, you don't offer these other adults any opening. If you don't go out of your way to meet them, they are left to make up their own picture of just who you are and what you stand for.[1] At the same time, these adults are not your teenager's counselors, either, so the trick is how to ask for assistance without overwhelming them. This usually means a face-to-face conversation so that you can make your best assessment of how much to share, gauging their reactions along the way.

I remember Stephanie—I taught her during her junior year. She was cool toward history, but since our personalities were similar, we hit it off on the first day and never looked back. As a result, she did well in my history class. Without wanting to sound arrogant, I knew that I was one of her favorite teach-

ers, which is about the highest compliment a high school teacher can get from a student—as long, that is, as you are the favorite teacher for the right reasons.

I'll never forget the first parent–teacher conference I had with her parents that November. Since Stephanie liked the class and was doing well, I was looking forward to the conference. The meeting was pro forma for the first few minutes—I was going over her various assignments while also commenting on her demeanor during the first few months. Then her dad interrupted.

"Heather, whatever you're doing with Stephanie in class, please keep it up. We've never seen her do this well in any class or show so much enthusiasm for a teacher as she has for you."

It was the kind of moment that most teachers live for, at least teachers like me. I was speechless—a rarity, I'm sure my students would say.

Her mom picked up the conversation. "But like most sixteen-year-old girls, Stephanie is pushing the limits at home—but we don't need to go into the details of that with you."

I was stunned by the direction this conference was taking, and I was relieved to hear that they weren't looking to me for advice on parenting issues. (Did I mention that I was single and twenty-six years old when this conference took place? This made me closer to Stephanie in age than to her parents.)

It was her dad's turn. "So what we're hoping is that in your interactions with our daughter you can reinforce some of the messages we're trying to get across to her that we fear she isn't hearing from us right now."

My heart began to race. Images of *The Stepford Wives* flashed across my brain. Then I said, "You mean you want me to offer her advice based on what you tell me to give her? Do you have some sort of script in mind?"

I couldn't believe I had said that last line aloud. But both her mom and dad looked at one another and smiled. Then her mom said, "I can see why Stephanie likes you so much."

"No, no, it's nothing like that at all," said her father. "It's just that she trusts you and you've got an excellent reputation at the school, particularly with the other parents."

Wow. Two major compliments in one parent–teacher conference.

But now I was suspicious—I try my best to not trust flattery.

He continued, "It's not that we want you to say anything specific to Stephanie. We would just like you to encourage her to take more risks, not to be so afraid of failing, and not to let her friends' opinions dictate what she does and does not do. Through elementary and junior high school she was fearless, and she totally trusted herself, but for the last couple of years this has all slipped. She seems to look to everyone around her rather than to herself."

"Well, you do know that she is a sixteen-year-old girl, right?" I was too far into blurt mode to stop now.

The parents answered in unison, "What do you mean?"

"That what you are describing is fairly typical behavior for girls Stephanie's age: tuning out parents, paying more attention to what friends think than what they think, and paralyzing self-consciousness that gets in the way of trying anything new for fear of looking bad."

The mother looked scared. "Yeah, we've heard that this is normal, it's just that it's not normal for Stephanie. We've never seen her like this before and it worries us."

I relaxed, leaned back, and said, "Oh, now I get it. You're afraid that what she's going through now is more than a phase, aren't you? You think it might be a permanent condition?"

They said in unison, "Yes, exactly!"

"Well, in that case, I'm more than willing to use my influence to help prompt her to trust herself more and more as the year unfolds. That'll be easy."

Now it was their turn to relax. And Stephanie's mom said, "Thanks, that's a bigger help than you realize."

Here are some points to remember when it comes to making use of the adults in your teenager's life:

- Acknowledge that this person has status in the eyes of your teenager. Believe it or not, this adult may not realize or appreciate this simple fact until you tell her.

- Do not burden her with all the details of what is happening at home, the "who says what and when" syndrome. All she needs is the general lay of the land. Remember, you're not going to her for counseling, nor is this person prepared to offer therapy.

- Do not prescribe exactly what you want her to say and do. Your teenager trusts this person because of who she is as a person, so don't put this at risk by overlaying the relationship with all your expectations.

- Back off. Once you've had the conversation, give their relationship space and time. That is, don't call this person every other day for a progress report.

- Do your research. Before speaking to the adult, find out a bit about her from other parents, teachers, and kids. This will help you ascertain how much to share and how much to ask.

- Trust your intuition about this person.

- Invite this adult to trust her intuition, too. That is, if she detects a change in behavior that is disconcerting, encourage her to contact you before there is any proof. A hunch will do. Because we live in such a litigious time, most teachers won't reach out with their suspicious feelings unless they have proof, so your best antidote is to reach out to them first, paving the way for them to call you should the need arise.

Terrorism in Our Neighborhoods

The previous section dealt with the optimistic and bright side of your teenager's relationships with outside adults, but this section, sadly, must address the darker and more nefarious potential of these outside adults. Sexual predators of young teenagers are the terrorists who live among us, and we cannot close our eyes to their very real existence, as witnessed of late by the spate of teenage kidnappings, random killings, and the shocking revelations about a small portion of the Catholic clergy. Because an adult holds a position of authority over and influence with teenagers does not make him or her automatically trustworthy. As it is everywhere else in the world, trust must be earned one relationship at a time, and fortunately this is something we can help our teenagers to learn. But first we must familiarize ourselves with the terrain and learn to tune our ears to what our teenagers are really saying and asking of us.

With the preponderance of media attention given to sensationalized stories of what I call neighborhood terrorism, it's easy to misconstrue reality. We need to strike a middle and realistic ground when it comes to our teenagers, which means our messages change from teenager to teenager and from context to context.

For instance, when your seventeen-year-old daughter is giddy over the guy she met earlier in the day at the mall and whom she is planning on going out with that very night, she needs you to instill some anxiety and restraint in her. *Remember our family guidelines: We need to meet all your potential dates before you go out. So what time is he coming by? And, of course, I know you remember that there are no dates with new guys when it's just the two of you. So who else is going out with you?* Though she will not like this line of conversation, she will appreciate it because at bottom she knows you have her best interests at heart—though it will feel nothing like that in the moment, for both of you. Even though it isn't warm and fuzzy by any stretch of the imagination, this is still an important moment of connection.

With a teenager, or any other human being for that matter, there is no simple rule to dictate every situation. We must instead look within ourselves and to our teenagers to discern what they need at any given time. In line with this are two complimentary practices that can minimize the anxiety you both have about the very real existence of sexual predators and evil in the world. Taken together, these ideas will make your teenager safer in any situation in which he finds himself.

First, help your teenager learn to assess people. When you meet people in the company of your teenager, get in the habit of giving voice to your impressions and encourage her to do the same. This exercises her intuition and her ability to pick up on nonverbal information. Thinking like an anthropologist, ask your teenager how she recognizes trustworthiness in someone. Ask her how she shows respect to friends and how friends show respect back to her. Ask her how she can tell when someone is disingenuous. In short, help her to develop a vocabulary to assess relationships with old friends as well as new. And, above all else, remind her to trust her intuition.[2]

Second, supplement the development of his intuition and thinking with some practical training in how to take care of himself physically—an ongoing martial arts class, a weekend self-defense course. In the end, you want him to have confidence in defending himself—which also includes knowing when not to fight and how to avoid fighting—and this deep confidence comes only from hands-on, supervised experience.

> When I teach self-defense courses, one of the most difficult concepts to persuade participants to act on is that this person is out to hurt them. Sure, they understand it intellectually, but that's a far cry from actually kicking someone's knee out, or kneeing him in the groin, or grabbing for an eyeball. It's almost as if they think that understanding is enough. And that's what we get them to do in the workshops: assess and act. They have the experience of getting attacked and fighting back, and once that kind of experience is in their bodies, they are much better prepared to deal with these types of situations in real life.

This practical approach to helping them learn how to take care of themselves in dire situations can easily extend to almost gamelike exchanges between you and your teenager.

> A few years back, a teenager was kidnapped and thrown in the trunk of a car. She escaped by doing something that her father had taught her—she played with the wires from the taillights and brake lights, turning them on and off. Sure enough, she caught the attention of another motorist, who called 911, and the police rescued her shortly thereafter. A few weeks after that, another girl was kidnapped, bound with duct tape, and left in a basement. Rather than panic, she chewed through the duct tape and successfully escaped.
>
> These stories got me to thinking about my own daughter, Rita, who had just turned thirteen. When I asked myself how she would have done in simi-

lar situations, I felt the bottom of my stomach drop out—she wouldn't have done nearly as well as these other two girls. That's when I initiated a game she quickly came to love; we called it *Worst Case*. In these conversations, one of us describes a James Bond–like predicament: "Okay, you're locked in a bathroom, the door is bolted from the outside, and the windows are barred. What do you do?" Then the other has to come up with ideas that range from outright escape to counterattacks. It's challenging and playful, and I know it's developing her resourcefulness.

In the long run, I'm not sure that any of this will make a difference, but what's important to me—and I think her, too—is that we feel we're making a difference, and we're having fun, too.

When it comes to our teenagers and our connection to them, we must not let fear get the better of us. If we resort to LoJack types of devices to monitor their every behavior for their own good, or always attempt to keep them within arm's reach, again, for their own good, then we risk letting the fear of terrorism get the better of the connection between our teenagers and ourselves. If our unchecked anxiety gets in the way of their love for life, of their growing up, of their learning to trust themselves, and of their desire to follow their curiosity, we and they are the collateral damage of the war on terrorism. But it needn't happen this way as long as we trust ourselves and have the courage to sort through all the propaganda to discern reality.

Approach this difficult topic with the same attitude you adopt when you purchase a lottery ticket. Everyone who buys a lottery ticket and waits to see whether he's a winner fantasizes about what he'll do if he hits the jackpot: quit his job, buy a new house, pay off credit card debt, get a new car, purchase a new wardrobe. At the same time, people do none of these things just after buying the lottery ticket; they wait until after they win, which is less likely than being struck by lightning. It's similar with these horrific acts against kids and teenagers. Don't forbid your teenager from walking to a friend's house for fear of kidnapping, or from using the Internet for fear of a sexual predator luring him into a life-threatening circumstance. In short, you need to prepare your kids to handle these kinds of incidents even though it's unlikely they will ever happen, and at the same time you and your teenager need to get on with your regular daily lives.

A Photograph Is Worth a Thousand Words

Nowhere is this sentiment stronger than in families, especially in photos that document family history. A major reason to keep old photo albums accessible is because of the past feelings they ignite—feelings that are often forgotten in the hustle and bustle of daily life. The images enable us to remember the old ways of being with one another; some have fallen by the wayside, others have come to dominate our relationships, and yet others we've all outgrown. But still, family photographs induce a kind of group regression in those viewing them that lasts long past the time actually spent looking at the photographs. This is when your sixteen-year-old son, who has disdained any sort of physical contact with you since the seventh grade, suddenly snuggles against your shoulder as you look at the photos from kindergarten. Most surprising is that throughout the viewing and the snuggling, he isn't the least bit self-conscious; it's as if he had become the five-year-old he used to be.

> We keep all our old family albums in a bookcase in the television room. And we've built the albums to be sturdy so that they can bounce from room to room and lap to lap. They include more than just photographs, though; we've also taped in artwork from school, newspaper clippings, even some favorite music—though I have no idea how we'll ever manage to listen to some of those old 45 RPMs!

And:

> All our bedrooms are off one hallway, and one side of the hallway is nothing but photos of our family and friends—vacations, Little League games, class photos, parties, weddings. It's our memory lane. What's really great is when the kids have friends over—the friends get engrossed in our memory lane (or wall of shame, as my husband calls it!) and start asking all sorts of questions about the various photos. Our kids get into explaining the photos, and I can see them experiencing again the memories and feelings that go with each picture. It's our way of keeping our family history alive.

Anything you can do to keep your shared history with your teenager around and available helps your connection with each other. Your visual history of your lives together sends a powerful implicit message: I've been with you from the start and I'll stay with you until the end, so any tough times we go through are just blips on the screen of our lifelong relationship with each other. This is why, periodically, it's great to text him an old photo from his childhood. It illustrates your history, tells him you are thinking of him, and deepens the connection.

High School Summers

Many teenagers have magical experiences during the summer (not every summer, but usually during at least one in their adolescent years). These are the times when they make leaps forward in creativity, emotional maturity, and responsibility. Typically, these magical experiences revolve around a unique opportunity or activity: an art or drama camp away from home, working as a counselor at a camp, a full-time job that comes with real responsibility. In short, experiences that open their eyes to some aspects of themselves to which they were previously blind. It is surprising, though only at first glance, that these discoveries almost never happen with your teenager's regular group of school buddies. Typically it's when our teenagers are around kids they have never met before or have never had substantive interaction with that these self-discoveries occur. It takes just a bit of backtracking to understand why this is so. But once you understand why these enchanted experiences happen this way, you'll have another subtle way to connect with your teenager.

Friends in school develop almost rigid expectations of one another and of themselves. They have a solid and known identity within the group, which is part of what provides security within the group of friends. They know how to behave with each other and know what to expect from one another. During seventh, eighth, and ninth grades, especially, this type of consistent security is paramount. But in tenth and eleventh grades, what was earlier felt as security is now experienced as constraining and confining. Here is what one tenth-grade girl has to say about this:

> It's like I'm changing in all sorts of cool ways, but my friends aren't changing at all. So when I'm around them, I feel fake, that I'm just pretending to be the way I used to be to fit in. And it's not that I don't like them, it's just that I'm bored when I'm around them—bored with them and bored with myself.

Of course, the huge irony here is that when one teenager in the group begins to think this way, it's often a sign that others are having similar thoughts or are on the verge of similar feelings—though they seldom voice them to one another for fear of hurting someone's feelings. And when they do, it's almost always in one-on-one settings, away from the group, which frees them up with one another but not with the group. Group think is powerful during the first part of high school—and even more powerful in middle school. This is why many friendship groups splinter and reconfigure—minus one or two old faces and a few new faces added—during the end of tenth grade and the beginning of eleventh grade. It's normal.

What this means for your teenager is that with his friends in school it is difficult for him to change or grow in substantive and surprising ways without sacrificing the security of those friendships and his ongoing identity within the group. This is why most teenagers who have magical experiences during the

summer, and feel that they change profoundly as a result, often have a difficult time bringing these changes back to school with them. Their friends don't
recognize the changes because they don't fit with their preexisting notions of
who your teenager is. This means that your teenager has to find new friends (to
maintain the changes), delay the changes (to maintain the security that comes
from these friendships), or figure out a way to do a little of both.

I spent six weeks of the summer away from home, working at a summer camp
as a counselor with little kids. It was the best summer ever. I discovered that
I'm really good at it, even to the point of realizing that I want to be a teacher
after I go to college—something I had never suspected before this summer.
Just seeing how their little minds work was a real turn-on for me. By the end
of the summer, I had a lot of responsibility and the kids came to count on me.

When camp ended, some of them didn't want to leave and they kept hugging me around the waist and telling me that they loved me. They made me
cry. So now I've got fifteen kids I promised to stay in touch with over the
school year.

But the hard part is that because I changed so much over the summer,
school and my friends just aren't the same anymore. I used to live for parties
and the whole high school social scene, but now it just feels kind of lame. You
know, *been there, done that* kind of thing. But my friends are still totally into it
and just roll their eyes whenever I bring up the summer and what it did for me.

I feel like I'm living two lives now. In one, I'm going through the motions of
finishing high school, going to parties, playing soccer, doing my schoolwork,
and all that stuff. But my heart's not really in it. In my other life, I'm planning
activities for camp next summer, staying in contact with some of the camp-
ers and other counselors, researching colleges that have good education pro-
grams, and volunteering two afternoons a week at the local YMCA—coaching
a little kids' soccer team. It's not what I expected of senior year, but it's the
best I can do right now.

You now have a wide-open opportunity to connect with the part of your
teenager that went through major changes during the summer, the part of him
that his friends aren't connecting with. There are lots of ways to do this. You
can acknowledge how it is difficult to go through change away from friends
and then to integrate those changes into the old friendships. Often an example
from your life opens the door.

Sophomore year in college I spent the second semester studying in Spain. Far
and away it was the best semester of college. But it made for a tough junior

year because none of my friends could relate to all that I had gone through. It took a while, and I admit I was lucky, but I managed to keep my old friends and to make some new ones who were more in line with some of the changes I had undergone while studying in Spain. But for a while there, a couple of months, in fact, I was pretty depressed and definitely lonelier than I had ever been before in my life.

You can go out of your way to bring up his summer experience at different times in the year. It's a way for him to reflect on the summer and a way for him to realize that you recognize the changes he has gone through. Sometimes, you do this directly: *Have you thought anymore about some of the insights you had this summer? You know, about teaching after you finish college.* And, *How is it volunteering at the YMCA compared to working as a counselor at summer camp?*

At other times you work behind the scenes to create coincidences: *I was just clearing out the "Favorites" file on my web browser and noticed that your camp put up a bunch of new photos on its website. Want to take a look?*

And at yet other times, you feed this emergent part of your teenager by pointing out various articles or television specials: *Did you see that article I left on your desk about that summer program that hires high school students to teach elementary and middle school students over the summer? Seems like an incredible place.*

The point is that although his friends may ignore the changes he went through, you don't. Instead, you come back to the changes that have occurred, not every day, but at least once or twice a month. This validates the changes and tells your teenager that you've noticed, which matters more to him than he can ever tell you.

It's weird, but since I did summer theatre this summer, my mom and I are closer than ever. My friends don't get what it was about, but my mom does. Turns out that she loved acting when she was in high school and college—she even thought about moving to New York to act—until she met my dad, that is. Turns out I can talk with her more about this than with my friends, who haven't acted. Kind of strange, but nice, too.

Traditions and Rituals

Traditions and rituals are wonderful time markers in our lives. In our book *Field Guide to the American Teenager*, Joe Di Prisco and I called them memory mirrors because every annual tradition we go through serves as a reflection into all the past times we took part in that tradition. Thanksgiving with our mom and dad when we were twelve sits next to Thanksgiving when we were seven—our grandma's last—which sits next to the first Thanksgiving we were married, which sits next to the Thanksgiving our first child turned four, which sits next to that Thanksgiving last year when Ben, our sixteen-year-old bolted out the back door as soon as he had inhaled his turkey. They all blend and they are all separate. But, each year, they are sitting there waiting for us. As a result, we can mark the passage of time by remembering these times.

Family traditions reach their pinnacle when our kids are young, and then again when there are grandchildren with whom to share. In between, especially during adolescence, the sheen fades. Teenagers are famous for not wanting to leave their friends behind to travel for a family tradition. They are also famous for excusing themselves as soon as possible to go hang out with their friends. In other words, at many family traditions, your teenagers are an old-fashioned pain in the neck. Still, though, it's usually worth the effort it takes to persevere because, years down the road, your ex-teenager may surprise you.

> Every Christmas for as long as I can remember, our whole family visited my grandparents at their house in Virginia. They lived on a big old farm. As a little kid, I thought it was great, but as a teenager, it annoyed me. But the funny thing is that now that I'm about to have my first child, I really get it; more than that, I've come to love the tradition and really appreciate that my parents didn't cave in to my sister and me when we started our campaign to "Skip Christmas in Virginia."

Humor

As I mentioned in the introduction to this book, the humorist Victor Borge once said, "Laughter is the shortest distance between two people." And this is the gospel truth when it comes to staying connected to your teenager. Good humor and shared laughter are the foundation of a relationship that will hold steady no matter what magnitude of earthquake strikes.

> Both my parents are good at separating all the crap we have to deal with from just enjoying each day with one another. They have insisted from as far back as I can remember that we never go to bed angry with one another. And although I can't say we've always held by that one, we've done a pretty good job. If we do go to bed still angry with each other, it's a rare occurrence and it's because of something big, something that can't be worked out in a few minutes. Usually, it's one of those places where we end up agreeing to disagree.
>
> They always tell me that they fell in love with one another because they each think the other person is the funniest person on the planet. And I believe

it. Not that they're the funniest people around, but that each thinks the other is. No matter what, we all crack up with each other at least once a day. Sometimes, it's a crazy practical joke my dad plays; sometimes it's my mom getting off on one of her imitations; and others it's just quick exchanges with one another. It's probably why my friends love hanging out at my house, because we laugh a lot.

During the stress of normal adolescence, parents need to keep at the forefront of their minds, every day, the normal joys of parenting. More than ever you need to do this for yourself, because few teenagers will do it for you. This means exercising your creativity and your ability to keep things in perspective. Yes, perhaps your teenager flunked English class, stayed out past curfew, and came home with alcohol on his breath, and all in the past two weeks, but that does not mean you can't go out and enjoy a movie with him or a trip to the museum or the ball park. Don't think of it as rewarding his negative behavior; think of it more as making the effort to reconnect because this will help him make better decisions in the future.

Things had gotten pretty bad between Rory and me—her boyfriend was a bad influence on her and I had told her, repeatedly, what I thought about him. Those conversations now hung over our every interaction. Finally, I couldn't take it anymore.

"Rory, I hate feeling frustrated with you all the time, and I know you feel the same toward me. This has got to stop."

"The only way it can stop is if I stop seeing Lee, and I'm not going to do that. We've been over it a hundred times, so just drop it."

"How about a truce? Let's do something fun together and promise not to talk about Lee."

"Like what? Homework?"

"No, how about we go buy some new earrings?"

"You hate my taste in jewelry . . ."

"I know, and you hate mine, too. But I love you and like spending time with you. So let's just go, okay? Maybe we can get something to eat at that new restaurant."

"Let's take it one step at a time. If we get through shopping without fighting, then let's talk about lunch."

"Fair enough. Just no talking about Lee or schoolwork, right?"

"I'll believe it when I see it. So yeah, let's go. You're buying, right?"

"I'll buy the first pair—after that you're on your own."

In general, when you find yourself saying the same things over and over and having the same arguments again and again, it's a sign to get away from the problem for a while and instead focus your efforts on reconnecting. Because, in the end, your connection affects them more than your words or expectations.

The Prom

There aren't many people who don't remember their senior prom, even if they did not attend. It's a marker of the high school years. You may believe that the prom has escalated beyond reason—expensive dresses, limousines, hair stylists, after-prom outfits—but good luck in convincing your teenager. (Much as your parents felt way back when.) Still, though, when you're not arguing about the costs, curfews, and dates, the prom is a wonderful opportunity to connect with your teenager.

By its very nature, the prom is an extension of your teenager's comfort zone, which means it's your chance to step—briefly—into a role you cherish: advisor. Believe it or not, when it comes to shopping for a dress or renting a tuxedo, your teenager will appreciate your presence and the occasional well-timed tip. Knowing how to work with salespeople to purchase a formal dress is beyond the ken of most teenagers, and your assistance is appreciated and welcome.

> The first time Carrie went shopping for her prom dress, it was with three of her friends. She came home miserable. She was sure they were all going to end up buying the same style dress and looking like a gaggle of middle school girls at the prom. I just listened, and then nonchalantly offered to take her shopping at some of my favorite places and where I know a few of the salespeople well. I was shocked by how quickly she said *Yes!* followed by *When?*
>
> We ended up going on three different trips before we found her the perfect dress—her words, not mine. At first, I did most of the talking with the salespeople; but by that third trip, she was handling most of it herself, letting me observe and brim over with pride. She did a wonderful job. In fact, all the salespeople commented on what a wonderful young woman she is, even to the point of complimenting me on her manners and respectful way of interacting with everyone at the stores. I nearly fell over, and I know I wouldn't have believed it if I hadn't seen it with my own eyes. Best of all, I got plenty of photos during the trips.

Prom is a time of vulnerability, and you have to make sure you wedge yourself into the event. For instance, insist on having the date stop over for a bit, at least long enough to take photos. And prepare a special food treat to entice them. In short, this is a huge event in your teenager's life, so start the conversation about guidelines well before the prom so that it doesn't get in the way of prom night.

Sick Days

Anytime your teenager is sick to the point of staying home from school, you have an opportunity to connect. Most of us regress while ill, which means that your teenager will let you in, and in some surprising and almost childlike ways. Whether it is letting you take care of him, or spontaneously reminiscing about days gone by, or just watching him as he shuts down all his normal distractions to heal, you get to remind yourself what it feels like to nurse him back to health. Sick days are opportunities.

> When my daughter is sick, I do whatever it takes to stay at home to care for her, even if she assures me that she'll be fine on her own. I stay home, no matter what. In part to take care of her, but mostly just to hang out with her. Sure, she sleeps a lot when she is ill, but when she is awake all sorts of great things happen: She lets me take care of her; we watch old movies together; and sometimes she even lets me read books aloud from her childhood.

The same goes for your teenager as he reminds himself how important, understanding, and loving you are.

> I was out of school sick last week for the first time since elementary school, and I was really out of it. I missed three days of school. But it was cool; my mom stayed home two days with me and my dad one. I told them they could go to work, that I would be fine, but they didn't listen. I'm glad. I mean, I was totally zonked, but whenever I opened my eyes one of them was there to ask me if I needed anything. Then, no matter what I asked for, they got it for me. It really helped. We all kind of bonded.

When your teenager is ill, laid up with an injury, or recovering from some sort of surgery, do whatever you can to make the time to stay home and care for her. The payoff for your connection is huge, even though she probably won't tell you that.

The Child Within Your Teenager

No matter how old your kids are, whenever you look at them you see the ever-present five-year-old in them. No parent forgets that five-year-old, even when that child is sixteen going on twenty-five. It's a divisive kind of reality, but like most, it can either work for us or against us. If we see our teenagers perpetually at age five and treat them that way, they will recoil against us and overexaggerate their independence. But if we ignore the five-year-old in them, we lose our historic connection to them, which is the source of some of our best intuitive insights and warnings. Instead, I think we need to learn to appeal to that five-year-old when life is tough.

One day when my daughter was five (then an only child), my wife and I were upstairs doing some errand or other and she was in the living room playing on her own. When I finished what I was doing, I went downstairs to see what she was up to. She was lying on the floor playing with her dolls, and some paper and a variety of magic markers were off to the side. As I bent down to join her, I noticed a blue blur on the newly painted white wall to my right. I stopped to take a closer look. Sure enough, it was fresh blue marker, and it stretched along the wall for about seven feet. I was shocked, then furious.

"Elizabeth Ryan!" Then, pointing at the blue line across the white wall, I said, "Did you do this?"

She looked up, surprised. Then she looked at the wall, gulped, and said, "No."

I shook my head in disbelief. "Elizabeth, I want you to take a second to think about your answer. Remember, in our family, it's important to tell the truth. So, did you make the mark on this wall?"

"I already said I didn't."

At this point, I was about to point out the proof: the blue magic marker with the top off next to her dolls and the fact that the line was at her eye level. Fortunately, that's when my wife entered the room.

"What's up?"

"Somebody made this mark on the wall, and Elizabeth insists it wasn't her. Was it you, Mommy?"

"Don't be silly. Mind if I give it a try?"

Stepping aside, I said, "Sure. Good luck."

My wife got down to eye level with Elizabeth. "You know if you drew on the wall with the marker, I'll only be a little upset. What matters most is that you tell the truth, especially when it's hard to tell the truth. No matter what, we'll always love you. Any idea who made this mark?"

"No, Mommy. Can I play with my dolls now?"

"Not yet, honey. Just a couple more minutes. Is there maybe a small part of you that wants to tell me that you made the mark on the wall?"

"I didn't do it, Mommy. Why won't you believe me?"

"I want to believe you, Elizabeth; it's just that I can't imagine who else could have done this."

My wife looked over at me, clearly unsure of what to do next. At this point, I was just about to suggest that Elizabeth go to her room for five minutes to think about it all and decide if maybe she might want to reconsider.

But before I could speak, my wife reached out with both hands and put Elizabeth's tiny right hand between her two adult hands. Then she gently said, "Please look at me for a moment, Elizabeth."

They looked at each other for a couple of seconds before Elizabeth broke into deep sobbing and her eyes flooded with tears. Then they held each other tightly. A moment later, I joined them, and then somehow we were all in tears together.

All Elizabeth could say between sobs was "I'm sorry." Over and over.

No matter how grown up your teenager looks and sounds, down deep there is still a part of him that is five years old, and sometimes you have to persist until you can cajole that five-year-old out of hiding. When facing a difficult situation with your teenager, especially over telling the truth, remember what he was like at five. In other words, give him plenty of opportunities to change his first response. Be persistent with compassion. And although he probably won't let you hold his hand, figure out metaphorically what you can do to make that same kind of contact with him now, as a teenager. That contact is what the connection is all about. When the connection is on center stage, that gives your teenager added courage and makes owning up to misbehavior much easier all around. What matters the most is not the first answer he gives to the difficult question, but the last response. And what matters the most in between is how you bring your connection to him front and center.

The Big Secret

For years, I led workshops for teenagers, usually from two to four days long. During that time, we did a variety of exercises to help them see themselves and their lives with more clarity. Much of the time was spent discussing and building communication skills, both interpersonal and intrapersonal, and addressing issues of self-image. One of my favorite exercises was on commitment.

In this activity, the teenaged participants thought back over their lives and noted the big events and the priorities of their earlier years. Then they projected into the future, and finally came back to the present, at which point they made a list of their commitments—the football team, the fall play, academics, church, community service—in the end marking their top three. Then they talked about these three commitments with a partner—why this was a priority, what were the obstacles, and what were the rewards. The discussions were intimate. Finally, at the conclusion of all this, I asked them to circle the commitment that was most important to them at that moment. Then I announced that, one at a time, they were going to come up to the front of the room and tell their peers about their top commitments, along with the obstacles and rewards. As you can imagine, this is when their shoe tops got very interesting, everyone nervously looking down and hoping that someone else would volunteer. After ten or fifteen seconds, some brave soul eventually raised his hand and started us off. And always, no matter what type of school—public, private, rural, urban—the exercise went pretty much the same way. The first five to seven students who went in front of their peers talked about important topics: getting into college, the football team, community service, church. It was always beautiful to hear and see.

But then around the eighth student, the dynamics would change. Here's what one student, Ronnie, said during his time in front of his peers. He was a senior, about six feet four, built like a rock (I later learned he was an All-State football player), and, somewhat disconcerting to me, he was bright, sarcastic, funny, and cynical—the kind of person who can derail a workshop in seconds. Needless to say, when he stood at the front of the room, he had everyone's attention. He looked at the audience, shuffled his feet, cleared his throat, and began to rock back and forth on his heels. "Uh, this is a little weird. Strange with everyone watching. But the thing that I'm most committed to is . . . uh . . . ," he mumbled, then paused and bit down on his lower lip. "The thing I'm most committed to this year are my parents." The next moment was pretty much a chiropractor's dream: They snapped their necks as their heads popped up, they did double takes, then many of them picked up their pencils and circled *Parents* on their lists. From then on, close to 50 percent of the kids talked about their parents—and the kids who didn't speak of their parents didn't for two reasons: (1) It seemed that everyone was talking about their parents, so even if they wanted to as well, they chose a different topic to avoid repetition; and/or (2) their parents hadn't been there for them, so they talked about a different topic or discussed their parents in less-than-glowing terms out of disappointment in them. An amazing aspect of this was that you could see right before your eyes the kids in the audience completely update their sense and understanding of the person speaking. Suddenly they recognized the depth and pain of a classmate they had barely noticed before. And, of course, seconds after sitting down, these kids were besieged with well-wishers and supporters, often offering their own similar stories as only teenagers can. In other words, instant support groups. But back to Ronnie. "I'm pretty much a jerk to both my mom and dad. I'm not sure why, I just know that I am. So this year my commitment is to be nicer to them, to let them know that I appreciate all that they do for me." Then he returned to his seat amid light applause from his classmates. Seconds later, though, he was back on his feet. "Wait a minute. What I said wasn't quite right; can I say some more?" So he came back to the front of the room. "You know, if my parents heard me say what I just said they would have fallen off their chairs. Saying that I'm a jerk to them is a major understatement. Every night my mother is in my face about doing my homework, and every night I give it right back to her. But still, every night I do my homework. Sure, I'd like to find out if I would do it on my own, but one thing I know for sure is that my mom loves me, otherwise why would she put up with the hassle every single night? And my dad, well we used to get along real well, but these past six months have been tough. Couple of times we almost took swings at one another. But we never did. We always just walked away from one another. But no matter what, he still works an extra job to pay for summer football camp and he always shows up at my games and any practices that he can make, too. I know he loves me. But the crazy thing is that even though I want to go home and treat them better, I know that I won't. I'm not sure why, I just know that not much will change. Hey, I'm just being honest. So my commitment is that by the time I graduate, I'll let them know how much I appreciate and love them, even if I have to write it on a card."

Then Ronnie stopped and walked back to his seat. He received a spontaneous standing ovation from his peers. They understood deep in their hearts the dynamic he described: how much they love their parents and how difficult it is for them to translate this love into kind behavior.

*   *   *

No matter what else you take from this book, please take away this last point: You and your opinions matter deeply to your teenagers. During adolescence, they probably will never tell you this directly, but it's still true. And this is just another reason to focus on your connection with your teenager, because as the connection deepens you'll have more and more opportunities to see the truth in this statement—either through indirect comments or through the fleeting looks on their faces.

Conclusion

All parents of teenagers are besieged with setting limits, negotiating guidelines, and generally looking out for the well-being of their children. This is hard work. Worse, if the above becomes the focus of your relationship with your teenager, you will not have the influence you desire. Quite simply, the stronger your connection, the more influence you have with your teenager. When you pay the same attention to your connection as you do to limits and guidelines, everything becomes easier and more effective. But it takes work and creativity to foster this connection, most of it yours.

Let me offer you a wonderful tool to keep all this in mind and available when most needed. Marc Brackett is the director of the Center for Emotional Intelligence at Yale University, and when he spoke at our school he made a suggestion that I, and others, have found elegant in the way it keeps our focus on the relationship between us and our teenagers. Here is the idea. Think about the relationship between you and your teen and identify three words that you want to define the relationship—kind, loving, inspirational, respectful, trusting, honest, empathetic, etc. As you go forward, remind yourself daily of these qualities while asking yourself how your actions of that day impacted these three qualities in your relationship with your teen. If you make this a daily practice I guarantee your connection with your teen will get stronger. In fact, you will find yourself thinking of (and measuring your actions against) these three qualities in the moments of interaction with your teenager. More often than not, this will have an immediate impact on your behavior, for the better.

A friend of mine once had the opportunity to observe her twenty-something daughter at work as a third-grade teacher. This mother and daughter had a strong connection to each other through adolescence, which isn't to say that they didn't have their tough moments, those filled with doubt, resentment, and anger. But my friend, especially during the tough times, kept her focus on maintaining the connection. In the midst of a difficult situation, she would often choose to not address whatever was troubling her in favor of strengthening the connection, and then, after the connection was secure, addressing the contentious situation. When my friend's daughter went into the classroom, she introduced her mother to her second-grade students as her mom, which, of course, set the kids to tittering among themselves. But later that day, just before school got out, one of the little girls came up to my friend:

"Are you really my teacher's mom?"

"Yes, yes I am."

"Well, I just want to tell you that you did a really good job."

It took a long time for that circle to complete itself, but, in that moment, the importance of maintaining equal focus on the connection and setting limits was never more clear. Now, while your child is a teenager, is the time to wonder about how the circle between the two of you will complete itself. If you keep that connection vibrant, creative, and persistent, I wager it'll come together along the same lines as that of my friend and her daughter.

We all strive for consistency in how we treat and raise our teenagers, but in the end the highest and best consistency we can hope for is love. We hope that our teenagers never doubt or lose sight of our love for them, and the only way to make this happen is through that daily connection you keep with your teenager.

Finally, although this book is ostensibly about your relationship with and connection to your teenager, it's also much more. With just a bit of imagination and tweaking, you will see it's about all relationships, not just between parent and teenager. The daily connection you maintain between yourself and your spouse is what allows you to get through the tough times and flourish during the good times. Your connections at work are the difference between a positive work environment and a dreaded one. The same goes for friends.

In short, connections matter, and the best way to teach this to your teenager is through your connection to each other during these tough adolescent years. After all, one lesson we want our teenagers to learn and carry forward into the rest of his or her life is that relationships and connections matter. People on their deathbeds don't wish they had worked more; instead, most people wish they had loved more. This really means they wish they had learned to love and to stay connected when relationships became complicated and tough. And adolescence is about as tough as it gets, so staying connected now is the best training you will ever have or need.

Additional Reading

On Raising Adolescents

Bradley, Michael J. *Yes, Your Teenager Is Crazy! Loving Your Kid Without Losing Your Mind.* Gig Harbor, WA: Harbor Press, 2001.

Riera, Michael. *Uncommon Sense for Parents with Teenagers.* Berkeley, CA: Celestial Arts, 1995.

Riera, Michael, and Joe Di Prisco. *Right from Wrong: Instilling a Sense of Integrity in Your Child.* Cambridge, MA: Perseus Publishing, 2002.

Wolf, Anthony E. *Get Out of My Life, But First Could You Drive Me & Cheryl to the Mall.* New York: Noonday, 1991.

Teenagers in Their Natural Environment

Hersch, Patricia. *A Tribe Apart: A Journey into the Heart of American Adolescence.* New York: Ballantine Books, 1999.

Riera, Michael, and Joe Di Prisco. *Field Guide to the American Teenager: A Parent's Companion.* Cambridge, MA: Perseus Publishing, 2009.

Gender

Chodorow, Nancy J. *Feminism and Psychoanalytic Theory.* New Haven, CT: Yale University Press, 1991.

Gilligan, Carol. *In a Different Voice: Psychological Theory and Women's Development.* Cambridge, MA: Harvard University Press, 1998.

Gurian, Michael. *Boys and Girls Learn Differently!* San Francisco, CA: Jossey-Bass, 2001.

Pipher, Mary. *Reviving Ophelia: Saving the Selves of Adolescent Girls.* New York: Putnam, 1994.

Pollack, William S. *Real Boys: Rescuing Our Sons from the Myths of Boyhood.* New York: Random House, 1998.

Tannen, Deborah. *You Just Don't Understand: Women and Men in Conversation*. New York: Ballantine Books, 1990.

Kindlon, Dan, and Michael Thompson, with Theresa Barker. *Raising Cain: Protecting the Emotional Life of Boys*. New York: Ballantine Books, 1999.

Learning

Gardner, Howard. *Frames of Mind: The Theory of Multiple Intelligences*. New York: Basic Books, 1993.

Levine, Mel. *A Mind at a Time*. New York: Simon & Schuster, 2002.

The Sex Conversation

Basso, Michael J. *The Underground Guide to Teenage Sexuality: An Essential Handbook for Today's Teens & Parents*. Minneapolis: Fairview Press, 1997.

Roffman, Deborah M. *Sex and Sensibility: The Thinking Parent's Guide to Talking Sense about Sex*. Cambridge, MA: Perseus Publishing, 2001.

Sex and Sexuality

Bass, Ellen, and Kate Kaufman. *Free Your Mind: The Book for Gay, Lesbian, and Bisexual Youth—and Their Allies*. New York: Harper Perennial, 1996.

Shalit, Wendy. *A Return to Modesty: Discovering the Lost Virtue*. New York: Touchstone Books, 2000.

Woody, Jane DiVita. *How Can We Talk About That?: Overcoming Personal Hang-Ups So We Can Teach Kids the Right Stuff About Sex and Sexuality*. San Francisco, CA: Jossey-Bass, 2001.

On Being a Teenager—Books for You to Leave in Their Rooms

Bell, Ruth. *Changing Bodies, Changing Lives: A Book for Teens on Sex and Relationships*. New York: Three Rivers Press, 1998.

Madaras, Lynda, with Area Madaras. *The What's Happening to My Body? Book for Boys: A Growing Up Guide for Parents and Sons*. New York: Market Press, 2000.

Madaras, Lynda, with Area Madaras. *The What's Happening to My Body? Book for Girls: A Growing Up Guide for Parents and Daughters*. New York: Market Press, 2000.

Riera, Michael. *Surviving High School*. Berkeley, CA: Celestial Arts, 1997.

Shandler, Sara. *Ophelia Speaks: Adolescent Girls Write about Their Search for Self*. New York: Harper Perennial, 1999.

Notes

Chapter 1

1. "Emotion Revolution—Student," Yale Center for Emotional Intelligence, http://ei.yale.edu/what-we-do/emotion-revolution/.

Chapter 2

1. Daniel L. Schacter, *The Seven Sins of Memory* (Boston: Houghton Mifflin, 2001), 3.

2. Dan Ariely, "The End of Rational Economics," *Harvard Business Review*, 87 (7), July 2009.

3. Michael Riera, *Making the Most of Difficult Conversations*, National Association of Independent Schools (Washington, DC, 2013), 45.

4. Jerome Bruner, *Actual Minds, Possible Worlds* (Cambridge, MA: Harvard University Press, 1987).

Chapter 5

1. Daniel Goleman, *Emotional Intelligence: Why It Can Matter More Than IQ* (New York: Bantam Books, 1995).

Chapter 6

1. Nancy J. Chodorow, *Feminism and Psychoanalytic Theory* (New Haven, CT: Yale University Press, 1991).

2. Carol Gilligan, *In a Different Voice: Psychological Theory and Women's Development* (Cambridge, MA: Harvard University Press, 1998).

3. Lawrence J. Cohen, *Playful Parenting: An Exciting New Approach to Raising Children That Will Help You Nurture Close Connections, Solve Behavior Problems, and Encourage Confidence* (New York: Ballantine Books, 2008).

4. Michael Gurian, *Boys and Girls Learn Differently!* (San Francisco: Jossey-Bass, 2001), 31.

5. John Gray, *Children Are from Heaven* (New York: HarperCollins, 1999), 331.

6. Ibid., 232.

7. On the Internet at www.medialit.org.

8. Jane DiVita Woody, *How Can We Talk About That?: Overcoming Personal Hang-Ups So We Can Teach Kids the Right Stuff About Sex and Sexuality* (San Francisco: Jossey-Bass, 2001).

Chapter 7

1. Marshall P. Duke, Amber Lazarus, and Robyn Fivush, "Knowledge of Family History as a Clinically Useful Index of Psychological Well-Being and Prognosis: A Brief Report," *Psychotherapy Theory, Research, Practice, Training*, 45 (2): 268–272.

Chapter 8

1. Joan Ryan, "The Dirt on Dirt," *San Francisco Chronicle*, September 24, 2002, http://www.sfgate.com/health/article/The-dirt-on-dirt-2767494.php.

2. Michael Riera and Joe Di Prisco, *Right from Wrong: Instilling a Sense of Integrity in Your Child* (Cambridge, MA: Perseus Publishing, 2002).

3. Victor E. Frankl, *Man's Search for Meaning: An Introduction to Logotherapy* (New York: Touchstone, 1959), 76.

Chapter 9

1. William Bridges, *Transitions: Making Sense of Life's Changes* (Cambridge, MA: Perseus Publishing, 1980).

2. Michael Riera, *Surviving High School* (Berkeley, CA: Celestial Arts, 1997).

Chapter 10

1. Noah Goldstein, Steve Martin, and Robert Cialdini, "Which Single Word Will Strengthen Your Persuasion Attempts?" In *Yes! 50 Scientifically Proven Ways to Be Persuasive* (New York: Free Press, 2008), 150–154.

2. Jennifer Langston, "What Tech Usage Rules Would Kids Make for Their Parents?" University of Washington, March 8, 2016, www.sciencedaily.com/releases/2016/03/160308135122.htm.

3. Monica Anderson, "Parents, Teens and Digital Monitoring," Pew Research Center, January 7, 2016, http://www.pewinternet.org/2016/01/07/parents-teens-and-digital-monitoring/.

4. Amanda Lenhart, "Teens, Technology, and Friendships," Pew Research Center, August 6, 2015, http://www.pewinternet.org/2015/08/06/teens-technology-and-friendships/.

5. Ibid.

6. Ibid.

7. Nicholas St. Fleur, "Playing Video Games Can Help or Hurt, Depending on Whom You Ask," August 8, 2014, http://www.npr.org/sections/health-shots/2014/08/08/338855459/playing-video-games-can-help-or-hurt-depending-on-who-you-ask.

8. Rachel Dunifon and Lydia Gill, "Games and Children's Brains: What Is the Latest Research?," Cornell University, College of Human Ecology, Department of Policy Analysis and Management, 2013.

9. Neil M. Malamuth, "Pornography's Impact on Male Adolescents,"*Adolescent Medicine: State of the Art Reviews*, Vol. 4, No. 3, October 1993, http://www.sscnet.ucla.edu/comm /malamuth/pdf/93AM4.pdf.

10. Philip Zimbardo, *Man Interrupted: Why Young Men Are Struggling & What We Can Do about It* (Newburyport, MA: Conari Press, 2016), 101.

11. Ibid., 105.

12. Alexandra Katehakis, "Effects of Porn on Adolescent Boys," *Psychology Today*, July 28, 2011, https://www.psychologytoday.com/blog/sex-lies-trauma/201107/effects-porn-adoles cent-boys.

13. George E. Vaillant, *Triumphs of Experience: The Men of the Harvard Grant Study* (Cambridge, MA: Belknap Press, 2015), 126.

14. Robie H. Harris, *It's Perfectly Normal: Changing Bodies, Growing Up, Sex, and Sexual Health* (Somerville, MA: Candlewick, 2014).

15. Tori DeAngelis, "Web Pornography's Effect on Children," *Monitor*, Vol. 38, No. 10, November 2007, American Psychological Association.

Chapter 11

1. Sylvia Rimm, *See Jane Win* (New York: Three Rivers Press, 2000).

Chapter 12

1. Charles Shields, *The College Guide for Parents*, 3rd ed. (New York: College Entrance Exam Board, 1995).

2. https://magellancounseling.com/wp-content/uploads/2016/02/tips-for-parents-nacac .pdf.

3. "The Common Application," http://www.commonapp.org/. The Common App website has good information on financial aid and scholarships, and is a good place to begin your research.

4. "Naviance," http://www.naviance.com/.

5. Frank Bruni, "How to Survive the College Admissions Madness," *New York Times*, March 13, 2015, https://www.nytimes.com/2015/03/15/opinion/sunday/frank-bruni-how -to-survive-the-college-admissions-madness.html.

Chapter 13

1. This reminds me of what the head of one school I've worked with in the past says to new parents at the beginning of each school year: "I want to reach an agreement with you: If you promise to believe only 50 percent of what your kids say is happening at school with teachers and administration, we promise to believe only 50 percent of what they say is happening at home with their parents."

2. As a testament to this intuitive form of reading someone's intentions through careful observation, there was a wonderful piece in *The New Yorker* (August 5, 2002) by Malcom Gladwell titled "The Naked Face: Can Experts Really Read Your Thoughts?" In the article, the author describes the work of Paul Elkman and others on the art of reading the emotions on a person's face. In short, with the proper training we are capable of reading one another's emotions through careful observation. While you don't necessarily want your teenager to become an expert in this area, a little attention may help him more than you imagine.

Index